KAMALASHILA

MEDITATION

•

THE BUDDHIST WAY

•

OF TRANQUILLITY

•

AND INSIGHT

•

WINDHORSE PUBLICATIONS

Published by Windhorse Publications
Unit 1-316 The Custard Factory
Gibb Street, Birmingham, B9 4AA

Reprinted 1995

Cover design Dhammarati
The cover is a detail from a thangka owned by Mike Yates
and reproduced by kind permission

Printed by Biddles Ltd
Guildford, Surrey

British Library Cataloguing in Publication data
A catalogue record for this book is available from the British Library

ISBN 0-904766-56-X

PUBLISHER'S NOTE: Since this work is intended for a general readership,
Pali and Sanskrit words have been transliterated without the diacritical marks
that would have been appropriate in a work of a more scholarly nature.
In general, Buddhist technical terms are in Pali unless otherwise indicated.

MEDITATION

·

THE BUDDHIST WAY

·

OF TRANQUILLITY

·

AND INSIGHT

·

CONTENTS

PREFACE

INTRODUCTION

11

Part One

FIRST STEPS

13

Chapter One

MINDFULNESS OF BREATHING

The gift of attention

The method of the Mindfulness of Breathing

The stages of the Mindfulness of Breathing

General advice on the Mindfulness of Breathing

23

Chapter Two

MEDITATION ON FRIENDLINESS

Where friendship begins

Valuing human life

The stages of the Metta Bhavana meditation

37

Chapter Three

ESTABLISHING A MEDITATION PRACTICE

Daily practice

Getting in the mood

Mindfulness

How to work in meditation

Some auspicious signs

61

Part Two

PRINCIPLES

63

Chapter Four

HIGHER CONSCIOUSNESS

The process of integration

Getting to know the dhyanas

79

Chapter Five

TRANQUILLITY AND INSIGHT

Our conditioned nature

Modes of cyclic existence

Introducing insight meditation

The universal characteristics of existence

101

Part Three

PRACTICE

103

Chapter Six

THE CONDITIONS FOR MEDITATION

Influences

External conditions

Internal conditions

121

Chapter Seven

MEDITATION POSTURE

Good meditation posture

Principles of meditation posture

How problems arise

Posture as a meditation method

The ideal meditation posture

Posture setting-up routine

'Feeling right' may not mean that it *is* right

Pain

Ways to make sitting practice easier

Exercises

147

Chapter Eight

WORKING IN MEDITATION

Activity and passivity

A setting-up routine

Working in meditation—a review

Working in dhyana

Taking dhyana further

177

Chapter Nine

REFLECTION

Hungry for the truth

The nature of thought

Levels of insight

Creating conditions for insight

191

Chapter Ten

TYPES OF MEDITATION PRACTICE

The five basic methods

Samatha

Vipassana

Other methods of meditation

235

Appendix

METHODS OF WORKING ON THE FIVE HINDRANCES

Sense desire

Ill will

Restlessness and anxiety

Sloth and torpor

Doubt and indecision

263

NOTES AND REFERENCES

269

INDEX

ABOUT THE AUTHOR

KAMALASHILA WAS BORN Anthony Matthews in England in 1949 and grew up in Tunbridge Wells, Kent. He studied art and drama from 1966 and intended to devote himself to fine art before discovering Buddhism in 1972.

In 1974 he was ordained and given the Buddhist name Kamalashila. He began teaching meditation at what was then the main centre of the Friends of the Western Buddhist Order in Archway, North London. He continued teaching for the next five years while establishing a new centre and community in West London.

In 1979 Kamalashila decided to leave the city and focus more on his own meditation and mindfulness practice. With a team of builders, he spent a year renovating a remote Welsh farmhouse to house a semi-monastic meditation community, named Vajraloka. At first the community spent their time deepening their experience of meditation. Then, after some years, they began to teach meditation on retreats.

Kamalashila has become popular both as a speaker and as a meditation teacher. In recent years he has led retreats in India, New Zealand, Finland, Estonia, Russia, and the USA. To encourage the practices of reflection and insight meditation he recently founded a Dharma studies centre close to Vajraloka, where he intends to spend most of his time for the forseeable future.

PREFACE

Not much to offer you—
just a lotus flower floating
In a small jar of water.[1]
  Ryokan

I first realized the need for a comprehensive introduction to Buddhist meditation in 1975, while I was studying Chi-I's *Dhyana for Beginners*.[2] Sangharakshita, my teacher, had drawn my attention to the text—he led a seminar on it, though unfortunately I wasn't able to attend. Yet I was attracted by the material, and as transcriptions of the tape-recorded seminar became available I continued to reflect on Chi-I's text, and tried to put its methods into practice.

At that time I was newly ordained as a Buddhist, and not in a position to devote all my attention to meditation, but my life changed radically when I joined a semi-monastic community dedicated to meditation practice. We meditated together for some years, but after a while it became clear that we must do more than simply get on with our own practice. There were now many visitors to our meditation centre, and we needed to give more of an emphasis to *teaching* meditation.

It also became clear that we needed a book to explain our approach, since (and this is still the case) very little has been written about Buddhist meditation practice. Though the art of meditation has been very thoroughly developed in Buddhism, only a comparatively small proportion of its literature is specifically devoted to techniques and principles. The finer points of meditation teaching have always been handed down orally, from teacher to disciple—not out of any desire to preserve esoteric secrets, but because it is a practical matter that cannot be expressed adequately in words. Meditation is really something to be practised and experienced—and *then* discussed on the *basis* of experience—rather than read about.

Nevertheless there *is* a need for clear written information about meditation. There are many people who will look to meditation—and, very likely, a *book* on meditation—to provide a direction for their aspirations. So I hope some of them will find this offering useful. I would like this book to be two things: an introduction to the basic meditation practices of Buddhism and the ideas underlying them; and a reference manual to help meditators deepen their commitment to practising the Buddhist Path.

Many people have helped me in this. I am of course immensely grateful to Sangharakshita, whose example ignited my interest in the Dharma in the first place, and who provided a number of useful suggestions for the book. But I would like to thank many other friends and companions in the Sangha who commented on my drafts from the early editing stages. There was Satyapala, Kulaprabha, Ruchiraketu, Dharmaghosha, Ken Robinson, Subhadra, Dhammadinna, Parami, Ratnabandhu—and Dhammarati, who also took the photographs (of Harriet Tipping, Joe Chandler, Paramartha, and Danavira) and designed the cover. I hope no one has been forgotten. Maitreyi advised me about the Alexander Technique; special thanks are also due to Robyn Alton for her editing work towards the end of the process, and to Shantavira for his compassionate exposure of my mixed metaphors, tautologies, and *non-sequiturs*. Above all I am indebted to Nagabodhi for his consistent encouragement and useful comments over the years, not to mention the hard work he put in at several points during the evolution of the text. It's good to see his dedication to Windhorse Publications bearing fruit these days.

Kamalashila
Vajraloka Meditation Centre
North Wales
August 1992

Introduction

THE GREAT TRANSFORMATION

*The different headings employed in this book, such as ... transcendental-
powers and wisdom, tranquillization and reflection',... are all derived from the
same source.... If you trace out this source and terminus, or should trace out
the practices and attainments of the Buddhas, they would all alike be found in
this practice of dhyana [meditation].... Briefly speaking, the dhyana which our
Master Chih-chi [i.e. Chi-I] had practised, and the samadhi which he had
experienced, and the lectures which he had delivered with such eloquence, were
nothing but the manifestation of this [tranquillity and insight]. Or, in other
words, what the Master had been teaching us was simply the narrative of the
operation of our own minds; and the profound teaching of the T'ien-t'ai School,
and the voluminous literature to be studied, are no more than an elaboration of
this single subject.[3]*

Bhikshu Yuen-tso, speaking of his teacher Chi-I

THE AIM OF BUDDHIST MEDITATION

This book draws some of its inspiration from the teachings of Chi-I, a
great meditation master. Chi-I taught in the sixth century CE, on T'ien-t'ai
mountain in China, when Buddhist methods of human development like
meditation were just beginning to gain popularity.

Fourteen centuries later, in our own very different time and culture,
'meditation' has become a familiar idea. You will almost certainly have
some sort of impression about it already. You might well have tried some
form of meditation yourself—maybe you are even a regular practitioner.
So let us clarify what exactly we are talking about, for there are many different approaches to meditation. Some of these may appear similar to
Buddhist meditation practices—the actual techniques may, indeed, be
identical. However, their *aim* can be different. Consider the way meditation is recommended by some doctors: their view is usually that
meditation is simply a therapy for reducing stress. It is true that the ability

to *manage* stress is a likely fringe benefit of meditation. From a Buddhist perspective, though, the point of meditation is to stimulate a process of change and development towards the ultimate goal of Enlightenment.

Enlightenment is the perfectly developed human state—an attainment of wisdom and compassion to a degree that transcends all our ideas about what 'human' and 'existence' might mean. It's certainly a high ideal, though not an impossible one.

Nowadays it seems that every kind of group, from the 'alternative' fringe to establishment Christianity, teaches some form of meditation, but there are important differences between these and the Buddhist approach. For example, Buddhism has a unique *view* of the spiritual path. It says that all men and women can gain Enlightenment through their own efforts, without resorting to blind belief. And in terms of actual spiritual *practice*, Buddhism draws on a tradition of 2,500 years experience of meditation—experience that has passed from teachers to disciples ever since the Buddha gained Enlightenment. Western Buddhists thus inherit a tradition that remains very much alive. Since it is a communication of individual experience rather than a dogma, the teaching remains fresh; Buddhism finds new forms and expressions whenever necessary.

Buddhist meditation includes any method of meditation that has Enlightenment as its *ultimate* aim. We can't expect to gain Enlightenment all at once—we need to do some groundwork first. Some meditation practices, therefore, are of a more preparatory nature, while others are much more advanced.

In the *short* term, there are Buddhist meditation practices designed to provide a grounding in certain basic qualities. We must first of all become a happy, healthy human being—and at this fundamental level Buddhist meditation shares similar objectives to many 'growth' groups. Each of us needs to harmonize our life by working on our habits—the moral peccadilloes, the psychological problems, and the negative emotions that stop us from entering into our full humanity.

But this isn't enough—even being happy in the ordinary way isn't fully satisfactory, because such happiness is usually so conditioned by the circumstances of life. So even when someone has established a certain degree of positivity and self-confidence, they are advised not to rest on their laurels but to start looking at their life in more depth—for true happiness can come about only when we understand, through insight, the true nature of reality. That deeper, more essential happiness is the way to enter into the stream of Enlightenment, and entering that stream is the *long term* aim of Buddhist meditation.

Buddhist meditation offers such profound possibilities that words can hardly do them justice. Everyone is invited to participate in a tradition of imaginative adventure, a 'journey into vastness' that is still, after millennia of exploration, producing new insights and insightful people. Yet, imaginative and 'vast' though our tradition may be, there is nothing cloudy or vague about it: we find that the whole great journey is mapped out for us in an extremely clear, systematic, and practical way.

AIDS TO ENLIGHTENMENT

But meditation is not the only kind of provision for us to take on our journey, even though we may find it the most direct and inspiring one. If we are really going to change ourselves, every department of our lives must be involved in the enterprise.

Say, for example, that we would like to develop deeper and more positive emotional responses to others. To achieve this, let's say we decide to meditate on friendliness, otherwise known as *metta*, one of the main practices that the Buddha taught. This meditation will be much more effective if we also cultivate friendships, clarify our communication, and lead an ethical life.

Each of these activities is a spiritual practice in its own right. Indeed, we can view Buddhism simply as a huge collection of these aids to Enlightenment, from which we can choose what works best for us. We can learn to live very effectively, use every moment skilfully—and enjoy it more, too—if we take responsibility for our own actions and states of mind. There are many ways of achieving this kind of creativity. For example, people often find that an effective way of practising the *Dharma* (i.e. Buddhist teaching) is to share a house with like-minded friends; some Buddhists team up to earn their livelihood. Participation in the arts and culture can help, too, by providing inspiration. Generally, practising the Dharma should stimulate our ethical awareness, a special sense that will eventually influence everything that we do—influence even, for example, the way we shop. After all, every article we buy, including food and clothing, has some kind of effect on the lives of others, not to mention our own state of mind.

OUR MIND—THE DETERMINING FACTOR

Whatever we choose to do with our time, it is always our mental state that determines how creative we can be in our actions. Mind is the great determining factor in Buddhism. The state of our mind from moment to moment—its happiness or unhappiness, wisdom or ignorance, compassion or cruelty—is the key influence on our development. According to one of the earliest recorded sayings of the Buddha, our whole life is the creation of our mind—if we act with a pure mind, joy follows; if we act with an impure mind, suffering follows.[4]

In other words, our actions reflect our present state of consciousness: we act the way we do because of the mental states we are in. But what *is* the mind? If the mind is so vital to our development, then we need to understand something of its nature—to the extent that this is possible.

WHAT IS THE MIND?

Our mind is a strange and wonderful phenomenon that is, in the end, impossible fully to describe or define. Despite all mankind's efforts at philosophical, religious, scientific, and psychological thought, no one (not even Buddhist teachers!) can really say, definitively, what the mind actually *is*. We can only try to *describe* it. We can say a little about how it functions, we can tell that it has some connection with the physical brain and the nervous system, and we know that we experience memory, feelings, knowledge, perceptions, and thoughts. But we do not fully understand these phenomena. We cannot get beyond the framework of the mind and see, as it were from the outside, what is really happening and what these experiences really are. Nor can we understand what, essentially, the 'outside world' is, because, again, the world is always our own *perception* of the world, our particular experience of it. We can never get to 'the thing itself' beyond our own viewpoint on it.

To understand the mind, we need to enlarge the framework within which we have placed it.

> *Usually we think of our mind as receiving impressions and experiences from outside, but that is not a true understanding of our mind. The true understanding is that the mind includes everything; when you think something comes from outside it means only that something appears in your mind. Nothing outside yourself can cause any trouble. You yourself make the waves in your mind. If you leave your mind as it is, it will become calm. This mind is called big mind.[5]*
> Suzuki Roshi

We probably do not think very much about the nature of our mind. Most of the time we simply regard it as 'me', and this 'me' is what seems to control 'my' life. 'Me' is obviously very important to us. Yet this me-sense is a relatively small part of our mental experience—it's the tip of an iceberg compared to what happens below the conscious surface. Our dreams remind us of this. When we go to bed at night it can be fascinating to see the images arising as we sink into a half sleep—it is as though the dream world were always there, playing on continuously like a drama beneath the surface. By watching what happens as we go to sleep we can sometimes catch a brief glimpse of this deeper region of our mind as we cross the borderline of consciousness.

But being conscious is not just a question of being awake or asleep—we are only *relatively* conscious, even while we are awake. This is demonstrated by the fact that we rarely know precisely *why* we do things—we usually, rather vaguely, 'feel like' doing them, which shows that we are influenced by subconscious motivations. Spiritual development requires that we work to unravel the knot of our ignorance of ourselves. Occasionally, in the course of our investigations, we catch glimpses of such impulses as they prompt us, so to speak, from the sidelines of our awareness. As our experience deepens, we will discover aspects of ourselves that we never expected, some far nobler than we could have imagined, others very dark and disturbing. We develop through becoming 'larger', assimilating these different aspects of our mind into a deepening harmony.

LEARNING TO LIVE IN FULL COLOUR

The key to deepening, and broadening, our mind is the development of reflexive consciousness or self-awareness. This is the state of being aware *that* we are aware, and of knowing *that* we know. Reflexive consciousness is what brings colour and depth—and sometimes pain too—into our lives. Sometimes we can feel when this dimension is missing—life lacks its usual colour and interest, and our experience seems to be painted in unrelieved shades of grey. It may be that at such times we would really prefer *not* to be self-aware; sometimes we feel that awareness is all too painful, and so we retreat into ourselves, or deliberately distract ourselves.

But at those times when we *do* fully acknowledge our own existence, we start living in full, glorious colour. The colours we experience may sometimes be harsh and garish, but they can also be beautiful. It is in these moments of reflexive awareness that we are fully alive and fully ourselves.

Reflexive consciousness is natural to human beings—it is the distinctively human factor, the factor that gives us our sense of humour, our ability to think creatively and to empathize with others. But we certainly aren't self-aware all the time. We are often just absorbed in our thoughts and sense experiences, without reference to anything or anyone beyond them, in a state that has been called simple consciousness. It is sometimes said that animals exist on this wavelength. I do not know whether that is true, but it certainly seems that we humans can lapse into simple consciousness, particularly when we are somewhat emotionally 'off colour'. If we want it, self-awareness is not difficult to develop. We simply need to appreciate it in all we do, noting when 'something' seems to be missing from our experience—noting when *we* are missing from it!—and then getting back into contact with what we are really feeling and thinking at that particular moment.

BEYOND SELF AND OTHER

Compared to simple consciousness, self consciousness is a much higher dimension of development. But occasionally we may experience a higher dimension still. Perhaps as the result of some insightful reflection, or maybe in a spontaneous moment of illumination, we may see 'ourselves' and 'the world' in a deeper, more universal way, so that these words no longer fit what we are experiencing. Whenever, to any extent, we transcend this experience we call 'self', we experience a dimension known as *transcendental* consciousness.

Forest.
Thousands of tree-bodies and mine.
Leaves are waving,
Ears hear the stream's call,
Eyes see into the sky of mind,
A half-smile unfolds on every leaf.
There is a forest here
Because I am here.
But mind has followed the forest
And clothed itself in green.[6]
  Thich Nhat Hanh

MAKING CHANGES

The goal of meditation is the transformation of our whole existence from simple consciousness, through self consciousness, to transcendental consciousness. This transformation begins to happen, quite naturally, whenever we try to be aware. Like a softly glowing lamp, our meditation will begin to illuminate all the marvellous qualities that were previously covered over by confused emotions and attitudes. As awareness develops, the obstacles to our freedom gradually dissolve away—confusion begins to be displaced by clarity, ignorance by wisdom, and negative emotion by positive emotion. In this way meditation, and other aids to Enlightenment, will gradually change our whole life for the better.

No doubt to some people—at least in certain moods—all this grand talk of spiritual transformation will appear naïvely optimistic. Of course, it is important not simply to accept new ideas uncritically. Indeed, sincerely held doubts can be very useful for our growth, if we are really prepared to explore them. But sometimes doubt can be no more than a bad habit. I have met many people who are inclined to be sceptical in a way that is not only unrealistic, but very damaging to their own natural self-confidence. Perhaps we are only too familiar with the obstacles to our freedom; maybe we know, only too well, the chaos that our minds are capable of. But that is no real cause for doubt—in fact, our self-knowledge puts us in a good position to make progress. There are many, many more people who are *truly* naïve about themselves! We need to take heart in the Buddha's message that all the obstacles we experience—whatever they may be—really can be overcome, and that we—whoever we may be— really are capable of overcoming them. Confidence that *we can change ourselves*, at least by degrees, is the foundation of the whole spiritual life.

Spiritual change is most definitely worth the effort, for our development benefits not only ourselves, but also the whole of society. Those who are making that effort are an asset to everyone around them, not to mention themselves. In the longer term, over the course of one's entire life, there is no limit—absolutely none, according to the Buddha—to what a man or a woman can make of themselves. Very few people realize this. It is true that such change is a major task which will demand our very best efforts. But as a Tibetan saying goes, undertakings that place no demands on us are probably not particularly worthwhile. Spiritual development is said to be the most worthwhile possible use of human life; this book is meant to help you, the reader, begin the great transformation.

Part One

FIRST STEPS

·

THIS PART OF THE BOOK TEACHES TWO BASIC MEDITATION TECHNIQUES

·

AND ASSUMES NO PREVIOUS EXPERIENCE OF MEDITATION

·

Chapter One

MINDFULNESS OF BREATHING

THE GIFT OF ATTENTION

YOU PROBABLY KNOW how it feels when you are trying to 'get through' to someone whose mind is on something else: they can't or won't give you their attention, and it's a frustrating experience. Yet something of that frustration exists in our experience all the time, for we are rarely able to give our *undivided* attention to anything. Most of us have so many things on our minds that our attention easily gets dissipated. Distraction then becomes a normal part of our lives, a permanent feature of our consciousness. We become 'distracted from distraction by distraction', sometimes so side-tracked from our original purposes that we even lose sight of what is most important and precious to us. Sometimes the progress of our life is like one of those dreams in which everything conspires to prevent us from doing something, in which there is a frustrating sense that there *was* something that we really wanted to do—but we cannot remember what it is.

There is much that can be gained by developing our ability to concentrate. As we concentrate our attention, we begin to 'find ourselves'—to uncover something deeper and truer in our nature. The meditation practice you are about to learn is an aid to this kind of concentration. It shows how to relax the mind and focus it on a single object *without conflict*.

It is important to realize that we cannot *force* the mind to concentrate—at least not for long, and not very effectively. If we try forcibly to fix our attention, there will be a reaction from our emotions that will cause either mental instability or dullness. Real concentration of mind depends on our intellectual and emotional faculties being in harmony, whereas—in most people—these faculties often operate disconnected from one other. We can easily think about something without knowing what we feel, or just thoughtlessly go along with our emotions. This state of mental imbalance separates us from a fuller experience of ourselves, and so we can never fully concentrate.

We can often see this imbalance in others. Sometimes we say things like 'Be careful what you say—she's really not herself this morning', or, more positively, 'I'm sure you'll like old so-and-so—he's very much himself.' By considering whether or not this person is 'themselves', we are sensing their inner balance of reason and emotion. 'Being oneself', in the fullest possible sense, is the primary aim of concentration meditation.

Many factors contribute towards our ability to give attention. It's obvious that some people have more of a natural ability to concentrate, while others have their attention more scattered. People also find it easier to concentrate in different situations and at different times: external pressures, different emotions, even the time of day, all make a difference. Even a normally cool and collected person may lose their calm aura in a crisis, while an enthusiastic, motivated person may become anxious if there is nothing for them to do. But to some degree we all possess the faculty of concentration. Now, to make further progress, we need to deepen and balance this concentration so that it is less dependent on circumstances.

THE METHOD OF THE MINDFULNESS OF BREATHING MEDITATION

A beginner should first give attention to this meditation subject [i.e. the breath] by counting.… When counting, he should at first do it slowly (that is, late), as a grain measurer does.…

As he does his counting in this way, the in-breaths and out-breaths become evident to him as they enter in and issue out. Then he can leave off counting slowly (late), like a grain measurer, and he can count quickly (that is, early), as a cowherd does. For a skilled cowherd takes pebbles in his pocket and goes to the cow pen in the morning … sitting on the bar of the gate, prodding the cows in the back, he counts each one as it reaches the gate saying 'one, two,' dropping a pebble for each. And the cows of the herd, which have been spending the three watches of the night uncomfortably in the cramped space, come out quickly in parties, jostling each other as they escape. So he counts quickly (early), saying 'three, four, five,' and so on up to ten.

…For as long as the meditation subject is connected with counting it is with the help of that very counting that the mind becomes unified, just as a boat in a swift current is steadied with the help of a rudder.[7]

Buddhaghosha (traditional commentary, fifth century CE)

The essential method of this practice is very simple. We give continuous attention to the flow of the breath coming in and going out of the body, and whenever we notice our attention straying, we gently bring it back to the breath.

As we continue doing this we will find our attention becoming deeper and more constant, as the mental wandering tends to lessen. We will feel as though our scattered energies are being collected together—rounded up like stray cattle—as we persist in returning our attention to the breath. Experiencing the mind coming together in this way is uniquely satisfying: we feel increasingly peaceful, relaxed, and clear-minded. Once we are able to settle our attention constantly on the breath, we begin to feel completely absorbed. There is that tangible sense of integration, of being totally 'ourselves'.

In a way, there is no reason why we should not use any object as a focus for concentration. The breath is just one of thousands of possible concentration objects. For example, we could concentrate on a small visual object—perhaps a matchbox, a black dot, or an orange. The trouble is that people who are unused to meditation techniques can easily become bored with such things, or even hypnotically fixated on them.

The breath is especially good as an object of meditation, because it can engage our interest deeply whilst allowing a certain flexibility. This flexibility of mind is quite important, for if our attention is allowed to become stiff and wooden we will lose our energy and inspiration. Breathing is inherently interesting. It is a very tangible sensation with a certain rhythm and a soft sensuous quality that is naturally enjoyable and engaging. Breath is also a rather mysterious thing: it is the breath of life, something all creatures depend on in each moment for their existence.

Perhaps it is because breathing is so basic to our survival that the quality of the breath is so closely associated with our physical and mental state. When we are emotionally stirred, our breath quickens. As our body relaxes and becomes calm, our breathing quietens down; and as our breathing becomes still, so our mind becomes correspondingly collected, composed, and inwardly content.

But even though breathing can engage our attention in so many ways, a certain effort will still be needed to stay engaged with it for a whole meditation session. Now and again you will probably find yourself becoming distracted, and perhaps completely losing track of what you are doing. So in the initial stages of the mindfulness of breathing meditation, the method is to 'tag' each breath with a number, from one to ten, just to keep the mind on the task.

THE STAGES OF THE MINDFULNESS OF BREATHING MEDITATION

I will describe the four stages of the practice now. You can try the meditation right away if you wish—just make sure you are sitting in a position that will be comfortable for 15–20 minutes, and read right through the description of the stages before you begin.

THE FOUR STAGES IN BRIEF

Here is a brief description of the meditation stages, to give you an overall idea before you start.

Begin by sitting quietly for a minute or two, to relax and settle yourself down.

(1) Feel the sensation of the breathing as it flows naturally in and out of the body. Just after each breath leaves the body, mark it with a (mental) count. Count ten breaths in this way, then start again at one.

(2) After doing that for a short while (say four or five minutes), start counting each breath just *before* it enters the body, counting in the same way as before.

(3) After a few minutes of stage 2 stop counting altogether, and simply experience the flow of the breathing.

(4) Finally, direct your attention to the point where you most feel the air making contact with your body (this will probably be in or around the nostrils or the upper lip, though the exact location does not matter). Choose any point that seems suitable, and let your attention stay with the subtle sensations made by the air stimulating that point.

THE FOUR STAGES IN DETAIL

Here are the four stages in a little more detail.

**STAGE 1—
COUNTING AFTER
EACH OUTWARD
BREATH**

First take a minute or so to relax and settle down. Have your hands resting together in your lap or on your knees. It will help if you have already arranged everything you need to make a comfortable seat (though it will probably take some experimenting with different combinations of cushions and blankets before you get everything exactly right). It is best to close your eyes—but if you think you might become drowsy, have them half open.

Once you are settled, start to take your attention to the breathing. Just let each breath come as it will, without altering its natural flow in any way—some breaths may be short, others long, or sometimes the breathing may feel awkward, rough, or like a sigh; at other times it may be smooth,

Preparation	Make sure you are comfortably seated
	Sit quietly for a minute or two—relax, settle down
	Experience the sensation of your breathing
Stage 1	Count just after each out-breath
Stage 2	Count just before each in-breath
Stage 3	Stop counting and experience the general flow of the breathing
Stage 4	Maintain your attention at the point where you most feel the airstream

subtle, hardly perceptible. Whatever happens, experience each breath exactly as it comes.

Now, to establish your attention more continuously, start marking each breath with a count. Experience the overall sensation as one breath passes through the nose and into the lungs, and then out again. Then—just after the out-breath has finished—silently count: 'one'. Again, experience a breath as it comes in, and goes out: count 'two'. Once again breathe in, breathe out, and count 'three'. Continue experiencing and counting each out-breath until you get up to ten. Then return to one and repeat the sequence.

Repeat the counting sequence over and over again throughout this whole first stage. Whenever you notice that your attention has wandered, just bring it straight back to the breath and the counting. You need to get into a habit of returning to the meditation straight away, without wondering 'how did I get distracted?' or thinking any more about it. Thoughts of that kind are an unnecessary distraction that will waste energy right now (you can reflect on them later if you like). For the time being, keep returning patiently to the breath-sensation—as time goes on you will find it easier to stay fully focused on it.

Continue to count in the same way, after the outward breath, for the rest of the first stage. Then move on to stage 2.

Now start counting just before each breath comes in: anticipate each in-breath. This is only a slight change, but you will find that it alters the feeling of the meditation considerably.

**STAGE 2—
COUNTING BEFORE
EACH INWARD
BREATH**

So count 'one', and experience the flow of a breath as it comes in and goes out again. Then count 'two'; again feel the inward and outward breath. Count 'three', and once again feel the inward and outward breath. Keep marking each in-breath with a count like this, until you get to ten, then return to one, just as before.

You will probably find that your attention sharpens up a little at this stage, because in anticipating each breath you have to take a slightly more active stance. Generally, this stage serves to establish the concentration more firmly. Keep counting in the same way, still patiently bringing your attention back to the breath-sensation every time it wanders. Then, when another few minutes have passed, move on to stage 3.

STAGE 3—JUST EXPERIENCING THE FLOW OF THE BREATH

After practising the previous two stages, perhaps for ten minutes or more in total, you will probably have built up a certain degree of concentration. Even if this does not seem to have happened, you should still move on to the next stage. The change may not be very noticeable (it is likely that distractions are still present) but now it is less important to count each individual breath.

So now stop counting altogether and follow the natural flow of your breathing as continuously as you can. Feel it flowing down into your lungs, expanding the diaphragm, and causing the abdomen to rise and fall slightly. (Be aware of this in a general way—don't get caught up in the physiological details.) Pay special attention to the turning points between the breaths, the points at which the direction of a breath turns around from out to in, and from in to out, like the turning of a tide. This will help you to be aware of the whole of each breath, so that your awareness is completely continuous from breath to breath to breath.

Allow the breathing to quieten naturally, and allow both your mind and body to quieten with it. As you continue into this stage, your attention and your physical posture are both likely to become calmer and more refined in quality—allow this to happen.

Stay with the breath for a few minutes, still patiently bringing your attention back if it wanders. Keep bearing in mind what you are trying to do, otherwise you will forget and become distracted. Then go on to stage 4.

STAGE 4— EXPERIENCING THE SUBTLE SENSATION OF THE BREATH

Now focus on the subtle sensation just at the point where you feel the air entering and leaving your body. Choose any point that seems right—it will probably be in or around your nostrils or upper lip, but it could be further in towards your throat—and then stay with it.

As your breath passes this point, you may feel it as a soft, brushing sensation, cool as it comes in, warm as it goes out. Remain with that single point of sensation as continuously as you can, and rather than forcing your attention on to the sensation, try to be receptive to it. Feel all its details, all the slight changes in sensation—at each of the different phases of the in-breath, the out-breath, and the turning points between. Focus in so closely that you almost 'listen' to the sensation.

Doing this will require extremely close attention, because the sensation is subtle, and its quality changes at each moment. Eventually it may become so subtle that it is almost imperceptible—it may even seem to disappear completely, so that you cannot perceive it, even when you try. When this happens, you can be sure that the breathing has not really disappeared—it has just become very quiet. So now you must look for it again, by softening and quietening your concentration in a new way. At this stage the mind needs to become more subtle to re-establish its correspondence with this more subtle object.

As the breathing becomes increasingly fine and delicate, the mind is able to achieve an unprecedented depth of calmness, a calm that is joyful and blissful.

ENDING THE MEDITATION

When you are ready, gently bring the practice to an end. Bring it to an end gradually: slowly open your eyes, and sit quietly for a while before getting up. Don't get up too abruptly, even if you feel like doing something energetic straight away, because that could easily jar your mood—it may perhaps make you over-sensitive later on in the day.

It is important to make a smooth transition from a session of meditation to the rest of the day—don't immediately get involved with the hustle and bustle but do something quietly, just for a few minutes. Gaze out of the window, take a short stroll, make a hot drink—do something reflective that will help you to assimilate the experience, even if nothing special seems to have happened in the meditation.

Remember that the way a session of meditation has affected you may not be obvious all at once.

GENERAL ADVICE ON PRACTISING THE MINDFULNESS OF BREATHING

Here are some basic points about how to approach this meditation practice.

HOW TO SIT

Once you have found a suitable place, it is important to set yourself up in a comfortable sitting position. Remember that you will be sitting still for twenty minutes or so, and even minor discomfort may eventually become a drag on your attention.

Essentially, you need a stable and comfortable posture with an upright back. The way you achieve it does not particularly matter; you can sit on a kitchen chair, kneel astride a pile of cushions, or sit cross-legged in the traditional style.

In Chapter Seven there are details of the different ways of sitting for meditation, and some of the illustrations at the beginning of that chapter will provide ideas for experimentation if you need them. If—like most people—your hips are stiff and you can't sit cross-legged for very long, then the best posture is probably to kneel, on a thick blanket, with a *high* pile of cushions between your legs. The blanket under the legs helps prevent them getting numb, and the high pile of cushions is important for most people in helping to prevent the back from slumping.

These points apply to cross-legged positions too—use plenty of cushions. And have a folded blanket under your legs if possible.

Certainly use a kitchen chair if it seems better, but don't lean your weight against the backrest (unless you actually have back trouble) because of the tendency to slump.

ENSURING THAT YOU HAVE PEACE AND QUIET

You need a quiet place for meditation, and it is best if you can be certain that no one is likely to disturb you. For example, if you think someone may ring you up while you are meditating, it is a good idea to unplug the telephone.

Guaranteed quiet will make a considerable difference to your ability to relax and 'let go' into the meditation, and it is worth going to some lengths to get it. The effort of concentration can make you extra sensitive to distractions, so music or a conversation in a nearby room is likely to be a source of irritation. But don't be too fussy about this—there will always be external distractions of some kind. Even alone, in the depths of the countryside, there are all kinds of distracting noises for one's mind to latch on to. So once you have eliminated the distractions that you are able to deal with, try to be patient. Relax, let go! Just allow the distracting sounds to come and go 'in the background', while you focus on your breathing.

UNDERSTANDING WHAT TO DO

Spend a little time reading the basic instructions. Make sure you understand clearly what you are supposed to be doing in each stage, so that you will not have to stop in the middle and check.

If you intend to take up meditation as a regular practice, then you will soon need more personal guidance than this book can provide. Find out about Buddhist meditation classes in your area.

MOVING FROM ONE STAGE TO THE NEXT

Timing the stages on your own can be tricky. I have heard of people recording their own audio tapes with a five- or ten-minute bell to mark the stages, which sounds as if it could be a good idea. But it is not necessary to have exactly equal stages, and you can soon learn to time them approximately using a wrist-watch. Some people find it distracting to have to open their eyes, even for a moment, to look. If that is the case with you, then simply move on to the next stage as you feel ready. Once you feel your concentration is sufficiently established in one stage, or that enough time has passed, you can then go on to the next stage.

Even if, after some time, you don't seem to have become particularly concentrated in one stage, move on to the next anyway, even if you don't feel ready. Don't get attached to the stages—use them to work on your concentration from different angles. It is useful to gain experience in all four stages. Sometimes, even after a difficult start, you may find that a later stage has a more concentrating effect once you get to it.

CONFIDENCE IN THE TRANSFORMATION PROCESS
You should not be too dismayed if you sometimes get very distracted. The process of spiritual change is definitely not a linear one! Progress towards a more concentrated state is often reached by a rather roundabout route.

It is quite common for meditators, even experienced ones, to have phases during which—for example—they cannot count even three successive breaths without becoming completely distracted. So take heart, this is an adventure for all of us! This particular meditation practice is very effective in countering the mind's tendency to distraction, and there is often a reaction of some kind. Over a period of time, these disharmonies will all be resolved if you apply yourself consistently.

Remember that meditation is addressing the whole mind—that a transformation is taking place at a subconscious level. You need to 'trust the process' at such times. Be patient. Above all, continue to meditate as regularly as possible, discussing it with your teacher—it's best if you can keep in touch with someone experienced with whom you can discuss your practice—and eventually your state of mind will improve. Even if there is a lot of distraction, you will usually find that your state of mind after a meditation session is an improvement on what was there before.

ENJOYING THE PRACTICE
It is important to see meditation as something to be enjoyed. The long-term results of meditation practice will be pleasant and happy, even if you don't always experience that pleasure and happiness as you actually sit there.

You will experience two things: the state of mind you happen to be in then—which may be pleasant or unpleasant, depending on what is happening in your life generally—and the effect of the activity of your meditation on that state of mind. For example, if you meditate when you are very emotionally overwrought the experience probably won't be pleasant; but the activity of bringing the mind back to the breath is likely to calm you, and it may even resolve the conflict then and there. Or the improvement may be more gradual, spread over a number of sessions.

Overall the effects of meditation are extremely beneficial, and the more you appreciate those benefits the better. Such appreciation will affect your attitude to meditation, and your expectations of it—you will generally tend to feel good about your practice. If you meditate in this more positive frame of mind it will naturally tend to be enjoyable, and you will look forward to practising again another day.

Chapter Two

MEDITATION ON FRIENDLINESS

May beings all live happily and safe
And may their hearts rejoice within themselves.[8]
From the Buddha's Discourse on Loving Kindness
(*Karaniya Metta Sutta*).

The early records of the Buddha's life show him teaching a wide variety of spiritual practices. He introduced many of his friends and disciples to meditation, along with thousands of the other people that he met. When teaching, he would always vary his instructions according to the temperament and spiritual needs of each individual person. But out of all the different methods he taught, there were two that he particularly emphasized. One was the Mindfulness of Breathing. The other was known as the *Metta Bhavana*,[9]—'the development of friendliness'.

This quality, friendliness, is at least as important for our development as concentration. For many of us, it may be even more important. Certainly the Buddha's own first step towards Enlightenment was taken in a spirit of friendliness—in his desire that people should find true happiness. There is probably no worthwhile human development without that spirit.

We would naturally expect to find happiness and friendliness in a Buddha's wisdom, not unfriendliness and aversion. A hate-filled person can never become very wise. We know from our own experience that when we are in a grumpy, irritable mood, our understanding is at its most narrow and limited. And we know that it is easier to feel friendly towards others when we are in a healthy state of mind ourselves.

By meditating on *metta*, or loving-kindness, we can cultivate healthier states of mind whenever we wish.

WHERE FRIENDSHIP BEGINS

People are often struck by the way this meditation starts: right at the beginning, the meditator develops loving-kindness towards himself or herself. The implied message seems to be 'If you really want to befriend others, you must first learn to befriend yourself.' There is some very deep practical wisdom in this simple idea.

But right there, a problem may arise. Many people find it extraordinarily difficult to love themselves—they are unappreciative of their own virtues. This is quite common. It can be interesting to ask a friend what *they* think their good qualities are—some people seem strangely uncomfortable with the idea. I have a number of friends who appreciate the merits of *other* people very much, but who will only very reluctantly accept that there is anything good in themselves!

No doubt this sometimes arises out of politeness or modesty—real or false—but more often it seems to stem from a genuine lack of self confidence. And, unfortunately, this tendency seems to have become ingrained in our (Western, Christian-based) culture—it's almost as though we aren't *supposed* to like ourselves. Consequently many people nowadays have a poor self-image. Some even feel they must keep up a pretence of self-confidence in order to be accepted by others, which can make life extremely complicated.

SELF-CONFIDENCE IS FUNDAMENTAL TO GROWTH

This is a very great pity, because self confidence, faith in one's own potential, is absolutely fundamental to growth—no one can develop unless they actually believe that they can do it, or at least believe in themselves to some extent. It is clear that the majority of people need to appreciate themselves far more than they do. The Metta Bhavana is especially valuable for our psychologically difficult times—it enhances our appreciation of ourselves, our potential, and our world.

VALUING HUMAN LIFE

The Metta Bhavana meditation begins by nourishing self-confidence, but this does not imply arrogance or a merely selfish self-confidence. It is the ability to appreciate one's own existence as a part of the wider context of human life, with all the promise that human life offers. We see that it is a wonderful and precious thing to be a human being—though most people encounter many difficulties in their lives, each of us also has much that we may rejoice in.

The [human body] is called precious, because it is similar to the
Wish-Fulfilling Gem, as difficult to obtain, and very useful....

This human body ... has the power to reject evil and to accomplish good, to
cross the ocean of samsara, to follow the path towards Enlightenment, and to
obtain the perfect Buddhahood. Therefore it is superior to other forms of life
such as gods and serpent demons, and it is even better than the Wish-Fulfilling
Gem. It is called 'precious' because of the difficulty of obtaining this human
body and because of its great usefulness.

Yet, though difficult to obtain and very useful, it easily breaks down, because
there are many causes of death, and without waiting it passes on to the
future....

Therefore, because of the difficulty of its attainment, of the easiness of its
breaking down, and of its great usefulness, we should think of the body as a
boat and by its means escape from the ocean of samsara.[10]
Gampopa (Tibet, 1079–1153 CE)

By samsara or 'conditioned existence' Gampopa broadly means the
restrictive states of mind that condition cyclic, repetitive ways of living.
He is actually saying that life gives us the opportunity to develop positive, creative states of mind—and that this is the best use of it. It is an inspiring vision of human potential. If we cultivated such a view of the
significance of our life we would have little difficulty in liking ourselves.
No doubt we would also have a truer sense of the value of others' lives—
and therefore feel a more heartfelt friendliness for them.

THE STAGES OF THE METTA BHAVANA MEDITATION

This is a good point at which to introduce the Metta Bhavana meditation
itself. If you would like to try it now, read through the brief description of
the stages first, and make sure you are comfortably seated.

(Note: Because of its nature, far more words have been needed to
describe this meditation practice fully than the Mindfulness of Breathing.
So if you just want to try the practice out, all you need to read is the brief
description that follows.)

THE SIX STAGES IN BRIEF

Prepare for the meditation by sitting quietly for a minute or so—settle   **PREPARATION**
down, collect your thoughts, and get in contact with whatever you hap-
pen to feel at this moment. Then...

(1) CONCENTRATE YOUR ATTENTION ON YOURSELF

Experience your body, your emotions, and recollect your life generally. Now—and this is important—how does it feel when you do that? Be aware of any emotional responses that you have, like joy or sadness. Just feel them—you may or may not be able to describe them in words, but don't even try! Just experience whatever is there.

Develop a response of friendliness and kindness towards yourself, wishing yourself happiness. If it helps, you could say to yourself 'May I be well and happy.' (Don't just repeat the words, though—feel their meaning.) Keep your attention as constantly as you can on that friendly response, and patiently bring it back when it wanders. After a few minutes…

(2) CALL TO MIND A GOOD FRIEND

Concentrate your attention on a good friend (you may have a visual image of them, a feeling, a general impression, or even a scene from some past event). At this stage, don't choose someone for whom you might have 'parental' feelings (they shouldn't be too much older or younger than you are), or sexual feelings. Experience your response to your friend—just as they are—and try to generate strong feelings of friendliness towards them. Establish and deepen the friendly feelings as much as you can. After a few minutes of the good friend stage…

(3) THINK OF A 'NEUTRAL' PERSON

Think of a 'neutral' person. A 'neutral' person is someone for whom you don't have any particular liking or dislike. Again, notice how you feel when you bring them to mind. The feeling will probably not be very distinct, but stay with what's there and look for a more friendly, interested response. Wish them happiness—and work particularly to maintain your attention, because with a 'neutral' person it is naturally less easy to keep interested. So keep it up—continue developing the metta for several more minutes. Then…

(4) TURN YOUR ATTENTION TO A DIFFICULT PERSON

Turn your attention to a difficult person. This 'difficult person' is someone you are not getting on with at the moment. Anyone whom you dislike, or who dislikes you, is an appropriate choice. Once again, experience how you actually respond to them in the meditation. Don't let assumptions about how you *think* they will make you feel get in the way of your actual response. Try to cultivate a fresh response, based on understanding and well-wishing. Without making any false compromises, try to let go any feelings of animosity that you may harbour. Keep your attention on that well-wishing response. Then…

Concentrate on all four people—that's yourself, your friend, the neutral person, and the difficult person—and develop metta equally towards each of them, so that you feel no less friendliness for any one of them. If you like, imagine them all sitting around you. Spend a minute or so doing this (don't forget yourself!) and then…

(5) CONCENTRATE ON ALL FOUR PEOPLE

Allow your metta to expand outwards—eventually expanding it out to include the whole world. Start with the people nearest you, perhaps in the same room or the same building. Then imagine everyone in the locality, then everyone in the town, city, or geographical area in which you happen to be. Keep expanding the metta outwards like this in ever-widening circles—include everyone in the country, the continent, the other continents, the whole earth, the whole universe. Think about all those people, all the experiences they are undergoing right now, even as you are meditating. Include all animals, all sentient beings. Try to think of them all with an equally strong love and kindness.

(6) ALLOW YOUR METTA TO EXPAND OUTWARDS

METTA BHAVANA—THE SIX STAGES IN MORE DETAIL
Here are the stages of the Metta Bhavana meditation in more detail.

Start by sitting in a comfortable position. Also, try to sit as physically still as possible—that will help tune you in to how you are feeling.

PREPARATION— TUNING IN

This 'tuning in' is an important preliminary to the Metta Bhavana. It can also be done at any time outside meditation.

TUNING IN WITH MINDFULNESS

Tune in to your present experience. Whatever you are feeling, experience it just as it is—experience the pleasantness, or the unpleasantness, or just the nothingness! If there are painful feelings, don't pretend they don't exist—but on the other hand, try not to get angry or despondent because of them. Just experience, disinterestedly, what is there. Do the same with pleasant feelings, too—recognize them, experience them, enjoy them—but try not to get too involved (by fantasizing, for example).

This way of tuning in to experience is called *mindfulness* (it's the same 'reflexive' awareness that was mentioned in the context of the Mindfulness of Breathing meditation). If you practise with mindfulness, you will be able to stay tuned in for longer periods. At least a little of this ability is necessary as a foundation for the Metta Bhavana meditation. Once something of a foundation is there, you can start building on it, with more creative and aware emotions.

If you don't feel anything at all, you need to re-establish contact with your senses. Sit very still, and simply 'listen', receptively, to the overall experience, even though there may seem to be nothing there. Keep your attention within your body, concentrating mostly on your overall posture —experience the relaxation or tension in your muscles and the general flow of physical energy. Be aware of your breathing, too. When you give attention to your body like this, you gradually re-establish contact with the senses, and from that basis you will eventually begin to experience your feelings—either pleasurable or painful.

Don't worry if it is all rather weak. Feeling is often quite subtle—it doesn't have to be overpoweringly strong before it can be worked with. One can build up the metta very effectively when feeling is 'low level', yet steady.

**DEVELOPING METTA
—STAGES OF THE
MEDITATION**

Continue developing awareness of feeling in this more 'receptive' way as you add the following, more 'active', aspect of the practice. Using your imagination, develop a response of kindness and friendliness—first of all towards yourself.

(1) YOURSELF

Human experience is rarely all pleasure or all pain—it is usually bitter-sweet. When the feeling that you get, as you tune into your experience, is pleasant and enjoyable, it may be quite easy to cultivate kindness and friendliness. But when the basic feeling is painful or neutral, you need to avoid, as far as possible, reacting with emotions like indifference, ill will, frustration, or self pity, because these can all become obstacles to metta.

**Getting the positive
emotion to flow**

Instead, just continue experiencing, and patiently understanding, exactly how you are at the moment. Continue to practise mindfulness, understanding that your feelings are temporary and can change. The pain we create by our own reactions to pain is often far worse than the pain itself. Mindfulness is a creative response that can create a new trend in our consciousness—one that can even, eventually, grow into pleasure.

Patience can be a 'way in' to a more definite response of loving-kindness. This response may be weak at first, but there are ways of strengthening it once you get started.

For example, it may help to say to yourself 'May I be happy and well', or another phrase that, for you, evokes a friendly emotion. Don't just repeat the words automatically but consider their meaning, and allow yourself to respond to them. Another approach is to recollect a time when you were very happy, and recapture, in imagination, what it was like. That could start a positive emotion flowing. Or you can consider the potential which you have—and which, with a little more self-respect and confidence, you could actually realize. You can explore and use any method that you find helpful in creating metta.

Metta Bhavana employs the principle that thoughts and feelings are made stronger the more we concentrate on them. So once you have contacted a feeling of friendliness through the 'evoking' approach described above, you should focus upon it, putting all your energy behind it. As you do this, the metta will gradually deepen and become more established. Don't get caught up in fantasy or distraction—first use your thought and imagination to contact the metta, and then dwell on it wholeheartedly. The 'dwelling', or focusing, is the main part of the practice, the part that goes deep—everything else is preparation.

Focusing on metta

If it helps, you can give the focusing a 'direction' by using a mental image—one teacher I know, for example, introduces this practice by describing a flower opening. Perhaps you could imagine a bright summer's day. Or you could visualize your body being filled with a beautiful light, or a cooling liquid, representing the love and kindness that you are generating. An image can often evoke metta where words or thoughts alone can have little effect.

Using images

By the end of this first stage you are likely to feel more happy and contented with yourself. But moods come and go—if nothing much seems to have happened, don't be deterred. After four or five minutes, go on to the second stage anyway—don't linger in the first stage hoping that 'something will happen'. Bear in mind the fact that you have only just begun to meditate—for that reason alone, the first stage will normally be rather cooler in feeling than the others; you still need to 'warm up'. And in the Metta Bhavana generally, it is best to tackle each stage as it comes, without judging your performance in any particular stage. (The only really objective way to assess the effects of meditation is to see if there have been significant improvements in your life over a period of time.)

Now develop metta towards a good friend—somebody you already like and have friendly feelings towards. Choose your friend quickly, so that you don't lose your concentration in between stages. (This advice holds good, by the way, for each stage.)

(2) A GOOD FRIEND

Concentrate on your friend. Your imagined impression of them may be visual, or a thought-impression, or perhaps something else—but in whatever way you imagine them, stay as steadily as you can with that impression, and return to it every time you notice that your mind has wandered.

In developing metta towards your friend, you can use the same principles as in the first stage. As before, you can say 'May he (or she) be happy, may he (or she) be well,' or use any other method that deepens, and refines, your desire for their happiness. But be emotionally truthful—even though this is a friend of yours, you may not always feel the way you are 'supposed' to feel towards them. To develop metta, you need to experience how you are actually responding to them now, in this particular meditation session. If, perhaps to your surprise, you find difficulty developing metta towards them, the experience will be just as valuable—perhaps more so—because you have to adjust to the circumstances and create something new. You can expect to learn a lot about yourself—and your friendships—from discoveries like this.

(3) A 'NEUTRAL' PERSON

Now, in the third stage, develop metta towards a 'neutral' person. This is somebody for whom you have no particular feelings at the moment; you neither like them nor dislike them. They may be someone you hardly know, perhaps someone you often see but never speak to, yet have an impression of. What about the postman, for example? Otherwise it could be somebody you know very well, but for some reason you have never been interested in them.

Just as before, develop metta in response to the way you actually feel about them, at that very moment. Of course, the most likely difficulty with the neutral person is that you feel very little. The way to find more feeling is to concentrate on them as continuously as you can. This strategy acts in the same way as the 'tuning in' mentioned earlier. It will eventually reveal subtler feelings of pleasure or pain, to which you will feel more able to respond.

The 'neutral person' stage is designed as a challenge to our emotional sensitivity. Since we don't feel anything for this person—not even dislike—there doesn't seem to be any basis from which to develop the emotion. We feel that we must create a mental connection with them, and this forces us to expand or 'stretch' our capacity to feel and to imagine. This should have a very good effect on our relations with others. After all, there's a whole world full of 'neutral' people out there.

(4) A DIFFICULT PERSON

This 'stretching' of our emotional capacity is continued in the fourth stage. Anyone you dislike, or who dislikes you, is an appropriate choice for a 'difficult' person. Or you could pick somebody you are not getting on with at the moment, with whom there is some misunderstanding or habitual non-communication.

If it seems appropriate you may choose an out-and-out enemy—someone you really hate—but perhaps at first it is wise not to make things too difficult for yourself. If your negative feelings towards this person are very strong, you may end up completely distracted, perhaps even making the relationship worse. Remember that the whole point of the exercise is to generate loving-kindness! Choose the people for each stage primarily as a means to that end, rather than as a way of 'working something out' with them.

As in the previous stages, remain aware of the actual feeling that you have for them. Whenever you get distracted, keep returning to that impression of them in your mind. Reflect that even though you find this person difficult to get along with at present, things can change. Remember that the way they experience their life is certain to be different from the way *you* perceive it. Thinking in this way, wish that they may become happy and well. You could try reflecting that if they were actually happy, they would be different from the way they seem at the moment—perhaps they would even be more likable!

In the fifth stage, imagine each of the four people in the practice—yourself, your good friend, the neutral person, and the difficult person—all together. Remaining with the feeling of metta which you have been building up, work to equalize it between all four persons. Try to feel metta equally strongly towards your good friend and your neutral person, towards both yourself and your difficult person, towards your difficult person and your friend.

(5) ALL FOUR PERSONS

This requires quite a close awareness of how you feel about each—all together—and so needs plenty of practice. It may therefore be helpful occasionally to spend some extra time tuning in to this stage, comparing how you feel in relation to each person.

A simpler approach to this part of the meditation is to let your metta flow equally towards each person without too much analysis or comparison. Simply imagine that the metta *is* equal towards all. This is a good method when you are first learning the Metta Bhavana, or when time is limited.

Having equalized it, our development of metta is at its fullest and strongest. In the final stage we send it out to the rest of the world, far beyond ourself and our three companions. There are various ways of doing this—you can use your imagination freely—but here is the usual method:

(6) ALL BEINGS THROUGHOUT THE UNIVERSE

Begin by developing loving kindness towards yourself and anyone else

Stages of the Metta
Bhavana meditation

Preparation	Sit comfortably and still
	Tune in to your experience
Stage 1	Develop friendliness towards yourself
Stage 2	Develop friendliness towards a good friend
Stage 3	Develop friendliness towards a neutral person
Stage 4	Develop friendliness towards a difficult person
Stage 5	Develop friendliness towards each person equally
Stage 6	Extend friendliness to all beings everywhere

in the room that you are in. Then start expanding the friendliness to include everyone in the house, building, or wherever you happen to be. Then include the area round about, and then the whole town or city. Next imagine the county or state, the country, and expand your friendliness to include the whole continent. Then include the other continents too, until your wish is for everyone in the world without exception to be happy, well, and free from suffering.

Whatever beings there are—human, animal, or whatever—try to imagine their lives and wish them happiness. Moreover, don't stop even with our own world, for there are likely to be other life forms in the universe too—this is the Buddhist tradition—so wish them well too. Finally, develop the metta not only towards all present life throughout the universe, but also towards whatever living beings there might be in the future. So, using your imagination, expand the emotion of metta beyond all conceivable limits.

MEDITATION AND OTHER PEOPLE

If, in the state of Dhyana … we practise realizing the good qualities of other people, there will come a feeling of great compassion for all sentient life. In this connection we will have vision and recollections of our parents, our close kinsmen, our intimate friends, and our hearts will be filled with inexpressible joy and gratitude. Then there will develop similar visions of compassion for our common acquaintances, even for our enemies, and for all sentient beings in the five realms of existence. When we rise from the practice of dhyana after these experiences, our hearts will be full of joy and happiness and we will greet whoever we meet with kind and peaceful faces.[11]

Chi-I

PUTTING METTA INTO PRACTICE

A person's inner attitude is naturally expressed outwardly in their actions. To the extent that we feel metta, that feeling will be shown in an appreciation of others' points of view, in caring for their welfare—and, above all, in friendly actions. In Buddhism, friendship is regarded as a spiritual practice. The Buddha went so far as to say that, for his disciples, friendship is the whole of the spiritual life. Friendship offers many opportunities for overcoming negative emotions—and developing positive emotions.

Many people think of the spiritual life exclusively in terms of purification, in terms of getting rid of sins and faults. Of course by practising Buddhism one becomes increasingly free from such obstacles. But it is far more useful to view one's development in terms of creating positive qualities. If you try to develop positive qualities, negative emotions tend to dissolve naturally—but if you think always in terms of 'getting out of negative patterns', that point of view may actually encourage *more* negative patterns!

The Metta Bhavana meditation gives us a unique way of developing positive emotion. It is only in meditation that we have the opportunity to experience our response to someone deeply, without the complications which can arise when they are actually present. Often 'real' interactions with people give us no time to experience our feelings—sometimes we react to them almost before we know what we feel. But in meditation we have the mental space to reflect, consider, and work with the reactions. It is an extremely effective way of getting to know oneself more deeply. **BEFRIENDING OTHERS**

But friendliness cannot exist in a vacuum—it also needs to be expressed. As well as meditating, we should make efforts to befriend others, treating each communication that we have with another person as a possible opportunity for friendship.

Friendship doesn't mean always agreeing, or pretending that emotional difficulties don't exist. Our relationship to a friend is not superficial. We are prepared to be ourselves, ready to be truthful with them—not just truthful with the facts, but emotionally truthful too. When we are with a friend, we will usually try to be more aware of the emotions we are experiencing and expressing.

Our emotions drive us. Look at all the people that you know, and consider the extent to which they are governed by moods and emotions. You can often see that all the clear, reasoned explanations that people give for their actions are only a part of the truth. Emotions are extremely powerful forces, often complicated and difficult to work with. We certainly don't seem to have much control over them. Sometimes we are in a good emotional state, sometimes not—and that, very often, is simply the way our life goes. **WE'RE DRIVEN BY EMOTION**

RESPONSES TO OTHERS

We can change this somewhat passive state of affairs, but we must be ready to acknowledge what we most *invest* in emotionally. Notice, for example, how often our emotions are responses to other people. Our lives are very closely bound up with others' lives: we live with other people, work with them, read about them, know about them—it's no wonder that people are constantly in our thoughts and in our dreams.

You may be a little reluctant to admit how strongly your responses to people affect you. But the fact that a certain person 'makes us feel' inspired or relaxed (or jealous, or irritated, or whatever) often matters deeply to us. These responses can be almost entirely habitual. We all have pre-existing tendencies to excitement, boredom, or fear, that can very easily be triggered by some external factor.

NOTICE THE CHANGES IN THE WEATHER

Emotional influences keep building up and dispersing again. They are sometimes as changeable as the weather. Moods affect the content of our thoughts, our level of energy, and our creative ability. If we are to develop and become more emotionally mature we need to become more conscious of this emotional 'weather'. Yet the weather can be so changeable and uncertain—perhaps stormy—that we may well feel disinclined to take any risks.

We may also have a sense of alienation, of being cut off from emotions. Our society is so complex, and we have so many different, strong, experiences, that people often lose touch with their feelings about things. We may not think that we have much feeling, because we don't experience it very consciously. But, nevertheless, it's there somewhere.

EMOTIONAL TRUTH

The way into a deeper engagement with your emotions begins when you acknowledge pleasure and pain, the most basic of all feelings. These strong, simple signals are often ignored or hastily covered up; it's important to own them. They are the points where emotions originate. You need to acknowledge pleasure and pain in the moment when you are feeling it. Make it a constant practice to ask yourself whether you like this experience or not, whether you feel anything or not. And if you can feel something, is it a pleasant feeling or is it a painful feeling?

This emotional truthfulness—or mindfulness, to use the word we used earlier—is a very good habit to get into. If you are truthful with yourself about what you feel, then you will become more clear-minded and self-confident—you will not be pretending that you are enjoying something when you are not, or convincing yourself that some experience will be unpleasant when you know that you will enjoy it. If you don't pretend, you give yourself more freedom of choice in your emotional reactions.

Awareness gives you power to act, more leverage over your conditioned responses.

If you practise emotional truthfulness, you will begin to see that people never *simply* get angry, or jealous, or possessive, or secretive, or grumpy, or insecure. Such emotions don't arise without causes—they happen in response to certain situations. At some point, *we* allow the emotions to happen. A negative emotion is a habit that we have somehow got ourselves into (perhaps recently, perhaps long ago in our childhood). It is a habitual response that we release when certain triggers are pressed.

WE LET NEGATIVE EMOTIONS HAPPEN

Of all triggers, pleasure and pain are the most powerful, hence the importance of acknowledging them. We naturally want pleasure and don't want pain—it's the basic human conditioning. But if we are unaware of how we are reacting emotionally, we may do almost anything—to anyone—in order to get the pleasures that we want and avoid the pains we don't want. In this way, our unawareness causes us to exploit one another in an infinite variety of ways.

A friendly mind will never knowingly exploit another person. As well as being a positive emotion, metta is an ethical quality that is based on the desire not to impose our will on others. It is definitely a *desire*, a quality of the heart—it's not a mere idea about love, or an unattainable, over-idealistic notion of 'loving everyone'. It is something that one actually feels, a tangible feeling that can influence one's whole attitude to life. Essentially, metta arises out of the realization that everyone wants simply to be happy—whatever they seem to be doing, however good or evil they seem to be. All beings are seeking happiness, even if they might often seek it in the wrong quarter. Metta is therefore a strong desire for people to become *truly* happy.

TRANSFORMING THE IDEAL OF METTA INTO A REALITY

This desire has to be genuine, of course. It must be based on emotional truthfulness. It is no use simply going around smiling all the time (though there's nothing wrong, in itself, with doing that—maybe it will help!). What we need, and what other people need of us too, is metta which comes from the inside. People can be suspicious of those they regard as naïve, or as 'do-gooders'. Perhaps they were once hurt or let down by someone they trusted. But perhaps we, too, can sometimes doubt the value of our development of metta. Perhaps the deliberate attempt to change ourselves can seem unnatural, as though it were just a badge pinned on to our otherwise unchanged persona.

Real, deep change takes a long time, so your efforts may well seem superficial at first. They *will* be superficial—but don't let that be a cause for self-doubt. The process of spiritual change is happening outside our conscious control. It is like a rock being gradually worn down by drops of water: by practising the meditation regularly we are gradually opening up to a new understanding of things. Somewhere, we are questioning our habitual attitudes towards others, and this is where the deep changes, the changes that matter, are taking place.

For example, you may have your own feeling—perhaps not a very clear feeling—about what constitutes happiness. But you cannot assume that you know what someone else needs in order to be happy. If you really wanted someone to be happy, that would have to be on their terms, not yours. But you may discover that you have a subtle vested interest in the other person's happiness—yet surely, ideally, you should simply want them to be happy, whether you will get something out of their happiness or not. This sort of enquiry will probably reveal inner conflicts as paradoxical as a Zen koan. But if you stay with the questions, you will eventually be transformed from within. So keep practising!

Chapter Three

ESTABLISHING A MEDITATION PRACTICE

If we are practising right dhyana , there will come into development and manifestation all kinds of meritorious qualities.... The body will become bright and transparent, fresh and pure; our minds will become happy and joyous, tranquil and serene; hindrances to our practice will disappear and good thoughts will spring up to help us; our respect for the practice will increase and our faith in it will deepen; our powers of understanding and wisdom will become clear and trustworthy; both our body and mind will become sensitive and flexible; our thought will be less superficial and more profound.[12]
   Chi-I

The first few months after taking up a meditation practice are often characterized by a general 'freeing up' of energy. You will probably enjoy a general sense of calm and clarity, and feel inwardly refreshed. You may experience a happy, confident feeling of 'being yourself' and find that you are able to approach life in a more open-hearted, creative way.

Other people, also, will notice that you are changing, and (provided all this does not go to your head!) they will enjoy your company more, since you will tend to be more communicative and friendly.

DAILY PRACTICE

These improvements are the direct result of meditation, so they depend on our actually doing it. To experience lasting results, we really do need to meditate regularly. It is best to practise every day and build up a routine. Then our practice will develop a momentum of its own, the positive benefits of meditation will stand out more clearly, and we'll generally feel more like doing it. Motivation is important. If we are to keep up our interest, we need to see that our meditation practice is effective—something that is working for us. All this regular meditation is going to require a little self-discipline, but that doesn't mean forcing ourselves—it just means finding ways to make regular practice enjoyable and satisfying. We need to look for creative approaches to our meditation.

MAKING REGULAR PRACTICE ENJOYABLE

One simple idea is to make a habit of meditating at the same time every day—any part of the day or night will do for a start. Think of that time as your meditation time.

For many people the early morning is the best part of the day for meditation—the mind feels more calm and peaceful. I have known people who always get up before the rest of the household, being careful not to wake anyone, in order to meditate. They find that practising at this quiet hour gives them a fresh start to the day, whereas there may be disadvantages to meditating later. In the evening they may be tired, or people may want to visit; there may be other distractions too, like television.

Others will find it impossible to get any peace in the morning at all. They find that everyone around them is usually in a rush, and at that time of day all they can think about is what they have to do later on. For them, the evening can be an excellent time to meditate: the day is over—they can relax peacefully and forget about their work. In the city it can also be pleasant to meditate very late at night, when everyone is in bed and the street noises die down.

MEETING OTHER MEDITATORS

If you do decide to meditate regularly, it's a commitment, and that needs support. Meditation practice benefits from the encouragement and inspiration that you can get from others. I hope that reading this book will give you some confidence, but it will not be enough, on its own, to support your practice. This is why some teachers say that meditation cannot be learned from a book. I agree with them. Live instruction is far more meaningful than the printed word—it is easier to grasp the essentials when you see the *manner* in which someone is teaching. A meditation class provides an opportunity for discussion and questions. Meditating with others now and again is also stimulating and inspiring. If you only practise on your own, the way you assess your meditation may lack perspective.

Contact with more experienced meditators can show more clearly what is happening in your practice. Most people have occasional periods when their meditation seems to be getting nowhere. At such times, contact with more experienced meditators is very helpful—they can provide inspiration and vision just by 'being themselves'—you can learn something important from them even if you don't have any particular questions to ask. It also helps to make friends with other new meditators, because you can see how meditation is changing them, and see that they sometimes experience similar difficulties.

So if you like the approach of this book, try to find a Buddhist centre near you that teaches these basic practices. If you live too far away, it could be worthwhile making contact by letter or telephone. Simply making a connection could make all the difference to your sense of engagement with meditation. And you may discover that a teacher is visiting your area, or that a meditation weekend or a longer retreat is available.

MEDITATION RETREATS

A retreat involves going somewhere quiet, getting away from the bustle of day-to-day life, and spending more time meditating. Once you have been meditating for a month or so, an event like this will give you a deeper experience of what meditation can be like, and so help you to establish your practice on a firmer footing. The retreat will be organized by a local Buddhist centre. It may be of any length, ranging from a day or a weekend to a fortnight or more. Different kinds of retreats cater for different levels of experience and needs. But the essential point of all retreats is to provide a complete break in order to concentrate on meditation practice. The improved conditions will allow you to connect more deeply with your meditation. The event will be held in the country, or at least somewhere fairly quiet, and the opportunity to meditate undisturbedly can make a very great difference. On retreat you can meditate at your best and experience your mind at its best. It is worth making the effort to get to one as soon as you feel ready.

GETTING IN THE MOOD

PREPARATION FOR MEDITATION

Sometimes we seem to be in the mood for meditation, and at other times we don't. But there are ways of encouraging a more meditative frame of mind.

Preparation can make all the difference to our ability to concentrate. If you leap enthusiastically on to your meditation cushion immediately after a lively conversation, or directly after work, or last thing at night when you are tired, it will probably be much more difficult to meditate than usual. If you try to meditate with a full stomach, or straight after a physical work-out, you will not be properly ready; the result, again, is likely to be a difficult meditation.

You can only meditate properly if your state of mind enables you to put aside the rest of your life and concentrate just on the present moment. You need to be able to 'let go' unfinished tasks, matters you want to discuss with people, and preoccupations of every kind. Unless you can let those things go, they will linger in your mind and interrupt you when you are trying to concentrate. So every time you sit, you need to be able to isolate yourself—as much as possible—from your current preoccupations. You need to create something of a 'gap'—a space between the ordinary activities of your life and your meditation practice. This can be achieved through taking a break with a cup of tea, or going for a brief walk—anything that you find calms you down and brings you 'back to yourself'. During this period, try to become as aware as possible of your body, your feelings, your emotions, and your thoughts, so that when you actually start to meditate you are fully present and in harmony with yourself. If you always make some space of this kind, you will find that when you sit to meditate, your energies will be more available for the practice.

FINISHING A MEDITATION SESSION

The way you say 'goodbye' to a friend can affect the whole future of your relationship with them. Similarly, the way you leave a meditation session can have a strong effect on your overall practice. It matters that you finish off a session of meditation properly.

It is important, for example, to conserve any calm and clarity which you gain in a session by leaving gently and quietly. Getting up abruptly, and immediately involving yourself in some stimulating activity, will at once scatter the concentration you have developed. Of course, if you have a busy schedule it may be more difficult to avoid this sort of thing. But if you really want to, you can always avoid haste—it's just a matter of commitment and clear time-management. If you plan things that way, you can always leave your meditation cushion gently, with time to spare before the next activity. You could perhaps make a habit of spending a few minutes quietly, uninvolved, before entering into the hustle and bustle of the day.

Leaving meditation abruptly can have a jarring effect which can create a feeling of resistance to further meditations. But if you take care to leave with a good feeling towards your practice, you will find it a pleasure to return for the next session.

ENJOYMENT AND INSPIRATION

Meditation practice is a living thing that needs your care and protection. A caring attitude will help to avoid arousing too much resistance to the meditation. There may often be a certain amount of resistance to be overcome, especially at the beginning of a meditation—this isn't normally a big problem, but when the resistance becomes strong it can be difficult to deal with. Remember that, as a general rule, you should be enjoying your meditation. Apart from the occasional 'write-off' something is amiss if you are consistently not enjoying meditation, and you need to redress a balance somewhere. Perhaps it is the way you are working in the practice, or perhaps it is a lack of preparation, that is to blame.

Such a difficulty could have something to do with the environment in which you meditate. External conditions can make an considerable difference to your concentration, so make sure you give yourself the best conditions available. If your surroundings are very noisy, making it difficult for you to get concentrated, it is worth doing something about it—if you can. Perhaps you could try talking to your neighbours; consider earplugs, double-glazing your room, or even moving house! You could perhaps spend more time at meditation classes and retreats, where it will be quiet and where other people will be supportive.

If you can, set up your sitting cushions and blankets permanently in a special meditation place—a corner of your bedroom, perhaps. A permanent spot can give you a sense of stability in your practice, and will remind you about meditation. It can help if you decorate this area in a way that evokes a peaceful atmosphere. You might arrange a few houseplants, interesting pebbles, driftwood, or other objects. You could place anything in this space that inspires you—I have an image of the Buddha on my small shrine, with candles and sometimes a few flowers. When you actually sit down to meditate, fresh air, and the fragrance of smouldering incense or essential oils, can produce a serenely calming effect on the mind. Setting up an environment in this way prepares the mind for concentration.

GIVING MORE TIME TO MEDITATION

If you give your practice the conditions it deserves—both internally and externally—it will begin to flourish. You can help this process further by giving more time to meditation. When it is going well—and you can sit fairly comfortably—try meditating for longer periods. Meditate for as long as you feel creative in the practice you are doing.

There are a number of benefits to be had from extending the length of your meditation sessions. Giving yourself a longer time-span may enable you to be more relaxed and therefore capable of putting aside distractions. It can often take a long time to become fully absorbed in the concentration—and even to get in touch with your feelings. Don't force yourself beyond your limits, but when you do feel like it, meditate for a little longer. Over a period of time, gradually extend the duration of your sittings. If, after a month or two, you are able to sit—and sustain your interest in the practice—for forty minutes or more, you will be doing very well.

MINDFULNESS

ARE YOU READY?

'There is a poem', said Mr Chen [the yogi], 'where preparation is mentioned before eating'. He smiled and referred to his notes, and then began to read. After hearing the first line, the listener and the writer also smiled, for this is what they heard:
'"A loaf of bread," the Walrus said,
"Is what we chiefly need:
pepper and vinegar beside
Are very good indeed.
—Now if you're ready, Oysters dear,
We can begin to feed."'[13]
Mr Chen laughed heartily, an infectious laugh in which we both joined.
'But', he continued seriously, 'a question is here being asked: "are you ready?" Upon examination, our whole life seems to ask this question. Even in very hurried moments, as with a boy crouched on the grass before a race begins, what question is asked?—"are you ready?"—Even in a moment like that there is preparation.'[14]

Are you ready to meditate? If you haven't prepared for a meditation session—if you haven't managed, for the time being, to put aside the rest of your life—you may find yourself spending the greater part of that session coping with the consequences. All the energy that you could have been using for concentration may get caught up amongst all the ideas and emotions you are still holding on to in your mind.

Most people experience this pattern time after time. We spend our meditation period planning what we are going to do today, working out 'what really happened' yesterday, or mentally continuing the conversation we were engaged in five minutes before. Eventually, we have to acknowledge how important it is to make ourselves ready. We may also look at our life more broadly, and realize that being *fully* prepared for anything at all—let alone meditation—is a stage we still have to reach. This is why each moment of our life is asking the question, 'Are you ready?'

One Saturday morning I make a decision. I decide that it is high time I went into town to buy that special part for my bicycle. It has been on my mind for weeks, but so far I have done nothing. The local bike shop closes at one o'clock every Saturday afternoon, and today is my only opportunity, since on weekdays I work in another town. But still, it's early and there is plenty of time—I sit down to watch some morning television. The programme is not very interesting, but somehow it holds my attention for a whole hour—in fact I am pulled away only by the sound of the telephone ringing in the hall. On the other end of the line is a friend who I have not seen for some time, and there is a lot to say. Half an hour goes by very quickly, and by the time I replace the receiver I have completely forgotten about the trip into town. So, not knowing what to do with myself (and with a nagging feeling that there *was* something I had meant to do), I wander aimlessly into the kitchen. Standing there, in a state of bewilderment, I come to the conclusion that I ought to do *something*, anyway. Eventually, inspiration comes—I decide to make a cup of coffee. I fill the kettle with water and put it on the stove to boil. Then I hear a faint sound coming through the wall. It is a human voice. A shiver goes down my spine.... *Who can be in there?* Then I realize that the television set is still on in the living room. I go to switch it off. However, this time the programme really is interesting, and I stay watching, my attention glued to the screen. Some time later—I could not say exactly how long—my concentration is violently interrupted by a loud knock at the front door. It is a friend, who offers to take me out for lunch. I am pleased and become very excited. Before we set out, I offer her a cup of coffee. But all at once I remember, with growing apprehension, that the kettle was put on some time ago. My mind races. How long ago *was* that? And is it really lunch time already? Confused and in a mild panic, I quickly enter the steam-filled kitchen. I furtively replace the water in the kettle, which has boiled almost completely dry. My friend, probably noticing the expression on my face, has insisted on following me into the kitchen. She sees what has happened and laughs. I laugh at the joke too—but somewhat embarrassedly. I am too ashamed to admit what her arrival has forced on my attention: the fact that it is one o'clock, that I had meant to go into town this morning—and that the bicycle shop is now closed.[15]

This (somewhat exaggerated) account may illustrate how much our lives consist of distractions from yet more distractions! If we are not 'ready', we'll have to deal with the consequences of distraction when we sit for our meditation practice. But we don't have to be distracted—if we really want to, we can be mindful and aware much more of the time.

FOUNDATIONS FOR MINDFULNESS

It seems that it would help us to be 'ready' if we brought more concentration and purpose into our lives.

The *idea* of mindfulness certainly sounds good—if we could be less distracted, our minds would be clearer and we would be better prepared for our meditation practice. That would tend to make the meditation itself more concentrated and the concentration would carry over into our actions outside meditation. Generally, we would be more effective people— indeed, our whole lives would be transformed.

But when we actually try to be mindful of what we do, we may become uncertain. Of *what*, exactly, should we be mindful? After all, so much goes on, even in a single second. Out of all the events taking place in our mind and body—not to mention the world around us—to which of them are we supposed to pay attention? The problem is that our experience is too complex to grasp all at once. We need to know—in immediate, practical terms—how mindfulness is to be developed.

The Buddha isolated four key aspects of human experience which he called the 'Foundations of Mindfulness'. They are the body, feelings, emotions, and thoughts.[16] Applying our awareness in these four areas of experience is like laying the foundation for a building: we are constructing a new kind of life, based on awareness.

THE BODY

The expression of a wellmade man appears not only in his face,
It is in his limbs and joints also … it is curiously in the joints of his hips and
*   wrists,*
It is in his walk … the carriage of his neck … the flex of his waist and knees …
*   dress does not hide him,*
The strong sweet supple quality he has strikes through the cotton and flannel;
To see him pass conveys as much as the best poem … perhaps more[17]
    Walt Whitman

Some people behave as though their bodies did not exist. They ramble around preoccupied by their thoughts like so many absent-minded professors. Yet it can be such a joy to be physically aware. If we concentrate on what we are doing physically even the simplest sensations— our feet on the ground, the air on our skin—can become rich and absorbing. Indeed, experiencing the movements of walking can become a form of meditation (which we'll explore later on).

When we bring awareness to the body, our actions begin to assume a certain harmony. Our bodily expressions gain grace and dignity. We become calm and relaxed—our whole approach to life slows down. But though we slow the pace, we don't get less done—in fact we achieve more, because this is a more efficient way of working. Paying attention to 'the basics' makes us effective; it puts us more in control. Bodily awareness brings us into the present moment. It allows us to address ourselves more fully to what is happening, right now. So it makes all our time available for use.

Whenever we lose this sense of 'being in the present', our bodily movements become clumsy and muddled. Sometimes children are delightful examples of this. We may see them chattering, standing on one leg, the other curled around it, writhing their hands or rubbing their ear at the same time. Running headlong through a room in pursuit of something, they may suddenly stop in mid-flight as a new idea occurs to them. They may even trip over themselves, attempting to do two things at once. They hardly seem to know what they are doing with themselves physically. (Adults are not so different; we are often just better at disguising our confusion!)

Without losing our natural spontaneity, or becoming robot-like, we can aim to cultivate deliberate, clear movements in all our everyday actions. Awareness of our physical movements can bring a more aesthetic sense into anything we do. Whether we are opening a drawer, closing a door, rising from our seat, picking something up or putting it down, physical awareness produces a calming, maturing effect on the mind. We can always choose to act in this clear way if we want, even if we are very busy. Mindfulness of our body will enable us to develop bodily skills—postural awareness and ways of moving—that will preserve our health as well as our state of mind. In some circumstances, such skill could even save our life. Unawareness can be dangerous—accidents are usually caused by unawareness of one kind or another. Through mindfulness, we can avoid straining our back by thoughtlessly trying to lift a heavy weight; we can save ourselves from catching a chill through not noticing that we are feeling the cold.

Body and mind are of course closely linked; we can learn something about our mental life simply through observing our bodily movements. Our body has its own 'language'—its physical expressions communicate directly how we are emotionally. Perhaps facial expressions give out the most obvious messages, the ones we are most likely to notice. But the way people hold themselves physically can also communicate moods—we immediately sense their joy, their affection, interest, uncertainty, or aggression. If we see the joyful spring in someone's step we know instinctively, without thinking, that they are happy. We immediately sense that something is wrong when a friend is bowing his head and rounding his shoulders. Sometimes we 'don't know what to do with our hands', feeling restless without knowing why. So we may put our hands in our pockets, strike a 'cool' pose, or fidget. We don't usually notice these things consciously, but if we observe ourselves, we may begin to see that our body language is expressing feelings and emotions that we had not even realized were there.

> *Know Thyself.*
> Inscription, Temple of Apollo, Delphi.

FEELINGS AND EMOTIONS

It is through exploring our feelings and emotions that we really start getting to know ourselves deeply. We looked at ways of doing this before, in the chapter on Metta Bhavana. We saw there that the key is to acknowledge what we actually feel. Feelings are simple—just pleasure or pain, strong or weak. Our emotions are responses to feeling. Emotions can be more difficult to observe since they are so often complex, not to say complicated! But if we carefully watch our inner reactions to things, we'll see all the habitual tendencies operating—the continual pattern of feeling–response, feeling–response, feeling–response. We'll see the basic attraction to whatever gives us pleasure. Then we'll see our joyful (or perhaps greedy) response to the pleasurable thing. (That is, if we can have it!—If we can't have it, we might start getting grumpy or depressed.) We'll see our basic repulsion from anything that gives us pain, and then maybe experience hatred—or perhaps a more serene, detached response. Attraction and repulsion, then, are the basic emotions—they are 'motions', urges to move either towards or away from an experience.

The human tendency is to 'cut off' if we feel inadequate to deal with an emotion. It is natural to feel uncomfortable with strong emotions like anger or sexual desire, and we may sometimes even pretend to ourselves that we do not experience them. Sometimes people become chronically distanced from their experience in that kind of way. Few of us are fully aware of our emotions. Each of us has a great deal of potential energy that is lying dormant, trapped in a web of unacknowledged emotions, energy that could be made available by 'owning' what we feel. But, liberating though it can be, experience of emotion is not enough on its own. The purpose of this kind of mindfulness, apart from simply getting more in touch with ourselves, is to cultivate skilful, creative responses. Through awareness, we can learn how to develop love and compassion in all that we do, and how to avoid the impulse towards negative emotions like craving or hatred. We can't change our feelings—pleasure and pain happen to us whatever we do—but we can learn to change the way we *respond* to our experiences.

One way that we can learn to be more emotionally creative is through awareness of our thinking. Thoughts and emotions are inseparable; each is a key to the other. And thoughts are far more than just ideas: **THOUGHTS**

> *Thought, I love thought.*
> *But not the jiggling and twisting of already existent ideas*
> *I despise that self-important game.*
> *Thought is the welling up of unknown life into consciousness,*
> *Thought is the testing of statements on the touchstone of the conscience,*
> *Thought is gazing on to the face of life, and reading what can be read,*
> *Thought is pondering over experience, and coming to a conclusion.*
> *Thought is not a trick, or an exercise, or a set of dodges,*
> *Thought is a man in his wholeness wholly attending.*[18]
>   D.H. Lawrence

Where do our thoughts come from, where are they going—and what *are* they? Very often we do not know what we are thinking, even though we spend long periods of time in thought. Thoughts are elusive things. They seem to come and go as they please, sometimes billowing forth like majestic clouds across the sky, or darting past us like tiny fish in a stream. With mindfulness practice, however, we can develop our ability to know what we are thinking—to spot specific thoughts, and know the direction our thoughts are pursuing. We can also learn to see how our thoughts are based in emotional attitudes—see how often, for example, our opinions are rationalizations of desires. This is what Lawrence means by 'testing statements on the touchstone of conscience'.

The clarification of ideas is vital to anyone's spiritual development. Because it develops our faculty of concentration, meditation practice brings us into closer contact with the ideas that already exist in our mind. We can then ask ourselves what we *really* think. When we observe our thoughts deeply, we will probably find that most of them are second-hand—they are a mishmash of other people's ideas (which are mostly second-hand too). We all take ideas from our parents, personal contacts, and from the media. Being aware of the 'mishmash' is the first step towards thinking more clearly and independently.

TUNING IN TO MINDFULNESS

This description of the Foundations of Mindfulness has had to be brief, but at least we now have some principles for creating better conditions for meditation. If we are aware of ourselves, we shall always be ready to meditate—in fact, we shall be ready for anything! And when we do sit to meditate it will be easier to establish concentration, because we will be in touch with our experience right from the beginning.

In practice, though, our experience can often seem 'all of a piece', and at first it isn't that easy to distinguish the different aspects of body, feeling, emotion, and thought. So a good method is to start with the most concrete part of ourselves—our body—and work 'inwards' to the subtler aspects of mind. Try the following, just as an exercise.

Take a little of your attention away from this reading, and focus it on your body. Take your awareness through the different parts of your body and experience whatever sensations you find there.

Feel the skin on your face, and the variety of different physical sensations there. You will probably find tensions and tinglings. Experience these sensations for a while, in a general sort of way. Then allow your attention to shift from the sensations in the eyes to those at the lips, then to the forehead and scalp in turn. As you do this, you may feel other parts of your body relaxing 'in sympathy'. Next, move down to your shoulders, upper arms, forearms, wrists, palms, fingers and thumbs. Then take your attention minutely down through the rest of your body—first the chest and abdomen, then round to the back and down the spine, then the hips, buttocks, thighs, knees, calves, ankles, feet, and toes, experiencing the sensations right down to the tingles on the soles of your feet.

Bodily awareness provides a 'way in' to awareness of feelings, emotions, and thoughts. When you are in touch with your body you are much more able to experience what you feel in terms of pleasure or pain. The physical sensation of sitting here, for example, may be quite pleasant. See whether it is or not. We also experience mental feelings—we find ideas pleasant or painful. You could ask yourself what feelings you are getting from reading this.

So let's say, to continue the exercise, that you are sitting here, aware of your body. This awareness leads you to realize that you are hungry—not ravenously so, but you are definitely a little peckish. There is almost no feeling connected with the hunger, but you can recognize a subtle unpleasantness. As you acknowledge this unpleasant feeling, you may also notice that you have a definite emotional response to it: one of easygoing contentment. Despite the slight discomfort you feel, you are quite happy to continue reading. Perhaps in other circumstances you might have responded with craving and thoughts of food. Or, unaware of your basic feeling, you might have become confused without knowing why, and lost your concentration on the reading. But, right now, you're perfectly happy to continue.

So the fact that you are in touch with your *body* allows you to tune in to your feeling; the fact that you are in touch with your *feeling* allows you to tune in to your emotion; the fact that you are in touch with your *emotion* allows you to tune in to your *thoughts*.

Mindfulness of emotions is intimately connected with mindfulness of thoughts. You might tend to regard thoughts as existing in their own purely rational sphere, but that is not so. According to the Abhidharma (the ethical psychology of Buddhism) our thought always has some emotional connection. When we get angry, we have angry thoughts. When we are greedy, we have greedy thoughts. When we are hungry, we tend to have thoughts about food. If we are relaxed and patient, the mind is flexible, and we are able to choose our thoughts.

Awareness of our emotions and thoughts are the two most important Foundations, because emotions and thoughts are the parts of our experience that we can change. We cannot change the fact that we have a body, or the nature of the body we have. Nor can we change our feelings. (We can choose what to experience through our senses but we can't determine how those experiences will feel.) But we *can* change our responses and we *can* clarify our thinking. Since our thoughts are themselves emotionally toned, it is emotion that provides the main working ground of mindfulness practice. Awareness of emotion teaches us how to respond in new ways, ways that promote our happiness and our development.

HOW TO WORK IN MEDITATION

APPRECIATING CONCENTRATED STATES OF MIND
We have considered some external factors that will help you establish an effective meditation practice. Now it is time to consider the meditation itself.

THE NATURE OF CONCENTRATION

Even if you have only tried the Mindfulness of Breathing once, you will probably have discovered something about the nature of concentration. Even if it was just for a split second, you probably experienced some clarity of mind. You therefore know what it *means* to be undistracted— what it is like to be without all the distractions, images, and thoughts which usually clatter away in the mind. A concentrated mind is happy; it is clear, like a blue summer sky. The more concentrated you become in meditation practice, the more you will find these distracted thoughts dissolving away. In fact when one is very absorbed in meditation there may be almost no thought at all.

We usually identify mental experience with thoughts. But the experience of meditation shows us that thinking is not necessarily the most important activity that happens in our mind. We may discover that our mind can be at its clearest, richest, and most refined when there is virtually no thought at all.

Sometimes when people with no experience of meditation hear of this they jump to the conclusion that it must be some kind of vacuous, blank state. A popular myth about meditation is that it involves 'making your mind go blank'. But thought-free awareness is a very positive and natural thing. It is certainly not confined to meditation—people sometimes experience it in activities which they love doing. Take gardening or painting, for example, or simply looking at something beautiful. We can get so happily absorbed, so 'wrapped up' in an activity, that thoughts simply do not arise—or, at least, very few thoughts arise. Our attention is partially withdrawn from the outside world, to the extent that we may not even notice when someone speaks to us. Awareness and thinking are distinct processes: we can be intensely aware of what we are doing, but hardly thinking at all about it. The same happens (in a more direct way) in meditation: we may be closely aware of the object of the practice, yet not be thinking about it.

THE ELEMENTS OF MEDITATION

This aspect of meditation has led to another myth—that it is about 'getting rid of thoughts'. It is true that irrelevant thoughts often distract us. But trying to get rid of thoughts, as a deliberate method, is not usually effective. There are many better ways of dealing with distractions.

But before we start looking at possible distractions and hindrances, it is useful to know roughly what we are aiming for. When we meditate, we should be looking for an absorbed, balanced, happy, concentrated state of mind. And it's helpful to have some expectation that this happy state of concentration is somewhere 'just round the corner', or 'just beneath the surface'. We may not actually come across it all that often—our mental states may be rather unpredictable—but nevertheless concentration is always there potentially. In fact there is always *some* degree of concentration present, even when we are distracted! If we have this attitude it is much more likely that deeper concentration will arise.

Meditation is like flying a glider, sailing with the wind, or surfing. We need to take the opportunities offered by the elements of meditation. We

need to ride the warm air currents, use the power of the wind, launch ourselves skilfully in and out of the waves. And if we are to do so, we must
be on the look-out for the wind and the waves. In other words we need to
be aware of the positive potential of the states that arise in our mind. We
need to be ready to 'ride' our mental states as they arise.

One example is pleasure and enjoyment. If we notice that we are experiencing a pleasant state of peacefulness—even if it is very slight—in
the midst of an otherwise dull or distracted state of mind, this feeling is to
be encouraged. We can allow this feeling to continue, and simply experience and enjoy it, as we concentrate on the object of our meditation.
We should avoid getting distracted by the feeling—perhaps 'hooking' it
on to some pleasant fantasy—and simply use it as a support for our concentration. There is a bright energy in pleasure that we can learn to channel into our practice, rather than allowing it to divert our attention.

Similar to this is inspiration—the deep joy and excitement we feel as a
result of developing through meditation—which can even be felt physically, in the form of 'goose-pimples' and 'rushes' of pleasure. Again, we
can encourage this, include it as an aspect of our concentration. Another
kind of recollection that can aid our concentration is the more sober,
patient kind of determination—we feel deeply that we want to meditate,
that we don't want to be distracted, that we want to grow and develop.
This kind of motivation can be profoundly moving. Another such aid can
be the sense of concentration itself. As they grow, concentration and
clarity of thought have their own distinct feeling-tones which we can
learn to recognize and encourage.

We shall be looking at these elements in more depth later on. We need to
get to know these allies of meditation—to anticipate them, to utilize their
aid, and to ride upon their positive influence. The more use we make of
these allies, the less we shall have to be concerned with the hindrances to
meditation.

HINDRANCES TO MEDITATION

Paying attention to just one thing, as we do in meditation, is not always
easy. There is often a semi-conscious resistance from those parts of ourselves which want to stay in the ordinary sense-world and do other
things. There are five recognizable kinds of hindrance to concentration,
and everyone experiences all of them from time to time. If you know what
they are, you can recognize them when they arise—perhaps before they
take you over!

The five hindrances are: (1) desire for sense experience, (2) ill will, (3)
restlessness and anxiety, (4) sloth and torpor, (5) doubt and indecision.

(1) DESIRE FOR SENSE EXPERIENCE

Desire for sense experience is the most basic kind of distraction. We aren't particularly interested in the meditation, and so our mind keeps getting drawn back to the sense-world. We haven't yet learned how to find pleasure in concentration, so we can't help looking for it in pleasurable sense experiences. If we hear a sound, it seems so interesting that we start listening to it. We may open our eyes and start looking at all the amazing colours and textures on the wallpaper, or start stroking our limbs, enjoying the sensations. If an idea arises, it fascinates us and we want to explore it more.[19] We may have many pleasant thoughts about our world—about what we could be doing this evening, about what we could have to eat, or ideas we have recently read about. These impulses are perfectly natural in themselves—but they make concentration impossible.

(2) ILL WILL

Ill will is a variant of the previous hindrance: this time our interest is stuck in some *painful* experience. We are irritated—by something or someone—and we really can't let it go. We can't stop thinking about the way we have been mistreated and about what we'd like to say, or do, to even the score. Or maybe there is some external sound, or smell, which irritates us so much that we cannot stop thinking about it. Perhaps some idea or opinion has struck a wrong note, and we feel we must analyse all its faults in detail. So long as this is going on, it is impossible to concentrate our minds on anything else.

(3) RESTLESSNESS AND ANXIETY

Restlessness and anxiety gives us no peace—we cannot settle down and concentrate our mind. We need to slow down. We are 'speedy', going too fast. Either the body is restless and fidgeting, or the mind is anxious—or both are happening at the same time! A restless body and mind might be the result of insufficient preparation. Maybe we sat down to meditate too soon after some stimulating activity; or maybe there is a lot on our mind at present; perhaps there is something weighing on our conscience. If we can work patiently with this situation, meditation practice itself will eventually harmonize such conflicts.

(4) SLOTH AND TORPOR

With sloth and torpor the hindrance to our concentration is dullness of mind. We feel tired, and our body feels heavy. There is vacuity in the mind (that's the torpor) and heaviness in the body (sloth). Sometimes physical sloth can be so overwhelming that our head nods or we start snoring! The causes for this hindrance may lie simply in physical or mental tiredness, or our digestion may be coping with the onslaught of a recent meal. But it sometimes seems that psychological factors may be involved—perhaps the resistance has arisen due to some unacknowledged emotion. Again, it could also be a reflex of the previous hindrance, restless mental activity leading to exhaustion! We may sometimes alternate between restlessness and dullness, both in and out of meditation. If so, this demonstrates a need to find some new kind of balance.

Can *I*, with all *my* problems, hope to get anywhere with meditation—especially with *this* meditation? Is this *kind* of meditation practice really any good?—Can it actually do anything for me? Is this *teacher* any use?—Does he really know what he's talking about? And how would I know, anyway?

(5) DOUBT AND INDECISION

All this is doubt—and it is also indecision, since in this state of mind we cannot make up our mind and get on with the concentration. We end up prevaricating, 'sitting on the fence'—we lose our motivation. Doubt, in this sense, is a very serious hindrance to meditation.

There is nothing wrong with the sincere doubts that we are sure to have about meditation and its effects. There is bound to be a degree of uncertainty in our mind; some things can only be found out from experience. To a certain extent we have to take what we are told on trust and discover the truth through our own experimentation. But we can do that only by giving ourselves wholeheartedly to our experimenting. The doubting, over-sceptical frame of mind might often stem from *self*-doubt, or a rationalization of self-doubt. We can hardly expect to concentrate without some confidence that we will be able to do it—at least eventually.

BALANCING EFFORT IN MEDITATION

These five hindrances are a useful checklist for assessing how a session of meditation is going. Unless we are in a fully concentrated state, we can be certain that one or more of the hindrances is present. The most important thing is to recognize the hindrance *as* a hindrance, for once it is recognized as such we can take some action to counteract it.

LEARNING FROM THE HINDRANCES

Very often the act of recognition will itself weaken the hindrance, because it immediately reminds us that the aim of the meditation is to concentrate. However, there may be some tendency to avoid the recognition. Most people's hindrances have their own style of 'protection' built into them. Sloth and torpor, for example, may succeed in completely walling itself off from our recognition. It's like when we don't want to get up in the morning: our mind firstly doesn't want to know and, secondly, can keep finding good 'reasons' for lying in, just for another five minutes. When we're taken over by ill will, we probably won't want to stop picking on faults and running our minds over all the painful, unpleasant things that have happened to us. And our doubts can immediately fulfil their own prophesies: 'I can't do it' … 'There. I *knew* I wouldn't be able to do it!'

We need to recognize clearly that we are entertaining a hindrance to concentration. There are many 'tricks and tips' that can help us re-engage with the meditation—not to mention the earlier advice about looking for the positive qualities of concentration (see page 50). You can read about these in detail in the Appendix, but the basic principles are as follows.

PRINCIPLES FOR WORKING AGAINST THE HINDRANCES ACKNOWLEDGEMENT

The first principle is acknowledgement that the hindrance is actually there. It's no good carrying on meditating regardless, trying to ignore it and wishing that it would go away. That approach just leads to headaches and sloth and torpor! You need to take responsibility for the hindrance. You should accept that for the time being this is *your* hindrance and that you need to do something about it.

In meditation, you need to acknowledge each new mental state as it arises.

FAITH IN ONE'S POTENTIAL

Guilt can be a problem for some of us. Many people don't like to think that *they* could experience emotions like hatred, or animal-like cravings for food and sex. Yet when their meditation experience forces them to acknowledge that in fact they do, they may feel unduly bad about it. Such an attitude is not only extreme and unrealistic; it also blocks the possibility of progress. In meditation, particularly, we need to cultivate a positive view of ourselves, to have faith in our spiritual potential. This may require some reflection on our part. But since we have the power to understand life and to choose how to act—at least potentially—then how can there be any real doubt that, with the right kind of effort, we can make spiritual progress?

WORKING FROM THE GROUND UP

The principle of working from the ground up is connected with preparation—we can never make progress without having established a *basis* for that progress. If we want to concentrate our mind, we need to have established a *general* awareness of ourselves before we can generate a *particular*, more intense awareness of the meditation object. Then, if we lose our single-pointed concentration, we can establish it again by reconnecting with the more generalized mindfulness of body, feelings, emotions, and thoughts.

CREATIVE USE OF ANTIDOTES

There are a number of ways in which we can work against the hindrances.
The first is to **consider the consequences** of allowing the hindrance to

increase unchecked. What if we simply did nothing about our tendency to distraction, to hatred, or to doubt? Clearly, it would increase—our character would become progressively dominated by that trait. If we reflect on this, the importance of what we are doing may once again become clear, and the mind will be more inclined towards concentration.

The second is to **cultivate the opposite quality**. If there is doubt, cultivate confidence. If there is sloth, cultivate energy. If there is restlessness, cultivate contentment and peace. If the mind is too tight, relax it; if it is too loose, sharpen it. In other words, whenever a negative mental state gets in the way of our concentration, we try to cultivate some positive quality that overcomes or neutralizes it.

The third antidote is to **cultivate a sky-like attitude**. Sometimes the more we resist a particular mental state, the stronger it seems to get. If the previous two methods don't work, try the 'sky-like attitude': the mind is like the clear blue sky, the hindrances are like clouds. With this way of working, we accept the fact that the hindrance has 'got in', and simply observe it. We watch it play itself out in our mind—we watch the fantasies, the worries, the images—we watch whatever arises. We watch closely, but we try not to get involved. Getting involved only feeds the hindrance. If we observe patiently, without getting involved with the hindrance, it will eventually lose its power and disperse.

Fourthly, there is **suppression**. This is something of a last resort: we just say 'no' to the hindrance, and push it aside. This is most effective when the hindrance is weak, and when we are quite convinced of the pointlessness of playing host to it. If the hindrance is very strong—or if there is an element of emotional conflict—we may find that using this method creates unhelpful side-effects. Tension, lack of feeling, and mental dullness commonly result from an over-forceful approach. The best rule of thumb is therefore to use suppression only with weak hindrances. If we are in a positive, clear state of mind, it can be quite easy to turn such a hindrance aside.

Finally, there is **Going for Refuge**. Sometimes, we completely fail to deal with the hindrances; we spend the whole of a meditation session, or part of it, in a distracted state of mind. When this happens, it is important not to lose heart. We need to see that session of practice in the perspective of our overall development. Unconscious tendencies are strong in all of us, and sometimes there is bound to be struggle. We may need to remind ourselves that we did the best we could, that we made a sincere effort. Some good effects are certain to result from that effort, even though we didn't experience its fruits in that meditation! Going for Refuge is not so much a way of working against the hindrances as an attitude with which we try to connect *after* a meditation session. We need to reaffirm our commitment to our practice—in traditional terms, we need to go for Refuge—to our development of higher human qualities in the direction of Enlightenment (symbolized by the Buddha), to his teaching (the Dharma), and to all those who practise it (the Sangha).[20]

BALANCING YOUR EFFORTS

You will find more information later about ways of working in meditation. In the Appendix, for example, there is a detailed list of ways of counteracting specific hindrances. But you already have plenty of information to use. Just remember the basic points: recognize which hindrances are present, and when you work on them, do so in the spirit of the principles that have been mentioned, like acknowledgement and faith.

A MIDDLE PATH

You should make all these efforts in a balanced way—you need to tread a middle path between too much and too little effort. If you are too easygoing and lazy—if you don't make any particular effort to become concentrated, don't encourage positive qualities, don't bother to avoid the hindrances—you will tend to drift in a hazy, unfocused state of mind. That is one extreme. On the other hand, if you force yourself too hard you will tend to become rigid and inflexible. Later on, there will probably be some kind of reaction: force can lead to dullness or headaches. You can find a middle way between these two extremes by ensuring that there is just enough tension, and just enough relaxation. We need to sharpen our attention at some times, and relax it at others—relaxing when our mind feels too tight, sharpening when it feels too loose.

When we get beyond these hindrances and achieve a steady stream of balanced concentration, we will become especially relaxed and especially energized, both at the same time. When these two states—the bright, joyful energy, and the deep calm—arise together, we enter a state of absorption. This is a state of consciousness known traditionally as *dhyana* (Sanskrit, *jhana* in Pali). We shall be exploring the various levels of dhyana over the next few chapters.

SOME AUSPICIOUS SIGNS

Those who accomplish such good things as these
In every place unconquered do abide,
Moving in perfect safety where they will—
Theirs are the most auspicious signs of all.[21]
    The Buddha

If we practise regularly we will soon notice the benefits our meditation is having. We will probably see some signs of progress during our meditation itself—perhaps feeling unaccountably happy and peaceful. Ecstatic sensations of bliss may sometimes arise. We will also find outside meditation that we are happier, that our life seems to carry on more smoothly, more under our control. We will probably find that our thoughts and ideas are clearer, and that our outlook is more expansive and creative. We may even find that our dreams have become unusually vivid and colourful. These are all typical results of meditation.

Our progress may also show itself in less definite ways. We may simply notice that there seems to have been some kind of change, that an indefinable 'something' is happening. It may even be the response of other people that brings it to our attention—we may find people are more attracted towards us than before. Perhaps they can sense that we are more inwardly free and content.

These inner changes may also present us with some challenges. Meditation can stir up a wealth of rich new feelings and emotions, and we may be unsure of what to do with them. We may well start seeing our life very differently and may feel like making some fundamental changes. Such experiences are to be welcomed; they show us that we are breaking through some of our basic psychological limitations. It is important, though, that we understand what is happening. Meditation really can change people's lives, and we need to participate willingly and actively in the process of change—if that's what we want. If we don't actually want to change—perhaps we just wanted something to help us relax after work—no harm is being done, but we should be aware that the meditation we are practising is essentially about spiritual transformation, and that its effects will go deep.

SOME EXPERIENCES

A book about meditation might be useful, but it's no substitute for a teacher. So it seems a little hazardous to write about the variety of experiences that may arise in the course of taking up meditation. It could be rather like thumbing though a medical textbook. You might seem to have some of the symptoms—and you might then, perhaps, arrive at some rash conclusions! When you encounter something in your practice that you don't fully understand (which you will, sooner or later), it is best to consult someone who is more experienced.

But books, like this one, do have their uses. So as you read, just bear in mind that each person is unique, and that general statements can apply only in a general way.

What does it mean, for example, if we find ourselves experiencing beautiful colours, marvellous patterns, voices, or other sounds in our meditation? The general term for such experiences (which are common—*especially* for new meditators)—is *samapatti*.[22] Experiences like these can certainly seem very mysterious and exciting. Yet they are of no great significance. What seems to happen is that we achieve a good level of concentration, so that we are no longer aware of our body and sense-impressions. But it is as though our senses still insist on trying to operate, in spite of the fact that they are now disconnected from the physical world. So we experience strange distortions of sight, sound, smell, touch, or taste, as the sense-organs reel, deprived of their normal place in the world. Since there are many kinds of sense experience, there is a huge variety of these *samapatti* experiences. You may feel as though your body has become enormous—as large as a house, a mountain, or even a galaxy. Or you may feel tiny, microscopic. You may feel as though you have been turned upside down, or that you are now sitting facing the opposite way. Or you may experience your body in terms of some totally indescribable physical sensation. Usually these experiences are pleasant, if rather odd.

A *samapatti* experience like this is generally a good sign. At least it shows that your concentration has become independent of your sense experience—though you may equally well *not* experience any *samapattis* at that stage. Eventually these signs will pass, as you enter a smoother phase of the concentration.

For new meditators, the natural tendency is to get rather excited and think that they are about to gain some amazing spiritual insight. Perhaps this is Enlightenment! But actually they are experiencing a very ordinary stage of concentration. So acknowledge—and enjoy—the experience, while continuing to focus on the object of the practice. The occurrence of *samapattis* is a matter of temperament—many people never experience them at all. Apart from showing that a certain level of concentration has been reached, they are no indication of spiritual progress. So don't think in terms of encouraging them—*or* discouraging them.

SOME DIFFICULTIES

Sometimes people can lose interest in meditation—even though the practice seems otherwise to be going well. Let's say that your Mindfulness of Breathing meditation is fairly concentrated—you manage to count from one to ten every time, you never lose touch with the breath, even in the later stages—yet you don't actually *enjoy* it much—you don't find it particularly inspiring. In fact, you have started to find it rather boring—you practise harder and harder, but nothing ever seems to happen. You may feel both sad and irritated about this, because you really want to meditate, want to make progress—but it is all starting to become a chore.

This sort of difficulty can occur if you tend to see your practice rather narrowly in terms of concentration, and it has become merely an exercise in 'staying with the breath'. Or it may have nothing to do with the Mindfulness of Breathing practice specifically. It may be that your approach to any meditation practice has become somewhat dry and lacking in feeling—it's concerned with 'getting results' rather than engaging in the moment-by-moment process of the practice. At such times you need to appreciate the emotional side of concentration. You need to involve yourself in the concentration with more feeling—the Metta Bhavana practice could possibly help. Or maybe you need a retreat. You may simply need to talk to someone about your meditation. But however you do it, *inspiration* is what is lacking, and that is what you somehow need to regain.

Another common difficulty occurs if you start to view the meditation object as though you were an outside observer, thus distancing yourself from the process of meditation. Instead of the object itself (the tactile sensation of the breathing, for example) we experience only a *thought* about it. This is rather a dead-end, and a clear case for 'cultivating the opposite'. You need to concentrate on the experience, not the thought, of the breath. Perhaps you have uncovered a general tendency. Ask yourself whether this happens outside meditation as well. It may be that you are generally in the habit of mediating your experience through thoughts. Of course, in itself there is nothing wrong with thinking, but in this case the thoughts seem to be obscuring other aspects of your experience. So you need to develop more awareness of the basics—your bodily sensations, feelings, and emotions. Don't get stuck in your head! A little physical exercise can often help reassert this kind of balance. More contact with others, and Metta Bhavana meditation, will probably help too.

BEGINNER'S MIND
A man never flies so high as when he knows not where he is going.
Oliver Cromwell

This has been a practical chapter. In getting down to the 'nuts and bolts' of meditation practice it is possible that we could get lost in techniques and miss the essential spirit. While it is important to clarify what we are trying to achieve in the practice, at the same time it will help if we can retain our 'beginner's mind'. A newcomer to meditation often has an attitude of openness and faith which enables them to make very rapid progress. He or she has no preconceptions about what they are likely to achieve through meditation. Even advanced meditators need to find this kind of freshness in their approach—we all need to remain capable of learning something completely new.

If your mind is empty, it is always ready for anything; it is open to everything. In the beginner's mind there are many possibilities; in the expert's mind there are few.

…When we have no thought of achievement … we are true beginners. Then we can really learn something.[23]

Suzuki Roshi

Part Two

PRINCIPLES

·

THE PRINCIPLES OF TRANQUILLITY AND INSIGHT

·

IN PART TWO, THERE IS A CHANGE IN THE EMPHASIS OF THIS BOOK—THE NEXT TWO
CHAPTERS LOOK AT THE PRINCIPLES THAT UNDERLIE MEDITATION, RATHER THAN PRACTICE.
When you first learn to meditate there is no need for any special
knowledge, apart from understanding the basic instructions in
meditation. The important thing is simply to put what you have learned
into practice. Sooner or later you can decide whether or not you wish to
continue meditating indefinitely.
But once you have made a firmer commitment to your practice, it is a
good idea to learn a little of the theory behind Buddhist meditation.
Then, when you are ready to go more deeply into things, you will have
the necessary foundation of knowledge. An overview of the Buddhist
Path will help give you confidence in what you are doing.
This part of the book is therefore more concerned with the underlying
principles of Buddhist meditation. If you find some sections too technical
for your taste, then just skip them for the time being.
PART THREE deals again with practical methods—methods that are
relevant to more experienced meditators. Some of the ideas in
Part Three will make more sense if the principles explained here in
Part Two are understood.

·

Chapter Four

HIGHER CONSCIOUSNESS

THE PROCESS OF INTEGRATION

Here perpetual incense burns;
The heart to meditation turns,
And all delights and passions spurns.

A thousand brilliant hues arise,
More lovely than the evening skies,
And pictures paint before our eyes.

All the spirit's storm and stress
Is stilled into a nothingness,
And healing powers descend and bless.

Refreshed, we rise and turn again
To mingle with this world of pain,
As on roses falls the rain.[24]
  Sangharakshita

Sometimes when we meditate we may find blissful feelings arising spon-taneously. Such feelings can range from mild pleasure and joy to an almost overwhelming ecstasy—the experience can sometimes be so beautiful that we shed tears. People often blush, find their hair standing on end, or feel 'goose-pimples'. What is more, their ability to concentrate may enter a completely new dimension of lucidity and calmness. Whatever is happening? In psychological terms, they are directly ex-periencing what is known as the process of *integration*: somewhere, dis-parate parts of the psyche are combining into a whole.

  In spiritual terms, we are beginning to enter a higher state of conscious-ness—the first of four preliminary levels of dhyana enumerated by

Buddhist tradition—which is experienced as a deep inner harmony. It is the transition to this harmony which is so blissful.

Before I explain the nature of dhyana any further, it will be useful for us to understand how the process of integration takes place, to see the connection between dhyana and our day-to-day states of mind—which may not always be filled with bliss and inner peace! More often our mind resembles a battleground of contradictory likes, dislikes, hopes, and fears.

Practising mindfulness, whether in formal meditation or outside of meditation, is likely to reveal paradoxes and oppositions in our character. It's almost as though we are not one person—as though we have a number of different 'selves'. We may, for example, behave quite differently when we are at work, when we are at home, and when we are with particular sets of friends.

This is the case with everyone (to different degrees, and in different ways) and is perfectly natural. We probably even choose our activities and friends precisely because they allow us to express different sides of our personality. However, the fact that we do so indicates something of an imbalance, though we may not immediately see things that way.

Imagine you are walking along with a neighbour, someone with whom you are on friendly terms. On the way, quite by chance, you meet another friend from work. These two people have never met before; both know *you* quite well, but each knows you in a different context. The personality that your workmates see every weekday probably differs in certain respects from your 'off duty' personality around the home. Each friend may actually see you quite differently, and expect different behaviour of you. Such an encounter may feel rather odd, since you may find it difficult to live up to both sets of expectations at once.

This example illustrates a way in which we may sometimes detect a hint, at least, of hidden divisions within the mind. We do not usually notice such blind spots ourselves, unless they are pointed out to us. It is rather as though we have many different selves or, rather, different 'subpersonalities', which influence the mind in different ways at different times. Sometimes it is as if we had a whole coach full of these different characters, and each of them wants to take over the driving! Inconsistencies and conflicts like these are at the root of much of the psychological tension that we experience in day-to-day living. They can be very strong—so when the tension bound up in conflict is released through meditation, it's no wonder that blissful feelings and clarified concentration can arise.

However, these dhyana-like feelings, enjoyable as they are, are not the aim of meditation. At this stage they usually last for only a few sessions at most, so it may be tempting to chase them—we'll probably want to get them back! But such an approach is likely to stir up distracted meditations. Dhyana is a *by-product* of the integration process—it's what we feel when inner conflicts come to a head and are resolved. It is only natural that for a while afterwards we no longer experience quite the same intensity of pleasure, as the leading edge of our practice once again gets to work on the less integrated departments of our mind. For the time being our meditation will be more or less 'back to normal'. Yet the general tone of our practice, in terms of concentration and emotional engagement, will now be established at a new level. And, provided we keep practising, we should be able to maintain that new level.

BREAKING DOWN THE WALLS

Integration is an interesting phenomenon. It's as though our life used to go on in several different 'compartments' at once, and now the momentum of our practice has started to remove some of the separating walls. We have begun to harmonize the contrary aspects of our character, together with the thoughts and emotions that are associated with them— and which, no doubt, often arise as hindrances to concentration.

On the whole we can actually see the changes that are happening; they are all more or less at the surface of our mind, all on the same horizontal plane. But sometimes meditation can penetrate deeper than this. Sometimes we may go beyond the hindrances altogether and transcend the world of the senses and the ordinary mind. This is when we enter the state of absorption (dhyana) in the fullest sense. When we enter into absorption at this deeper level, some of the contents of our subconscious mind will come 'up' into our consciousness. This marks the beginning of a 'vertical' aspect to the process of integration.

HORIZONTAL AND VERTICAL INTEGRATION

This second aspect of integration is called 'vertical' because we are getting into contact with our heights and our depths—we are discovering our heavens and our hells. At this stage a completely new order of emotions, thoughts, and pictorial images may be released into our consciousness. They may be connected with significant past experiences: happy childhood memories, or perhaps painful experiences that have long been forgotten. They may well be vision-like: sometimes people see divinely beautiful or awe-inspiring forms such as gods, demons, Buddhas, or symbolic images. Such experiences have a very different character to the *samapattis* (distortions of sense-perception that can occur at the edges of deeper concentration, described in Chapter Three). These are more like visionary experiences—universal images coming from the heights and

Consciousness level	Characterized by	
Ordinary consciousness	• Desire for sense experience • Ill will • Sloth and torpor • Restlessness and anxiety • Doubt and indecision	• Mental factors in conflict • Energy blocked • Emotional clinging to hindrance
Access concentration	No gross hindrances present	• Enjoyment • Co-operation of mental factors • Concentration easier • More energy available • No strong emotional pull towards hindrances
First dhyana	(Described later)	(Described later)

depths in our mind, such as the archetypes described by Carl Jung, who particularly mentions the Shadow, the Hero, the Anima and Animus, and the Wise Old Man. Images like these are commonly experienced in deep meditation. Clearly, there is much hidden energy and creativity in the depths, waiting to be activated through meditation.

GETTING TO KNOW THE DHYANAS

ACCESS CONCENTRATION

Getting rid of these five hindrances is like having a debt remitted ... it is passing from a famine-stricken country into a land of prosperity. It is like living in peace and safety in the midst of violence and enmity...[25]
   Chi-I

The experience of dhyana begins to emerge at the point in our meditation when the five hindrances start to die away. This point is known as *access concentration* (Pali *upacara samadhi*): we now have 'access' to the dhyanas.

It is extremely useful if we can recognize whether or not we have reached this stage in our meditation. We will know that we are 'in access' when the concentration has become significantly easier. At this point our thoughts and emotions will start co-operating with our efforts to concentrate, instead of continually pulling us away from it. We will still experience some distractions, but these will not exert a strongly *emotional* pull, as do the five hindrances.

This new situation provides us with a significant opening. Since distracting thoughts now have less power over us, we have more free energy available. This allows us to notice distractions more quickly, before they have time to take hold; it is therefore easier to disengage from them. Reducing the level of distracted mental activity frees even more energy—which further sharpens our awareness. We are entering into an expansive, progressive phase; indeed, this is the beginning of meditation proper.

CULTIVATING HIGHER CONSCIOUSNESS

The term 'access concentration' doesn't just mark a cross-over point between the ordinary mind and dhyana. It describes quite a broad band of consciousness, ranging from the point at which we are concentrated but still frequently slipping back into distraction (i.e. almost in the hindrances) to a state in which concentration is extremely easy (almost in dhyana).

This stage is within the reach of everyone who meditates regularly—it is not so very far away from our ordinary state of mind. If we know how to recognize access concentration, we can then learn how to encourage and dwell in it for as long as possible. The longer we can *sustain* access concentration, the more we are likely to move on into full concentration—that is, into the first dhyana.

The first level of dhyana is, again, within fairly easy reach of anyone who meditates regularly. We are likely to experience at least a taste of it within the first few weeks of taking up meditation—particularly if we 'treat' our practice to some time on a retreat.

Just now we noted that it isn't helpful to cling on to the *pleasure* of dhyanic experiences, should they arise. But that does not mean that dhyana ought not to be deliberately cultivated. On the contrary, it is important that we do so. We should definitely aim to develop higher states of consciousness—the benefits, in terms of our growth in maturity and insight, will be considerable. We can cultivate dhyana in the ways that have already been outlined—by concentrating mindfully on the object of meditation, by acknowledging the hindrances, and by working with them with faith and confidence. As with the hindrances and access concentration, *recognition* is an important key. It will be very useful if we can learn how to recognize different aspects of the dhyana state, so that we can encourage them to arise.

So how *can* we recognize them? Perhaps it is easiest to communicate the experience through images—just as the Buddha himself described the levels of dhyana:

IMAGES OF HIGHER CONSCIOUSNESS

> *As a skilful bathman or his apprentice will scatter perfumed soap powder in a metal basin, and then besprinkling it with water, drop by drop, will so knead it together so that the ball of lather, taking up the unctuous moisture, is drenched*

with it, pervaded by it, permeated by it within and without, and there is no leakage possible....

His very body does he so pervade, drench, permeate, and suffuse with the joy and ease born of concentration, that there is no spot in his whole frame not suffused therewith.[26]

(1) The experience of the first dhyana is compared to soap powder and water being mixed thoroughly together—mixed until the soap powder is entirely saturated by the water and the water is completely pervaded by the soap powder.

(2) Being in the second dhyana feels like a calm lake being fed by an up-welling underground spring.

(3) The third dhyana feels as though lotuses and water-lilies are growing in that lake, soaked and saturated by its water.

(4) The fourth dhyana is like the experience of taking a bath in that lake on a very hot afternoon, and afterwards resting on the bank wrapped in a perfectly clean white cloth.

Notice how water, a universal symbol for the unconscious mind, links the images together into a series. In the **first dhyana** the water is perfectly mixed with its opposite element, dry powder. This image of opposites mingling perfectly together reflects the theme of integration; we have already seen how, in our consciousness, there are all kinds of oppositions in need of integration. Oppositions like our emotionality and rationality, 'masculinity' and 'femininity', consciousness and unconsciousness, introversion and extroversion, are now all beginning to co-exist in harmony.

Dhyana is an experience of pure happiness, pure in the sense that it has not been caused by anything external but comes from within our own mind. While it lasts, it makes us feel truly ourselves. We may feel the effects of this 'perfect mingling of opposites' for some time—hours, even days or weeks—after the meditation.

Yet dhyana may not necessarily arise as a result of applying a particular meditation technique. It is a state of mind that occurs naturally in anyone who is extremely happy. Under special conditions it may be possible to dwell in dhyana outside meditation for sustained periods of time. (We will discuss some of these special conditions later on.) As a general rule, higher states of consciousness will arise naturally in our meditation if we are quite happy and free from guilt feelings.

In the **second dhyana**, our concentration is so pure that we experience no thought whatever. Thoughts did occur back in the first dhyana, of course, but even there they were minimal, and they were mostly thoughts about the meditation object. So as we cross over from the first into the second dhyana we find ourselves in a far more lucid absorption which—apart from a subtle recognition of the state we are in—is completely without thought.

Outside of meditation, it is unlikely that the second dhyana will simply arise on its own, spontaneously—but it isn't impossible. Apart from meditators, there could conceivably be great artists, composers, or philosophers in the world who dwell in this sort of state frequently, even without meditating formally at all. The second dhyana is thus a very inspired state of mind—we are sustained by an inner flow of inspiration which wells up inside us, like the constant trickling of an underground spring beneath the calm surface of a lake.

In Classical times, artists and poets in need of inspiration would call upon the Muses, goddesses who personified different aspects of this higher nourishment. At times, inspiration may be felt as a powerful unification with forces that are normally viewed as 'outside' our conscious personality. So this dhyana level is also the mental state of the inspired prophet, who receives 'messages' from a deeper level of consciousness.

The **third dhyana** is compared to lotuses growing in the waters of the lake, completely surrounded by and soaked in the medium of water. In our progress through the dhyanas we become more and more integrated with the higher element of inspiration (which in the second dhyana is experienced as just trickling into our consciousness). By the time we reach the third dhyana the stream has greatly expanded until it has become our whole environment. This is a very rich experience of 'vertical' integration. In this third dhyana, we feel as though we are part of something much greater than our conscious self. It is a mystical state, in which we are completely surrounded, pervaded, and 'at one with' a higher element.

The **fourth dhyana** is the perfection of human happiness—or, at least, happiness this side of Enlightenment. This attainment doesn't endow us with any ultimate wisdom or compassion—we could still act unethically, even now, and fall back in our progress. However, even though we don't possess the fullness of insight, we are in the best possible state of mental health. In the fourth dhyana all the powerful energies that have been tamed and liberated through previous meditation co-exist in perfect harmonious peace. Notice how the Buddha changes his style of imagery at this point. A immaculate being appears, secure from harmful influences through being wrapped in the pure white cloth. It is as though the inspired state of consciousness, thoroughly purified through experience of the other dhyanas, is now ours to wear and to take with us, as both a protection and an outward influence upon the world. We are so happy

The spectrum of dhyana factors

Cognitive—'cool'	One-pointedness
	Initial thought
	Applied thought
Emotional—'warm'	Rapture
	Bliss
	Equanimity (in fourth dhyana)

that our positivity radiates outward, counteracting harmful influences—affecting others too, so that we become charismatic and even magical. This is why the fourth dhyana is regarded as the basis for the development of 'magical' powers (walking on water, passing through walls, etc. attributed to practitioners of many religions)—and amazingly acute faculties of perception.

RECOGNIZING HIGHER CONSCIOUSNESS THROUGH THE FIVE DHYANA FACTORS
THE SPECTRUM OF DHYANA FACTORS

Images like the underground spring may help us recognize dhyana from our own experience. But a checklist of its main 'component parts'—the mental states of which dhyana consists—will also come in useful.

As though it were a brilliant rainbow of higher consciousness, we can view dhyana as a 'spectrum' of positive mental states, all of differing hues and shades. Tradition enumerates five of these positive mental states, known as 'dhyana factors' (Sanskrit *dhyananga*)—plus a sixth which only emerges in the fourth dhyana. However, we should not think that dhyana consists only of these factors, for we will experience many other positive qualities too. These six are selected because they are characteristic of particular levels of dhyana.

We may imagine these dhyana factors as bands of red, orange, yellow, green, blue, and indigo light. Dhyana is both a 'warm' state of positive emotion and a 'cool' state of increased concentration—and within this spectrum there are three 'warm' and three 'cool' colours, indicating the three predominantly emotional, and the three predominantly cognitive, factors of dhyana.

In the 'cool' portion are the cognitive faculties of one-pointedness, initial thought, and applied thought. **One-pointedness** is our ability to pay attention (which is especially strong in the dhyana state). Initial thought and applied thought are aspects of clear thinking. **Initial thought** is thinking 'of' something. For example, out of all the millions of possibilities, we might think of our friend George. As we call George to mind, some kind of thought or image which represents him arises in our consciousness. **Applied thought** is when we think 'about' George. We explore our general idea of him more, perhaps wonder how he is, and what he might be doing now.

'Initial thought' and 'applied thought' are simple categories for analys-
ing the way we think. Like one-pointedness, they obviously occur outside
dhyana too—we are thinking 'of' and 'about' things all the time. But in
dhyana our thinking is wonderfully lucid and almost entirely under our
conscious control.

In the 'warm' portion of the spectrum are the feelings of rapture and
bliss that were spoken of earlier. **Rapture** is when we experience the
process of integration as it were 'reflected' in bodily pleasure. It is
predominantly physical, though not entirely so—we feel both physically
thrilled and wildly happy at the same time. Traditionally there are supposed to be five degrees of intensity of rapture! We will probably recognize the first stage, which is the sensation of 'goose-pimples'—when the
hairs on our body become erect with pleasure. The second stage is even
more intensely enjoyable: the rapture descends on us in little shocks, like
repeated flashes of lightning. In the third, it washes over us again and
again, like waves breaking on the seashore. The fourth quickly floods
every part of our body, like a huge volume of water suddenly invading a
sea-cave. The fifth, according to tradition, is so intensely joyful that it
transports us bodily into the air: it is the 'miraculous' phenomenon of
levitation.

So if rapture is such a powerful experience, what can bliss be like? **Bliss**
is more subtle than rapture—but though less dramatic it is, in its own
'quiet' way, actually more intense. Rapture is traditionally compared to
the delicious feeling of anticipation we experience when we know that we
are about to obtain the very thing we have always wanted; bliss is more
like enjoying the satisfaction of actually possessing it. Bliss thus marks a
deeper stage of integration, in which our mind has begun to tame the
somewhat wild, unrefined sensations of rapture. With experience one becomes less attached to these relatively coarse feelings, and begins to move
into a deeper, stronger—and even more happy—state of mind.

The occurrence of rapture and bliss show that increased concentration is
an intensely enjoyable experience. It is interesting to see how bliss arises
out of rapture. As absorption takes a firmer hold, the experience of bliss
becomes larger, as it were, so that it increasingly 'contains' the feelings of
rapture. This process of containment is known as *passaddhi*, and it is
through increased *passaddhi* that the concentration will deepen further.
The deepening bliss gradually assimilates the bubbly, thrilling energy that
is released in the experience of rapture. The process of *passaddhi*[27] makes
one's mind pliable, flexible, and very easily worked with. It is a maturing,
strengthening quality, very characteristic of higher states of consciousness, and important in meditation generally.

Stepping from the
hindrances to the
dhyana factors

This dhyana factor	is brought into existence through developing	and transforms this hindrance
One-pointedness	Interest	Sense desire
Initial thought	Energy	Sloth and torpor
Applied thought	Commitment	Doubt
Rapture	Enjoyment	Ill will
Bliss	Peace	Restlessness and anxiety

**DEVELOPING THE
DHYANA FACTORS**

Since each of the five factors—initial thought, applied thought, one-pointedness, rapture, and bliss—is a component of dhyana, we can encourage the dhyana state to arise by developing those factors that seem to be missing from the experience. By developing a dhyana factor, such as one-pointedness of mind, we are simultaneously counteracting one of the five hindrances—sense desire, in this example—as shown in the table above.

This is how it can work: if you try to develop **one-pointed concentration**, your interest in objects of sense desire will begin to hold your attention less intensely. It is obviously more satisfying and enjoyable to be one-pointedly meditating than it is to be sitting there, supposedly meditating, but with your mind continually tossed here and there by sense desire. And, likewise, any ill will will have no choice but to subside if—through your efforts—**rapture** starts to arise. It is simply not possible to be angry and, at the same time, feel so wonderfully happy! There is less possibility of restlessness or anxiety taking hold if you have some sense of **bliss** in the meditation. Such a sense of bliss will begin to bestow a certain contentment. As that contentment grows, you will feel increasingly calmed and pacified, and the hindrance will subside. If you begin to clarify the objects of your thinking—if, in other words, you start arousing clear **initial thought** in the meditation—any mental torpor, and even physical sloth, may begin to lose its foothold. In meditation your thoughts can sometimes acquire such an abundance of energy and clarity that their inspirational power can eventually cut through the heaviest resistance. Finally, doubt—which can so stubbornly prevent you from involving yourself in the meditation—can be dissolved by introducing an element of **applied thought**. Remember that the hindrance of doubt is not 'honest' doubt but negative scepticism; and remember that the faculty of applied thought is not mere distracted thinking.

If you apply your thinking truthfully, you can see irrational doubts in clearer perspective. It is the nature of this more investigative thought not to allow any 'sitting on the fence', but to drive on towards a clearer examination of the meditation object.

In practice, of course, it may take some time to move from hindrance to dhyana factor—this depends on the strength of the hindrance. But if you know that there is a pathway that leads from one to the other you can have more confidence in your efforts to create the dhyana factor. And as you work you may be able to find 'intermediary' factors, such as those suggested in the middle column of the table opposite. For example, trying to arouse interest in the *practice*—rather than in the objects of sense desire—could be a first step towards shifting the emphasis of your attention more towards one-pointedness. Remember that our inability to pay attention usually depends on some emotional factor. We certainly have some emotional *investment* in the particular hindrance that we are stuck in—otherwise we could simply drop it and forget about it. If we first allow ourselves to experience what this investment feels like—experience its character—and then recall the character of the dhyana factor, it may be possible to 'unhook' our emotional energies from the hindrance and point them in the direction of the dhyana factors.

As soon as each of the five factors is strongly present, we enter the first dhyana level. If our concentration deepens still further, we may gain access to the other dhyana levels too. Each progressive stage of dhyana has a different ordering of dhyana factors. As concentration deepens, the cognitive factors tend to drop away and the emotional factors become progressively 'contained', as already described. This process continues until, in the fourth dhyana, a new 'emotional' factor—equanimity—arises. We shall see in the next chapter how the fourth dhyana is also the basis out of which a further four dhyanas—known as 'formless' dhyanas—may be developed.

THE CHANGING DHYANA FACTORS AT DIFFERENT LEVELS OF DHYANA

The traditional classification of dhyana levels is useful for defining higher states of consciousness in the abstract, but it is essentially an artificial way of looking at our experience. The dhyana factors provide us with a better, more experiential framework. For example we do not really experience 'the first dhyana' as we become free from the hindrances. We simply experience various positive mental states arising—in particular rapture, bliss, initial thought, applied thought, and one-pointedness. What happens is that these factors become stronger and then—as we enter further into meditation—thinking (first initial thought, and then applied thought) is left behind.

This is because discursive thought requires a state of mind which, compared with a higher state of consciousness, is unrefined; it also takes up a considerable amount of energy. Now, the energy that was previously taken up with thinking is free to flow directly on to the meditation object. At this point we find ourselves in that state of lucid, conceptless concentration traditionally classified as the second dhyana. From this stage

Progress of dhyana
factors through first
four dhyanas

	1st dhyana	2nd dhyana	3rd dhyana	4th dhyana
Cognitive dhyana factors	One-pointedness	One-pointedness	One-pointedness	One-pointedness
	Initial thought			
	Applied thought			
Emotional dhyana factors	Rapture	Rapture		
	Bliss	Bliss	Bliss	
				Equanimity

onwards we experience 'vertical' integration increasingly strongly. In terms of the Buddha's simile, this is the point when an underground spring begins percolating its way up from the depths. The spring of inspiration expands and broadens until, in the third dhyana, it becomes the entire medium in which we experience ourselves. The process of *passaddhi* has by now absorbed all the wildness of rapture into bliss, so that the only dhyana factors remaining are this peaceful bliss and one-pointedness. This process of purification continues into the fourth dhyana, at which point bliss is transformed into equanimity (*upekkha*). At this stage our mind goes beyond any possibility of conflict, and reaches a peak of emotional stability and purity. Our one-pointedness of mind becomes unshakeable, so that we can maintain the concentration undistractedly for as long as we wish.

RECOGNIZING
HIGHER
CONSCIOUSNESS
THROUGH THE WAY
WE PERCEIVE THE
MEDITATION OBJECT

Another approach that will help us become familiar with higher states of consciousness is to notice how we experience the object of our meditation at different levels. As we progress into the dhyanas, the way we *experience* the breath, or the metta—or whatever it is that we happen to be concentrating on—will undergo several noticeable changes.

It may seem that the object itself changes, but of course we are really witnessing a transformation in our own state of consciousness. Any change in our subjective state is reflected in our experience of what is 'out there'—if we are in a good mood, we'll perceive the external world as beautiful. The same goes for meditation experience—our perception of the meditation object reflects our state of mind. Since everything is filtered through our subjective mental states, we cannot say whether or not we perceive our meditation object *as it actually is*. But we certainly experience something: we experience some kind of *image* of the object. The technical term for this image-object is *nimitta* (literally, 'a sign'). Let's look at what happens to the *nimitta* as we enter the dhyana state.

Changes take place in the perceived meditation object during every kind of meditation practice—including the Mindfulness of Breathing and the Metta Bhavana. However, it is easier to explain what happens in the context of meditation practices in which we visualize something. So let us imagine that we are engaged in one of the *kasina* visualization practices. These simple visualization exercises were originally taught by the Buddha. If you wish, you may try something like this for yourself, though it is given here just as an example.[28]

A kasina is a disc of colour which we visualize in our mind—traditionally, the actual colour is chosen according to our temperament. Since it is easier to visualize the kasina when its colour is really bright and vivid, tradition recommends that an actual physical disc is made first of all—often out of flowers of the appropriate colour. There are other types of kasina too, like the fire kasina, in which one begins by gazing, through a round hole, at some flames.

As we concentrate on one of these discs, our concentration will eventually pass through the three levels of consciousness that have been mentioned—we eventually transform our ordinary sense-based consciousness into access concentration, and that into full concentration or dhyana. At each level of consciousness our experience of the disc undergoes a definite change.

We begin by positioning a disc of the appropriate type about a metre in front of our meditation seat. We then simply look at it. With our eyes open, we try to keep our attention continuously upon it, returning to it every time we notice we are distracted. Whatever we perceive as we look at the physical object with our physical eye is called the preparatory image (*parikamma-nimitta*). Once we have gained a fairly undistracted perception of this, we are said to have reached the first stage, that of preparatory concentration (*parikamma-samadhi*).

Then, closing our eyes, we try to visualize, internally, a replica of the preparatory image. This may take many attempts. If we persist, however, we shall eventually be able to perceive the coloured disc 'in our mind's eye'. At this stage, our perception of the object is known as the 'acquired image' (*uggaha-nimitta*). We now place our attention on this internally visualized image. When we manage to establish our attention on the acquired image—again, this may require much practice—eventually the level of access concentration (*upachara-samadhi*) will arise.

In access concentration there will occur a subtle but significant change in the appearance of the object. It may become lighter and, as it were, transparent. It may acquire new qualities which are not easy to describe—and which will vary considerably from person to person. A traditional text says that the new *nimitta* appears 'like the moon's disc appearing from behind a cloud', or as 'cranes (silhouetted) against a thunder-cloud', or, again, 'like a crystal fan set in space'.

Level of consciousnes	Type of object (*nimitta*)	Description
	e.g. the breath, emotional quality such as metta, visualized object, etc.	How we experience the object at each level
Ordinary consciousness On first taking up a meditation object, our concentration is generally scattered and characterized by the five hindrances	**Preparatory image** (*parikamma-nimitta*)	The basic object of the meditation that we take up, experienced as separate from oneself
Preparatory concentration (*parikamma-samadhi*) The stage at which some continuity of concentration has been established. The object now becomes more internalized as the hindrances are weakened	**Acquired image** (*uggaha-nimitta*)	A subjective mental impression of the object, experienced internally
Access concentration (*upachara-samadhi*) Concentration has settled easily on the acquired image, though it is not yet completely stable. Now the object begins to acquire a more 'image-like' character	**Reflex image** (*patibhaga-nimitta*)	Indescribable (see text)
Full concentration (*apana-samadhi* or dhyana) Concentration is now very stable. The dhyana factors (which appear weakly in access) now become strong and constant	**Reflex image** (*patibhaga-nimitta*)	Indescribable (see text)

We should not expect literally to see anything like this—these images were chosen to give a feeling for what happens, rather than a concrete representation—though the *nimitta* may have a visual aspect. At this stage our perception of the object has become the 'reflex', or 'counterpart' image (*patibhaga-nimitta*): we are experiencing a *subtle counterpart* of the original meditation object. We should now concentrate our full attention on this reflex image. As we sustain access concentration with this as our object, the dhyana factors of rapture and bliss, etc. will arise, and then we will enter the stage of full concentration, or dhyana (also known as *apana-samadhi*).

Some form of *nimitta*, some *image* of the object of concentration, will be perceived as we progress through these stages in any meditation practice. It may, however, not be a visual image. In the Mindfulness of Breathing, for example, the breath may simply acquire a special subtlety at the stage of access concentration. That would be a type of *nimitta*. On the other hand, there could be some indescribable visual-aural-tactile counterpart of the breath. It is very difficult, even impossible, to describe reflex images because they are purely mental; since they are not experienced through the physical senses, the usual modes of factual description do not exist. A simile or poetic image is the best that can be offered—the Buddha's image of mingled soap powder describes this kind of experience well.[29] In access concentration we are entering a realm in which we experience only mental form, not physical form. We are moving from the realm of the senses (known as the *kama-loka*) into the realm of purely mental form (the *rupa-loka*). More will be said about these modes of experience shortly.

Chapter Five

TRANQUILLITY AND INSIGHT

MEDITATION IS PART of a spiritual path which leads beyond ordinary human limitations. This 'path' does not consist of a series of external waymarks for us to follow. *We* are the path; the path is our development, the unfoldment of our own life in awareness. And this path begins, at some time or another, with questions.

What are we? What is humanity? What *is* this experience we call 'life'—and what is the point of it? Does it have any meaning or purpose, or is it all some kind of dream? Why do people suffer? Does anything determine the future? What happens when we die? How did we get here? How is it that we were born in *our* particular set of circumstances and others were born in theirs?

Many people wonder about such questions from early childhood onwards—but they come up against apparently insuperable barriers. If we were really capable of exploring these questions in depth, and coming to conclusions based on our own experience, there would be no problem; we would very soon comprehend 'life, the universe, and everything'. But it is hard to imagine anyone really capable of arriving at such definite conclusions. So when people find themselves up against these barriers, they may either be forced into accepting a religion which simply tells them what to believe, or they may cynically conclude that such questions are a waste of time. Neither answer is very satisfactory—and the inner conflicts still remain.

Fortunately Buddhism has a point of view which avoids both these extremes. Firstly, it provides *methods of practice*—meditation, the development of awareness, ethics, and spiritual friendship—through which we can develop our minds until we can see into these issues for ourselves. Then there are deeper, more metaphysical *teachings*, which can provide us with a provisional framework for getting to grips with such issues. These ideas are not offered as fixed dogma but simply as operational concepts—they are suggested ways of engaging with our existential dilemmas. We have already looked at a number of Buddhist methods of practice, so now we are going to look at a few of its teachings. First of all, we are going to explore how Buddhism sees the nature of existence.

OUR CONDITIONED NATURE

Some questions may reveal vast areas of unnamed, uncharted territory. One such question is 'How did we get to be as we are?' Apart from a few biological and psychological facts, we don't know much about how we got here, or why we are the kind of person we are. Each of us has his or her own set of attitudes and responses, likes and dislikes; each of us has a certain way of speaking, moving, looking at things. But how did that come about?

We can see how the course of our life has been influenced by many things. We are conditioned, for example, by our nationality, our religion, class, and gender—there are a large number of such conditioning factors. We are fairly passive in relation to most of them—we simply get born into a set of influences, and these influences incline us to act in certain ways. Later, we may modify these 'inborn' inclinations in response to new events that happen in our life. Throughout our whole life, this ongoing process of adjustment has been forming and re-forming our attitudes, likes, and dislikes.

Buddhism, too, sees existence in terms of conditioning. It takes a broad overview of life, and sees that the inclinations we form provide the conditions for future sets of circumstances to arise. In other words, our interests and emotional drives tend to get us into particular situations. We can see how often our friends get themselves involved in incidents which are somehow 'typical' of them. (Our friends may see that we do the same.) Our life is very much defined, and limited, by our conditioning. And even though external factors influence us, it is *we* who respond, and who modify our responses, to those external factors. We ourselves *create* our own conditioning.

According to Buddhism each of us is subtly re-conditioning ourselves in every thought-moment, and that process of 'becoming now this, now that' has been going on since beginningless time. The momentum cannot be stopped: we cannot simply stop acting. Even when we seem to be doing absolutely nothing we are still acting—we are still thinking, still making tiny semi-conscious decisions. In the space of a single hour, we carry out hundreds of minute physical deeds and react to circumstances with countless thoughts and emotions. Most of them, viewed separately, may be insignificant. But they work together: like different currents combining in a single river, a momentum builds up which propels us in some particular direction—at least for a while. Buddhism asserts that unless we break out of this, there will never be an end to conditioned existence: we will be bound to becoming now like this, now like that, for ever into the future.

Yet it is possible to change, or re-channel, the direction in which our actions are taking us. And, if we want, we can develop the capacity to break through these limitations completely. According to Buddhism it is possible to reach a state beyond all conditionings. This is what is ultimately implied by spiritual development: a release from every kind of self-imposed limitation, and a new kind of freedom. The highest level of spiritual attainment is the unconditioned or 'Enlightened' mind of Buddhahood. We may begin to realize the first glimmerings of this through the insight that we are not something separate from this process of becoming: that we *are* this momentum, nothing more—and nothing less. Such an insight can free us from the tendency to grasp selfishly onto things as 'ours'. So here, at least, is a kind of answer to the first question that was posed at the beginning: 'What are we?' We can say that we consist of a self-modifying flow of action which we can choose at any time to direct positively or negatively.

While there is immense disparity regarding the *degree* of choice available, all living beings are like this. One Buddhist scripture describes existence in terms of innumerable beams of coloured light, all criss-crossing and penetrating one another. All beings participate in a universe—*are* a universe—consisting of the currents and counter-currents created by all their actions, simultaneously influencing and being influenced by each other.

WE ALWAYS EXPECT PERMANENCE

It is quite easy for us to understand—in theory—that everything is subject to impermanence and change, but it is actually very difficult indeed to accept it in our own lives. We resist the idea emotionally. Our resistance to the truth of impermanence is the basic reason why life is so often frustrating. We tend to expect things to remain just as they are. We never want the things we enjoy to come to an end, or even to change in any way—but they always do. When our expectations are so unrealistic, frustration is inevitable. When things change, we can feel insecure, hurt, angry, embittered, and cynical.

These emotions are painful, and they create the conditions for more pain, both for us and for others. They can cause us to lash out blindly, automatically, to defend dubious pleasures and ward off imaginary threats. Yet the anger we sometimes feel does nothing to heal the pain (in fact, it makes it even worse), and our increased desires bear no relation to our actual enjoyment of pleasure—they just increase our sense of insecurity.

LIVING IN AN IMPERMANENT REALITY

And there is no way out—there is no escape from reality. Unless we can learn to sit more easily with the fact of impermanence, we are going to keep hurting ourselves and others. We need to realize that ending, renewal, death, birth, and change continue endlessly—and that it's actually a very good thing that they do. If it were not for impermanence nothing could ever happen! It is because of the very fact that life is so changeable that we can change ourselves.

With that understanding we hold the key to happiness; we are in a position to participate creatively in reality instead of seeing ourselves as passive victims of circumstances. The activities of a Bodhisattva, a person whose life is dedicated to Enlightenment for the sake of all sentient beings, are referred to in some Buddhist scriptures as 'play'. This does not mean that he or she doesn't take them seriously. The Bodhisattva is said to play in the realm of Reality because he enjoys it. He has accepted impermanence, and is able to participate joyfully in the fact of change.

WHAT WE DO, WE BECOME

We will change anyway, in one direction or another, whether we deliberately try to do so or not. We should be aware of the changes that are taking place in us now, and consider what changes could take place in future. According to Buddhism there are no limits to the extent that we can change, and no limits to the possible kinds of change. The whole universe is our field of spiritual development—or degeneration. We cannot help changing with every tiny act, becoming now like this, now like that. Over time, we have the potential to become anything from an Enlightened Buddha to a psychopath or some harmless animal. Of course developing into some of these states of being could take a very long time, from our present position. Traditional Buddhism has a very broad time-scale indeed, viewing the process of development from here to Enlightenment—or other forms of life—as normally taking place over several lifetimes.[30]

MODES OF CYCLIC EXISTENCE

We may view this process in various ways. According to the Tibetan Wheel of Life we can enter any of six 'realms' of existence. Apart from our present human state, we can in time become an animal (due to wilful stupidity), a 'hungry ghost' (through intense craving), a competitive Titan (through jealousy), a suffering hell-being (through hatred), or a divine being (through good deeds).

You may find the idea of hells, gods, and heavens quaint, off-putting, and even out of touch with reality. But here Buddhism is speaking the language of myth and archetype to communicate some general truths; the traditional modes of expression do not have to be taken completely literally.

Yet there is no reason why these should *not* be viewed as objectively possible states of existence—why it should not be possible to be reborn, for example, as an actual animal, or in an actual hellish realm. We know, unfortunately, that many such situations exist, even in our visible world. According to traditional Buddhist teaching, divine beings exist in some objective sense, though invisible to normal consciousness. In the Pali scriptures, we see the Buddha spending a significant part of his time teaching the *devas*. This, of course, runs counter to the popular scientific world-view that we all inherit—but since our world-view is the product of particular historical, religious, and philosophical conditionings, it may be limited in its perspectives, and in this area could be wrong. The existence of higher life-forms cannot be proved or disproved by scientific methods. Here Buddhism does not take its evidence from ordinary sense data but from the experience of higher states of consciousness acquired in meditation. From a common sense point of view, if one looks at the variety of known life forms it does not seem unreasonable that there could yet be more to be discovered.

The six realms may also be regarded as the mental states predominating in a particular human life situation. Viewed in these terms, we could imagine our mental state becoming fixed in animal sensuality, tight-fisted meanness, jealous competition, paranoid hatred, or delight and bliss.

I then said to him: Even in the present we are transmigrating, we go from birth to birth even when we are awake and this succession of births continues when we sleep. When after awaking and sleeping we come to death, how then should it be any different? As there are dreams in the night following the experiences of the day, so at our death, owing to the store of deeds committed, our karma leads on from life to life. It is like this: When you are enjoying with your wife,

then your mind is at animal level; but if she makes some mistake and you should want to kill her then you have sunk down into the Hells; while after forgiving and restoring harmony if a beggar comes and you give him alms, then that is heaven worlds; but if [you] see someone else doing good deeds and thereby [become] envious, you go to the Asura-demons; perhaps in your life you did not do anything so good, [or] so bad, then you keep the human state; though if your servant gets only a little food and you do not pay him properly because of your meanness, that is the realm of the hungry ghosts. So many events of the day-time are stored in the sub-conscious and these same sorts of things are dreamed at night: and this goes on, day-night, night-day until death, and as the dream continues from the day-life, so life continues after death though there is nothing more real about this life than any other since we find upon examining it that it is composed of so many levels of existence.[31]
C.M.Chen

The message of the Wheel of Life is, of course, that each of these conditioned realms is a trap—whether we take them literally or figuratively we should avoid them altogether by striving to gain Enlightenment. Otherwise, we move a step towards one of the realms every time we reaffirm one of these basic tendencies. If our life is dominated by any one state, that tendency is likely to continue establishing itself more and more firmly, so that any future life will be strongly conditioned in that direction.

DHYANA IS THE REALM OF THE GODS

As an interesting application of this principle, just consider the lives of very good, happy, well-favoured, perhaps even famous people. Many people are highly creative and intelligent, well loved and respected—some people seem to have lives which are like those of gods in comparison to our own. And yet the Wheel of Life seems to present this state of the *gods* as something to be avoided. What is wrong with being good, happy, creative, and intelligent? Aren't these just the kind of fruits one might expect from living the spiritual life? That is certainly true. Spiritual development does indeed involve becoming a better, happier, more creative, more intelligent person. It really does mean becoming more god-like. The Wheel of Life teaching does not deny that such an improved quality of mental health is valuable; it simply says that certain dangers exist even for a very healthy person.

The main danger is complacency—the possibility of getting stuck on an enjoyable plateau in life, with no other perspective on existence. A distinction is therefore drawn between the devas (i.e. gods and goddesses) of the Wheel—who make no further spiritual progress and eventually lose

Plane of consciousnes	State of consciousnes as experienced		Consciousness embodied as
Kama-loka Plane of sensuous enjoyment			Hell-beings
			Hungry ghosts
			Animals
			Asuras
		Five hindrances	Humans
		Access concentration	Kama-loka gods
Rupa-loka Plane of pure form or subtle form	Four **rupa-dhyanas**	Access concentration	Gods of subtle form (various levels)
		1st dhyana	
		2nd dhyana	
		3rd dhyana	
		4th dhyana	
Arupa-loka Plane of no form or exceedingly subtle form	Four **arupa-dhyanas**	Sphere of infinite space	Gods of exceedingly subtle form (various levels)
		Sphere of infinite consciousness	
		Sphere of no-thing-ness	
		Sphere of neither identification nor non-identification	

The three planes of
conditioned existence

everything they have gained—and the devas of the Path. Since human development involves increasing happiness, one of the special dangers of the spiritual life is settling down as a deva of the Wheel. As we develop ourselves we may become happier, more satisfied, stronger, and more self-sufficient. The process of deepening happiness may continue for years. But eventually we may become so satisfied with the transformation in our life that we get complacent, stop making an effort, lose awareness of the plight of other living beings, and so come to a standstill on the spiritual path. It is the danger of this type of stagnation that is symbolized by the realm of the gods.

While taking to heart this warning about complacency, we can still use the 'realm of the gods' as a symbol for higher states of consciousness. From that point of view, it is very much to be encouraged.

OUR EXISTENCE REFLECTS OUR CONSCIOUSNESS

Tradition says that divine beings are in a state of *dhyanic* consciousness, and that when we reach the dhyanas in meditation, we too are temporarily elevated to the status of a divine being. In general, one's level of existence is said to be determined by one's state of consciousness: Buddhism sees the universe as made up of states of consciousness 'bodying forth' into the visible world at different levels of spiritual development. According to the quality of consciousness pertaining at each level, it distinguishes three great planes of existence. These are known as the *kama-loka*, or plane of sensuous enjoyment, the *rupa-loka* or plane of pure form (alternatively, subtle form), and the *arupa-loka* or plane of no form (or 'exceedingly subtle' form).

Each of the three planes may be experienced through developing the dhyanas in meditation—so here we have yet another way of describing higher states of consciousness.

Human beings, animals, and the more exotic inhabitants of the Wheel of Life—except most kinds of gods—are said to spend most if not all of their time on the plane of sensuous enjoyment. If we consider what we ordinarily think about and how we use our time, we may agree that this is, indeed, our usual state of consciousness. Our main interests are in all the kinds of enjoyment that we can get from material objects. When we enter the first dhyana, however, things change: the quality of that desire becomes subtler as we enter the plane of pure or subtle form. At this level of consciousness we perceive forms to be composed of fine or subtle material, as though made of light—perhaps because the mind itself seems light and, as it were, transparent. You may recall that in access concentration and above, one's meditation object appears in the form of a *nimitta* or subtle counterpart of the original material object. The Pali word *rupa-loka* may also be rendered 'the realm of archetypal form', for it is also here that we enter the realm of image and mythic symbolism.

FURTHEST REACHES OF HIGHER CONSCIOUSNESS— THE 'FORMLESS' DHYANAS

The four dhyanas that we explored in Chapter Four[32] all occur within the *rupa-loka*. On the highest plane, that of 'exceedingly subtle' form, the four so-called 'formless' absorptions—or *arupa*-dhyanas—may be experienced. These formless dhyanas may be developed on the basis of the fourth *rupa*-dhyana. We saw earlier that this state of concentration is the highest experience-point in conditioned existence. It represents the climax of individual integration. From this high point one is in a position to experience the infinities, and the subtleties, of space and consciousness. It is not, however, that we literally *see* infinite space and consciousness. The 'formless' dhyanas are inner experiences of infinite freedom and expansion that grow out of our complete attainment of integration.

The first formless dhyana is called *the sphere of infinite space*, the second *the sphere of infinite consciousness*, the third *the sphere of no-thing-ness*, and the fourth *the sphere of neither identification nor non-identification*.

The sphere of infinite space represents a state of consciousness in which there is no object, or at least our experience of 'objecthood' is exceedingly subtle—this is characteristic of the arupa-loka generally. All that remains of objecthood is the sense of our awareness expanding to fill the whole of space. This state is attained (after the fourth absorption has been reached) when the meditation object (the nimitta, i.e. our experience of the meditation object) expands to fill infinite space. The meditator transfers his or her attention from this infinitely large object to the infinite space which it is occupying. This may produce a further degree of concentrated harmony and tranquillity, and this provides access to the first formless dhyana.

The **sphere of infinite consciousness** arises when we give *attention* to the fact that we are experiencing infinite space. This implies that in some way our consciousness also becomes infinite—if we are aware of an 'object' of infinite space, then there is, as it were, a 'subject' of infinite awareness. Experiencing this fact, we then withdraw our awareness from infinite space, concentrating entirely on infinite consciousness. This is the point at which the second formless dhyana arises.

At the stage of the **sphere of no-thing-ness**, we concentrate our attention on the fact that within the context of our infinite consciousness, there are no particular things that can be distinguished. In this expanded state, we cannot identify any one thing as distinct from another, even though our mind is unprecedentedly clear and bright. Focusing on this produces an even more exalted state of consciousness which is the third formless dhyana.

When the **sphere of neither identification nor non-identification** arises, we go almost completely beyond the distinction of subject and object. We now concentrate our attention on the way that we are identifying, or recognizing, the experience of infinity. This causes one more final stage of dhyana to arise. At this point 'we' are hardly separate from the experience. There is, in a certain sense, no subject who identifies, so that the process cannot be described either as an identification or as a non-identification.

Since these dhyanas of the formless plane are subtler than the 'highest experience-point in conditioned existence' marked by the fourth dhyana, they are, in a sense, at an even higher level. They almost take us right out of conditioned existence, inasmuch as the distinction between subjective experiencer and objective experience becomes increasingly subtle. Yet these higher states of consciousness are still conditioned. They do not necessarily indicate any insight into the ultimate nature of reality. Being conditioned, they are also impermanent—we can still fall back into lower states of being and consciousness.

INTRODUCING INSIGHT MEDITATION

[Samatha] is a refreshment of the lower consciousness, while [vipassana] may be compared to a golden spade that opens up a treasure of transcendental wealth. [Samatha] is an entrance into the wonderful silence and peacefulness of potentiality;… while [vipassana] is an entrance into the riches of intuition and transcendental intelligence.[33]

Chi-I

SAMATHA AND VIPASSANA DISTINGUISHED

So far we have been talking about meditation in the context of higher states of consciousness. Now it's time to introduce the kind of meditation which develops transcendental or Unconditioned consciousness.

The meditations we have explored are of a type known as *samatha* meditation. The Mindfulness of Breathing and the Metta Bhavana are samatha practices. They are so called because they cultivate mental integration and mental health, as manifested in qualities like concentration, calm, and positive emotion. The term samatha has both a broad and a specific meaning. Specifically, samatha refers to any meditation practice aimed at developing higher states of consciousness. More broadly, it applies to any means of achieving higher states of consciousness, whether through meditation or otherwise. For example, the general notion of samatha also includes ethics, since ethical actions create a foundation for positive mental states.

The other kind of Buddhist meditation is directed towards wisdom or insight, and is called *vipassana* meditation. The aim of vipassana practice is to gain insight into things as they really are. Insight does not mean abstract understanding, but direct experience of the real, ultimate nature of existence.

THE METHOD OF INSIGHT MEDITATION

The nature of vipassana will become clearer as we describe how the meditation is practised. Vipassana meditation requires the ability to concentrate the mind, so it needs to be practised *on the basis* of samatha meditation. A session of vipassana practice is therefore best preceded by a session of samatha practice—unless a general basis of samatha has already been well established. The concentration and emotional positivity that is established through samatha meditation will act as a support for the activity of vipassana, which is more illuminating and penetrating in character. One could say that samatha meditation develops our mental potency, while vipassana uses this potency to penetrate into the truth of things.

We use our *thoughts* in vipassana practice. Not distracted thoughts, of course—the clarity of our thinking is sustained by the higher states of consciousness which we have developed through samatha practice. As we know, thinking cannot take place at all beyond the first dhyana. So to avoid distraction, vipassana meditation must be practised either in access concentration or the first dhyana, and preferably the latter. The dhyana factors of initial thought and applied thought, which are particularly strong and clear (see Chapter Four), are employed in a contemplation of the nature of reality. We take our attention to a basic truth—which could be in the form of an idea, or an image, or a phrase which encapsulates some universal truth—and focus our thinking faculty upon it. We *reflect* upon reality. Buddhist tradition uses many ideas, images, and phrases for this purpose. For example, there are said to be three universal characteristics of existence—impermanence, unsatisfactoriness, and non-selfhood.

We shall be exploring these universal characteristics shortly, but as an example of the basic method of practice, let's imagine that we are meditating on impermanence.

First of all we would develop the first dhyana—perhaps by spending forty minutes or so on the Metta Bhavana practice. Then we would take the general notion of impermanence, or perhaps some image which evokes impermanence for us, and 'turn it over' within a tranquil, concentrated state of mind.

In ordinary consciousness our mind is affected by the hindrances, which either tend to make our thoughts vague, or stubbornly hard and fixed. But in the first dhyana our thinking is very sharp. At the same time, it is pliant—easily workable—so that we can quickly direct our attention in exactly the way we want. We can maintain our reflection on the vipassana-object without interruption, since it is supported by the foundation of samatha that has already been established. The samatha also ensures that we stay emotionally engaged—we are interested and inspired.

This kind of thinking is more akin to initial thought ('thinking of') than applied thought ('thinking about'). In dhyana our mind is so receptive that we hardly need to do any 'thinking about'. In a concentrated state, we may only have to think *of* impermanence for a very short while, and a great richness of meaning will reveal itself. We may simply lay the thought or image of impermanence within our receptive mind, and remain with the experience as it unfolds further.

It is rather like gazing at a lovely jewel that has been laid on a piece of dark velvet cloth. We do not have to make any effort to see its beauty;

REFLECTION WITHIN TRANQUILLITY

THE NATURE OF THIS KIND OF REFLECTION

more and more beauty simply reveals itself as we become more accustomed to looking. At this stage we do not even try, actively, to understand anything; we simply allow ourselves to be affected by the truth, by the reality of our contemplation. For this to be effective, a basic understanding needs already to have been established—some study may have been necessary beforehand in order to clarify exactly what we are meditating about.

THE ROLE OF THE DHYANAS IN DEVELOPING INSIGHT

So to practise insight meditation effectively, we need at least a little conceptual understanding (see Chapter Nine for more about this). But insight itself is not an abstract understanding—it is direct experience of the real, ultimate nature of existence.

Before we can even begin to appreciate that depth of experience, we must acknowledge that we ourselves do *not* see things as they really are. This does not mean that we are being asked to regard things like trees, tables, and people as something else—it isn't that our senses misrepresent the world. Perhaps in certain respects we are sometimes misled by our sense experience, but that isn't important. The point is that we misunderstand the *meaning* of reality—we are ignorant of the real nature and significance of our existence. It is *this* kind of ignorance that restricts our potency, freedom, and happiness.

You may wonder how such fundamental misunderstandings can exist. If you have been practising meditation for some time, then you will certainly be aware of one thing that hinders people from seeing how things really are: our capacity for paying attention is limited. You will probably know from your own experience that even a well-organized, efficient person can have a relatively distracted mind. Even at its best, the mind can still be surprisingly chaotic.

Thus one very good reason for our lack of insight is our lack of samatha. We have seen how, through samatha meditation, we may gradually integrate our conscious mind with our unconscious—how it is possible to become stronger, more 'ourselves', as we work through the hindrances and increase our experience of access concentration and the dhyanas. We've seen that the general concept of samatha refers to a healthy state of consciousness: it is joy, strength, and power; it is calmness, tranquillity, receptivity and openness. We know that qualities that are normally opposed to one another may combine through deeper samatha experiences—as, for example, our more powerful, 'masculine' qualities may come to co-exist, in the same moment, with the peaceful, 'feminine' qualities of receptivity and supportiveness. We have seen that dhyana, in this sense, is a necessary basis for the arising of insight.

We have also seen that vipassana meditation can only take place in access concentration or, ideally, the first dhyana. This does not mean that the seven dhyana levels beyond the first have no relevance to the development of insight, because the stronger our basis in dhyana experience, the more effective this reflection is likely to be.

The ideal way of practising vipassana is first to develop as full an experience of the dhyanas as possible. Then, even if we have reached one of the higher dhyana levels, we should introduce some reflection on reality. Since this involves thought, the effect will be that we 'come down' to the first dhyana. But this should not be taken too literally. If we have just experienced the third dhyana, for example, the quality of the first dhyana will be far more peaceful and inspired compared to how it feels when we have just moved out of the hindrances—even though, technically, they are at the same dhyana level. Remember that the dhyanas and dhyana factors are broad categories used for describing states of mind; in experience, there may be different positive emotions contained within them. So in 'coming down to the first dhyana' it isn't as though we necessarily lose the concentration and inspiration that we were experiencing in the higher dhyana state. If we remain mindful, those qualities can remain with us, even though we are now—to some extent—using thought.

THE UNIVERSAL CHARACTERISTICS OF EXISTENCE

More will be said, in a later chapter, about the *method* of vipassana. At this point, with this outline understanding of what this type of meditation involves, we can explore the three universal characteristics of existence—impermanence, unsatisfactoriness, and non-selfhood—that we encountered a little while ago.

IMPERMANENCE AND UNSATISFACTORINESS

Impermanence, as we have seen, is the universal truth that nothing lasts, that everything changes. Since the principle of impermanence is inseparable from that of unsatisfactoriness, we'll explore them both together. The universal truth of unsatisfactoriness means that because no source of satisfaction lasts forever, we can never be fully satisfied.

This isn't really a very 'nice' fact. You must already have noticed that these reflections on the nature of reality involve us in an encounter with rather challenging truths. This is very characteristic of vipassana. Its practices draw attention to aspects of life which we normally try to ignore—facts which we may find difficult and confusing because they arouse anxiety. This is another reason why samatha meditation is a necessary basis for vipassana: the emotional stability it provides makes an essential buffer to vipassana's more ego-challenging aspects.

Our modern era has been called 'the age of anxiety'. But even if we lived in an age free from modern kinds of stress, we would still experience anxiety. We have deeper anxieties rooted in the fear of impermanence, in a fear of being separated from what we love because 'things change'. People always try to cling on to what they like, try hard to make any changes as painless as possible for themselves—all this is anxiety-provoking. Buddhism, however, asserts that our ignorance of the *significance* of impermanence provokes an even deeper sense of insecurity. If we really understood the significance of impermanence we would be liberated from our fear and a far fuller, far more enjoyable experience of life would be unlocked.

Our spiritual ignorance makes us incomplete beings, and it is mainly because of this incompleteness that we tend to feel so insecure. In spite of our continual searching for security in external things such as prosperity and personal relationships, we can never really expect any more than a temporary feeling of security. In fact, there is no security in life whatsoever—which, again, is not a very 'nice' fact to have to accept.

It is all *very* unsatisfactory, and because of our anxieties and insecurities, we try to hide from the implications of impermanence. Yet times will inevitably come when we are forced to acknowledge them. We may, for example, be deeply shocked by some great loss or bereavement, which may shatter our previous view of life. Sometimes people take up the spiritual life after such occurrences, because the experience has shown them the human situation so clearly. This serves to illustrate how powerfully charged these themes are. It also demonstrates the value of having a good basis in samatha whenever we contemplate them: vipassana can be very strong medicine. However, any potential dullness or depression will be counteracted if we develop the emotional stability and 'sparkle' of dhyana. Dhyana also helps us to accept and assimilate the experience afterwards.

Over a period of sustained vipassana meditation practice we may develop a general ability to acknowledge and accept the nature of impermanence. We may even become able to 'dance with it', to be active and creative in the realm of reality. For when it is practised correctly, systematically, and under the right conditions, vipassana meditation will eventually lead to a profound realization and insight into the meaning of our existence. It is an insight which opens a gateway to true freedom—for if we see things as they really are, we will no longer react blindly to circumstances. Through our understanding, we shall no longer suffer from emotional turmoil.

This is the ultimate liberation and a special source of inspiration. The qualities of this kind of inspiration are given many symbolic forms in the Tibetan Buddhist tradition. One such form is the *dakini* (Sanskrit), or 'sky dancer'. At first, her appearance may seem a little outlandish: she is completely naked, except for her ornaments—ornaments made out of human bone. Her hair is waist length and dishevelled, as though she really doesn't care about it. She is a brilliant ruby red colour—her whole complexion is flushed with excitement. As well as the other ornaments, she is wearing a necklace of human skulls around her neck. And she is laughing. She's dancing for joy, and she is drinking blood—out of another human skull, hollowed out specially for the purpose.

THE SKY DANCER— IMAGE OF LIBERATION FROM FEAR

The impression that the dakini conveys seems somehow like insight itself. She is very attractive—but at the same time rather frightening. But putting yourself in her place (which is partly the idea)—adorning yourself with the bones, dancing and drinking the blood from the skull—you may begin to feel how the dakini feels. She expresses such a joyous freedom from the fear of death. It has been said that all fear derives from our unconscious anxiety about death—from fear of the existentially unknown. The dakini, having realized the Enlightened consciousness, has completely overcome this fear. Because it stresses that acknowledging impermanence will free us from fear, Buddhism has been described as 'one great meditation on impermanence'.

NON-SELFHOOD

Nothing is fixed, nothing is independent. Like unsatisfactoriness, the universal characteristic of non-selfhood arises out of impermanence. Things have no 'self' (or essence) *because* they are impermanent. Every part of every material object, for example, is constantly changing; it therefore cannot have a fixed, consistent nature.

Nowadays we are used to the idea that matter is not as solid and fixed as it appears, because modern physics has revolutionized our conception of 'solid matter'. Even so, our *emotional* response to material objects is still very much as though they were fixed entities. We are always creating entities like this. We tend to think of our car, for example, not as a collection of components bolted and welded together, but as 'the car'. And if it is scratched, we think at once that *our car* has been damaged. Our emotional attachment creates an impression of this 'car' in our mind, an impression which differs from the objective reality of co-existing components.

We look at all material objects in this way, from the food on our plate to continental land masses, from hi-tech gadgetry to rocks and trees. We tend to think of them as things which exist independently of anything else—in many cases almost as though they had a kind of 'self', a separate existence. But actually, everything is created by conditions. Everything is defined by everything else and cannot exist apart from everything else.

To make sense, this all requires considerable reflection. Probably the unconscious assumption that there is such an 'essence' in physical things isn't that obvious. But it may become a little more obvious if you examine the way you see yourself and other people.

Our unquestioning attitude to ourselves tends to be that 'we are what we are'; we think that somewhere, behind the shifting façade of our daily life, we never really change. Something, somewhere deep inside us, seems eternal: we may well think that we have a soul which remains aloof and unchanged by the incidental phenomena of our life. We may also like to think of others like this. We may tend to feel that behind someone's changeable everyday persona is 'the person themself', pure and incorruptible. We think, 'old Fred hasn't changed a bit since I first knew him.' We may actually like this—it's rather a comforting notion. We may like to think of an essential, eternal Fred. It's rather similar to the way parents sometimes think of their grown-up offspring as though they were still small children.

But, says Buddhism, in reality, people *do* change. So why do we have this feeling that they don't? Perhaps part of the feeling comes from the degree to which we identify with our own habits. We may associate our feelings of 'me'—or 'them'—with the confirmed, ingrained habit patterns that we—or they—have. And since our behaviour mostly consists of such habit patterns, it appears that no one ever changes. But even the most ingrained habits do, in fact, alter over time.

THE ILLUSION OF THE 'ETERNAL SOUL'

The feeling of having a permanent essence or soul may be quite strong. It is possible that at some time in our life we became aware of a much deeper level of our selves, or of the nature of existence itself. Perhaps this happened in a momentary visionary or mystical experience. Perhaps it was even under the influence of drugs. Or maybe we have sometimes had a sense of some powerful personal myth, some archetype of the unconscious. Many people have experiences of this kind at one time or another; it may be that everyone does. But very few people recognize their value, and even fewer know how to respond to them.

Our religious or cultural conditioning usually provides us with ready-made labels for attaching to such experiences. For example, when a practitioner of one of the great theistic creeds like Hinduism, Islam, or Christianity has some deep experience they will usually interpret it as relating to God or an eternal soul. But if we employ the methods of samatha and vipassana meditation sincerely, we can test for ourselves whether particular religious ideas—including those of Buddhism—actually fit our experience or not.

Though Buddhism sees ideas such as the belief in a permanent self or soul as an illusion, it would be absurd to think that we have no self of any kind at all. From what I said about samatha meditation earlier, it would seem that self-experience is an extremely important part of a particular stage of our development. Whatever the ultimate truth about selfhood, we still have an *experience* of a self; and certainly for the time being we need to strengthen our individuality, to become confident and integrated. Samatha development is the stage of refining and strengthening the 'ego'. On a practical, day-to-day level the experience of a self ought not to be denied, even though insight may increasingly reveal that this is not ultimately how things are. We will only be ready properly to experience our non-selfhood—or, as we could put it, the infinite changeability of ourselves—when we are psychologically whole and healthy in the dhyanic sense.

RELATIVITY OF SELFHOOD

It is unfortunate, therefore, that the language of 'ego' can sometimes be used to suggest that spiritual development requires us to weaken and 'destroy the ego'. This terminology can be misleading. In Buddhism the idea is not literally to destroy, but to progressively refine, our experience of selfhood through the experience of higher states of consciousness in samatha meditation. At first we need to become *more* ourselves. Once that stage has been reached, vipassana meditation can refine our experience of selfhood still further, this time to induce an awareness of its relativity and lack of permanence.

SAMATHA, SUBJECT, OBJECT

When insight is fully developed, the apparent division between subject and object is completely dissolved and we see that in reality there is no distinction between what is experienced and what experiences. At present we experience everything within a subject-object framework. This means we experience a feeling of being separate, which reinforces our idea of 'me'. This feeling of separateness also strengthens our emotional attachments, so that we tend to want to 'fill the gap' with experiences of pleasant objects—and woe betide anyone that obstructs us from doing so!

Insight meditation is certainly the ultimate antidote to all this, but there is another, more intermediary, way. So long as one's overall goal is seen in the perspective of insight, the gulf between subject and object may also be narrowed, or at least begin to be narrowed, by the practice of samatha meditation. Through this practice we become mentally richer—more relaxed, contented, and inspired—so that our selfish needs diminish; we also become stronger, less easily threatened by the prospect of losing things. The more of this kind of integration we gain through our dhyana experience, the weaker becomes the urge to incorporate objects into ourselves (craving), and to destroy threatening objects (hatred).

In fact, although there is no permanent progress, the gulf experienced between subject and object generally lessens as we progress through the dhyanas. In the highest *arupa*-dhyanas, where there is only the very subtlest distinction between mind and matter, selfness and otherness *almost* become one. But it doesn't quite happen. On the subtlest level the delusion of self and other remains—with the possibility of its eventually hardening and becoming the cause of reactive, unskilful emotions once again. Even the highest gods are subject to backslidings. Samatha is thus the process which *attenuates* the subject–object distinction, while vipassana is the process which *dissolves* it finally and forever. Looked at in this way, the whole process of samatha and vipassana can be seen, not as two separate methods of practice, but as a progressive deepening of spiritual experience.

METTA AND INSIGHT   This is illustrated very well in the case of the Metta Bhavana practice. Metta Bhavana is not traditionally considered to be a vipassana practice; indeed, the commentarial tradition states that it can lead only to dhyana, not ultimate liberation. However, most samatha practices may also be approached from a vipassana point of view, and the Metta Bhavana is especially interesting in this respect.

In the Metta Bhavana we try to develop a disinterested emotion of well-wishing towards another person. 'Disinterested' doesn't mean that we don't feel anything, but that we want them to be happy on their own terms—there's no reference to any personal enjoyment that we might get out of their happiness. If we develop this kind of objectivity in our emotional life, then the Metta Bhavana will work both on ourselves as subject *and* on ourselves in terms of our attitude towards others. Metta can work with the tension which always exists between subject and object, and may eventually transform the way that we relate within the self–other, subject–object framework. This is, as we have seen, also the working ground of vipassana. When metta is developed to an advanced degree, there is no distinction experienced between ourselves and others: we wish happiness equally for all, quite unreservedly. The Metta Bhavana meditation and its associated practices, the *Brahma-viharas*—such as the development of joy and the development of compassion (which we shall soon be exploring)—

thus approach the realm of insight, and may even lead us into it. Further on, flowering out of the development of these Brahma-viharas, is a state known as Great Compassion. This is a state of fully developed insight. One who possesses Great Compassion experiences the non-selfhood of others as keenly as his or her own. Such a person's compassion is directed, not towards the fixed personalities of the people concerned, but towards their real nature, their non-selfhood. In plainer language we see their potential for development far more clearly than is possible without insight.

POETRY OF SHUNYATA

In Buddhism the great themes of impermanence, unsatisfactoriness, and non-selfhood were developed, over the first thousand years after the Buddha's death, into the comprehensive philosophy of *shunyata* (Sanskrit). The word means 'voidness' or 'emptiness', and is intended to be taken poetically rather than literally. To the Enlightened mind, things appear as it were transparent and 'empty'. Everything is seen to undergo transformation through the influence of everything else; things are 'empty' of any core or essence which holds them together. The word was never intended to suggest nothingness or negation—in fact, the intention was very much the opposite. It is an expression of the nature of reality in terms of a dynamic universe, not a dead, static one. Were it not for the fact that reality is *shunya*, there could be no growth or development of any kind. Realization of the truth of impermanence and non-selfhood will mean that we awaken to the full potential and power of life: since nothing is restricted by permanence and selfhood, anything is possible!

THE PRINCIPLE OF REGULAR STEPS

As we are sitting up and practising dhyana, especially by the means of insight, it is possible that all of a sudden we will be enveloped in a wave of intuition and intelligence, but as our power of concentration is still weak, our mind will be weak and fluctuating like a candle flame in the wind, so this measure of transcendental intelligence will not be lasting.[34]

   Chi-I

Compared to samatha, vipassana meditation is, in a sense, a higher form of meditation. For this reason we may find it supremely attractive and in-spiring. But our appreciation of its profundity may not necessarily mean that we can usefully practise it immediately. We cannot practise vipassana effectively unless we have a basis of samatha.

Someone who is trying to develop insight without any basis in concentration is like a candle in a draughty room. Because of the draughts, it cannot burn and light up its surroundings but gutters and blows here and there, sending out only a flickering light. If we close off the draughts, however, our candle will burn high and bright. Likewise, in a concentrated mind, vipassana intensifies and illuminates our experience. But without samatha, someone practising vipassana is likely either to be dull in energy or lost in distracted thoughts.

Sometimes it may seem as though we are able to force ourselves to contemplate impermanence—even though our mind is not really very receptive. But in doing so we may strain ourselves, perhaps ending up with a headache or, even worse in the long run, a wrong idea of what insight is. We should follow a path of regular steps in our meditation and not practise in ways we are not properly prepared for.

In spiritual practice there exists a path of regular steps and a path of irregular steps. People generally tend to follow the latter, and might begin at the second stage and then—since it looks much more interesting—go on to try a little of the eighth stage. Finding that a little too demanding, we then have to go back to the first stage. There we establish our foundation, and start back again on stage two. But after beginning the second stage, we try to practise some of the fourth stage—and are even able to make a little progress—but it is not long before we have to retrace our steps. Before we can go much further, we must return to our practice of the second stage until it is complete.

We will make the best progress if we can get ourselves established more firmly on the path of *regular* steps—starting by practising stage one, and once that is established, practising the second stage until that stage too is established. Then we begin on stage three—and eventually, stage by stage, go on to more advanced levels. This is the ideal way of making progress, and in theory it certainly sounds straightforward. However, in practice, we may find it impossible to organize ourselves in such a straightforward manner. To some extent we cannot but follow an irregular path, and in that irregular way we will make progress—but only at times when the stage we are practising actually rests on the basis of an already established stage. Higher stages of practice are dependent on the establishment of lower ones, just as each level of a ziggurat or pyramid depends for support on the previous level. Sometimes we can make a little progress beyond our seeming capability, but we will not be able to sustain it without a real foundation.

INSIGHT AND THE INTELLECT   Another common result of premature vipassana meditation is that we think we have gained real insight when what we actually have is an improved intellectual understanding of the teaching we have been meditating upon. An improved understanding is certainly a very good thing—but it is not insight. What is the difference? The characteristic of insight is that it turns us upside down and inside out—its impact is shattering. Intellectual understanding does not have this quality. Understanding something intellectually can be exciting and challenging, may make us feel clearer, but it does not imply radical transformation. Understanding which is not shattering is not vipassana. Vipassana is revolutionary—is, as the *Lankavatara Sutra* expresses it, 'a turning about in the deepest seat of consciousness'.

Part Three

PRACTICE

•

ESTABLISHING AND DEEPENING TRANQUILLITY AND INSIGHT

•

PART THREE IS GENERALLY CONCERNED WITH THE PRACTICALITIES
OF DEEPENING YOUR MEDITATION PRACTICE.
CHAPTER SIX is about how to create the best possible conditions
for both reflection and the dhyanas, especially on retreat.
CHAPTER SEVEN gives some guide-lines for meditation posture.
CHAPTERS EIGHT and NINE offer practical hints for developing
samatha and vipassana meditation.
CHAPTER TEN is a guided tour through a number of different applications
of the principles of samatha and vipassana.

•

Chapter Six

THE CONDITIONS FOR MEDITATION

What is meant by regulating and readjusting? It may be likened to the work of a potter. Before he can begin to form a bowl or anything else, he must first prepare the clay—it must neither be too soft nor too hard. Just as a violinist must first regulate the tension of the different strings—they must be in perfect tune—before he can produce harmonious music.... Before we can control our mind for the attainment of Enlightenment, we must first regulate and adjust the inner conditions....

If these lessons are learned and applied, then samadhi[35] can be easily attained, otherwise a great deal of difficulty will be experienced and our tender root of goodness can hardly sprout.[36]

Chi-I

INFLUENCES

The way that our meditation varies from one session to another might seem strange. How can it be so easy to concentrate one day, and so hard the next—why don't we make some tangible progress every time we meditate? This is a very good example of the 'conditionedness' of human life. We very rarely experience exactly what we would like to experience!—so much depends on the influences, the conditioning factors, that happen to be in operation at any given moment.

In the art of meditation it is important to understand what the main influences are and how they affect our mind. We may not always notice it, but our mental states are strongly affected by the place where we are living, the people around us, what is happening in our life, and many other things. All of these factors are contributing, in some way, to our ability to concentrate.

For example, when you are in ideal circumstances you may naturally find yourself feeling happy and in a mood to concentrate, but in other situations even relaxation may be out of the question, let alone meditation. If possible, try to create circumstances which help your concentration, and avoid anything that you find distracting.

Physical surroundings can make all the difference. Everything around you—the room you are meditating in, the house, and even the immediate locality and its inhabitants—is going to have some kind of effect. So, if you can, put yourself in quiet, peaceful surroundings, where there is no radio, television, or traffic noise. At least do this from time to time—it is much more likely to generate a mood of concentration.

It's also worth repeating what was said earlier about preparation for meditation. What you do *immediately* before meditation may affect your mental state very strongly—it can often make the difference between being able to concentrate and being distracted. But paying attention to your actions immediately before meditation is just one particular kind of preparation.

In a way, your whole life is a preparation for meditation. Every action has made a certain contribution to the mental states you are experiencing at this very moment. (Some actions, no doubt, have been less significant, while others have probably had a very far reaching effect.) So the state of your mind as you are about to go into meditation is partly a product of your *life-style*. You might find that if you made one or two changes in your life-style, you would be in the right mood for meditation more often.

Remember that everything you do influences your mental state. Generally speaking, whenever you act with awareness and positive feelings towards others, the overall result will be an aware and positive frame of mind. If you are in the habit of being kind and friendly, Metta Bhavana will come more naturally to you. If you pay attention to what you do, say, and think, you'll start the Mindfulness of Breathing practice with an edge that would not be there otherwise.

Increased kindness and mindfulness are, of course, effects that you want to bring about through these meditation practices. But you can also look at it the other way round, and generate these qualities as supporting conditions for your meditation.

You can create what Chi-I called 'external' conditions for your practice. Most of these involve making sure that practical arrangements—for example the kind of place where you meditate—are helping your meditation. Skilful attitudes towards other people that will tend to preserve a happy state of mind are also included in this category (see table). There are also 'internal' conditions which are essential if you are to develop higher states of consciousness (they may also be applied to meditation in any circumstances). Success in meditation entails an understanding of how to create the best possible internal and external conditions.

External conditions Relations with outside world as preparation for meditation	Internal conditions Developing the dhyanas in ideal meditation conditions
Ethical foundation • Acting ethically • Freedom from guilt • Positive stimulation	Speech
The place	Food
Material needs	Rest and exercise
Freedom to engage	Information
Communication	Activity

The clear understanding that all your actions will affect your meditation is—from a certain point of view—even more important than a willingness to concentrate in meditation itself. You may be very inspired and enthusiastic, raring to get going on your meditation practice. But what really counts, when you close your eyes and try to concentrate, is your preparation. If you have prepared well, your mind will be clear, flexible, and interested. But if you haven't, then, no matter how bright you feel when you first sit down, your mind will soon become rigid and distracted and you'll have to spend your time working with that unprepared state. No amount of good intentions can make up for a lack of preparation.

Sometimes meditators get into a habit of not preparing properly, even though they anticipate that they will be gaining insight, Enlightenment, or whatever from their meditation—perhaps quite soon! Despite these high ideals, they don't notice how their life-style is affecting their mental state. On the whole, it isn't very helpful to meditate with the aim of creating immediate, specific results. The important thing is to keep making sure that the *conditions* for meditation are as beneficial as possible. If you do that, you will find good results arising quite naturally by themselves.

In making the effort to create good conditions, you also need to remember that, practically speaking, it is often impossible to create *ideal* conditions. There is not that much peace and quiet available—unless you decide to live as a hermit. You will often find yourself in situations where, because of the external conditions, your mental state is distracted. All you can do then is acknowledge the situation and meditate as best you can. Unless you take this attitude you may become impatient, and impatience may make you feel that you must 'concentrate' in a hard and forced way. This kind of mood is easy to get into. It is then possible to start disregarding how you are feeling, and to ignore what is actually happening in your mind. If you do that you will just exhaust yourself—and still fail to achieve any calm or concentration.

EXTERNAL CONDITIONS

THE ETHICAL FOUNDATION

The first 'external' condition to consider is the ethical foundation. There is an important connection between ethics and concentration; it is only possible to concentrate fully when you are happy.

But what is happiness? Happiness does not necessarily mean feeling elated with joy—it seems to have more to do with confidence in oneself, for even someone who is under great stress may still be happy underneath it all. A person may feel great satisfaction in their life, and therefore be happy, even though there are many problems, difficulties, and pain. One way that happiness reveals itself is in an ability to be interested. If you are happy you will also be, to a certain extent, naturally concentrated. 'A concentrated mind is a happy mind; a happy mind is a concentrated mind.'

So to meditate at your best, you need to be happy. But how do you become happy and satisfied with your life?

ACTING ETHICALLY   Traditional Buddhist teaching says that an ethical life-style is a necessary condition for happiness. But for many of us nowadays the whole topic of ethics has become unclear. It may seem full of ambiguous 'grey areas'. What does it really mean to be 'good'? This word itself seems ambiguous.

Certainly, for a Buddhist, an ethical life is not simply a matter of doing the conventionally right thing. It is a question of developing an awareness of *the consequences of our actions*. Actions have consequences for others and for ourselves—not only material consequences, but also consequences in the form of mental states. Just as natural laws govern physics and chemistry, a natural relationship exists between what we do and our state of mind. An ethical life is based on the creative, beneficial use of this relationship. Ethical behaviour is about doing things that promote positive states of mind.

Certain actions affect our mind in certain ways; for example, some actions (e.g. generosity) are inherently worthwhile and satisfying. These are ethical or 'skilful' actions. The great characteristic of such actions is that they make us and others feel happy. There are other actions (e.g. malicious lying) that are inherently regrettable, and somewhere in ourselves we do not feel happy when we indulge in them. These are unskilful, or unethical, actions.

Such feelings of happiness or regret can provide a good 'rule of thumb' for assessing the ethical value of our actions. Generally, the more skilfully we act the happier we feel; and the more relaxed, flexible, and concentrated our mind becomes, too.

There are certain actions which inevitably lead to happy states of mind. We feel at our best when we are doing things which are of benefit to ourselves and others: when we give generously, when we are sexually content, when we speak the truth, and when we are clear-minded. Harming, stealing, sexual exploitation, lying, and muddle-headed confusion—the opposites of the above—inevitably lead to unhappiness. These principles are set out in five traditional Buddhist precepts:

(1) The principle of *ahimsa*, nonviolence, means **doing what is of benefit** to ourselves and others. Negatively it is the avoidance of causing harm. (This is the basic principle which underlies each of the other precepts.)

(2) The principle of *dana*, generosity, means **developing a giving, sharing attitude**. Negatively it involves not taking others' property, energy, or time unless they have been made freely available to us.

(3) The principle of *santutthi*, contentment, means **developing sexual self-control and contentment** with any sexual partner we have (or don't have!). Negatively, it means not harming through sex, and trying not to have sexual matters as the central factor in our life.

(4) The principle of *sacca*, truth, simply means **being truthful**. Negatively, it means not telling lies and correcting our own wrong thinking.

(5) The principle of *sati*, mindfulness, means **developing awareness** of our world, ourselves, and others, and trying to maintain a bright, clear, state of mind. Negatively, it means working to avoid clouded, confused, or intoxicated states—which also means avoiding intoxication through alcohol or other drug abuse.

FREEDOM FROM GUILT

We'll probably find that our happiest times are when we live according to principles like these—when we genuinely feel no guilt, no regrets. When we experience such freedom we can be completely wholehearted in everything—no part of ourselves is held in reserve. This is the essential reason why ethical living makes such a difference to meditation.

But for most of us, most of the time, such clarity of conscience is rare. We may have to acknowledge that we don't act in accordance with these principles at all times. We may need to recognize that there *is* guilt in our mind, and that often we are *not* quite happy enough to concentrate with our whole being. Parts of us are preoccupied elsewhere; there are inner knots which need loosening.

This honest recognition is an essential first step towards ethical growth. We need to recognize what we are really doing, what is really happening. It is essential to recognize the subtle signs that tell us when we regret an action or when we are pleased about one. Recognition of guilt feelings can then become an ethical tool for spotlighting those areas we want to change.

But we can sometimes feel guilty even when we have done nothing regrettable! So to use this tool properly we need to be able to discriminate healthy from unhealthy guilt feelings.

We can sometimes experience *irrational* guilt feelings. These are often stimulated when some 'authority' seems to dislike our action—or at least when we feel that they do. We feel disapproved of, unworthy, and probably sinful. People often feel this kind of guiltiness in connection with their sexuality—when there is nothing at all harmful in what they have thought or done.

There is of course such a thing as an *appropriately* uneasy conscience. We all act unskilfully in all kinds of ways. But harbouring irrational guilt is yet another form of unskilful action. Our first task is therefore to pick out this false kind of guiltiness, and—if we can—banish it from our heart. When we notice guilt arising, we should check what action it is connected with and see whether we truly regret that action. If it really does seem regrettable and harmful, then we must acknowledge that we are responsible for its effects, and try to learn from the experience.

The sorrow or regret that we feel when we have harmed someone or lowered our standard of behaviour is a rational feeling of guilt. We take the blame cleanly—in this case it's appropriate to feel regret. But if we feel 'bad', yet can find nothing truly regrettable in our actions, we should recognize that our guilt feelings have no basis. There is no real cause for concern and we should try to let go of the irrational emotion. It may well be difficult to do this in practice, since deeply ingrained habits are usually involved in these matters—but we shall certainly be doing ourselves some good if we try to clarify what is going on.

It is clear that meditation is directed towards happiness and the development of joyful mental states. But when we are actually practising it, we usually experience rather a mixture of emotions—we frequently experience the hindrances and other negative emotions standing in the way of our concentration. Where have they come from?

According to Buddhism all our moods, positive and negative, have been conditioned, at least partially, by our actions in the past, and future moods are conditioned by our actions in the present. As an example, let's say you give something to a friend, a gift they are delighted to receive. This act of generosity delights them—and it puts you in a good mood too! Moreover, the memory of your action brightens your mental state for some time afterwards. You may even remember it many years later, and feel 'I'm so glad I did that.' Even if you never think about it again, this action will have had a generally good effect on you.

In this way, each action somehow affects our state of mind. Whether we speak kindly or harshly to someone, that speech affects us, the speaker, at least as much. We may not be able to see any obvious connections between past acts of speech and our present feelings, but the link surely exists, and if we observe more closely we may recognize some of the processes that go on.

If we observe ourselves over a long period we may notice that our actions sometimes affect us more deeply than just for a few hours or weeks afterwards. Some actions carry a great deal of emotional power and may penetrate deeply into our mind, even into our unconscious mind, where they become part of a whole complex of unconscious and semi-conscious attitudes and emotions. This process of outer (and relatively conscious) action stimulating deep (and relatively unconscious) inner reactions is basic to Buddhist psychology. Buddhism clearly distinguishes the second part of this process, known in Sanskrit as *karma-vipaka* (effect of volitional action), from the initial *karma* (volitional action). The ceaseless interplay of *karma* and *karma-vipaka*, action and result, is the cause of all the mental states which arise so mysteriously both inside and outside our meditation.

None of us can be free from the effects of our past. However, we do have a certain degree of freedom to initiate more skilful actions in the present—and we can develop our initiative further. In skilful living, as in life generally, 'the more you do, the more you *can* do.'

We often go around in a whirl of general impressions, hardly aware that we are using our eyes and ears. Yet all these sense experiences can affect us very strongly indeed. Everything we smell, taste, see, hear, and touch affects our mental state. This is obviously important for a meditator trying to create good conditions for practice.

STIMULATION
GUARDING THE GATES
OF THE SENSES

If we wish we can choose, to some extent, the objects that we encounter. We can learn to monitor our sense experience and become more discriminating in our choice. We can look for the kind of stimulation which will help our meditation, and avoid whatever confuses, irritates, or unduly excites us.

This kind of practice is sometimes known as 'guarding the gates of the senses'. Here, 'guarding' doesn't mean being over-fastidious and 'precious' about preserving our fragile states of mind at all costs, afraid to put our head out of doors in case we see something shocking. It simply means that we care about our state of mind and take responsibility for it.

Naturally, each of us is affected differently by different experiences; what is helpful to one person could possibly even be harmful to another. Many people would find their meditation somewhat improved after spending time in an art gallery, but some might not. (No doubt it would depend on the art.) Many people are inspired by contact with their friends, but others need more time to themselves. Without the conditions that suit them, neither type of person can settle into meditation. As ever, the real test is the effect of these sense experiences on our mental states.

We must take responsibility for the consequences of our actions and decide what is best for us. This can take time to learn, and decisions are not always easy. Perhaps one weekend we start wondering whether we could attend a late night party and meditate the next day. Well, perhaps we could! Honest reflection might reveal, however, that this could have some detrimental effect on our practice. We have to be careful of the tendency to rationalize weaknesses, to make good-sounding excuses to ourselves. Our reasoning might be 'If I go to that party, I shall meet people—that'll be an opportunity to put my Metta Bhavana into practice!' or 'If I go, it'll be a good test of my mindfulness.' The party could possibly be very testing indeed. But do we genuinely 'need to test' our mindfulness, or do we simply want to go to the party regardless of its consequences for our meditation? For the sake of our own clarity, it's better to be honest. Though such reasons can sound very plausible when they arise, it may be that we are finding ways of obscuring, perhaps 'spiritualizing' our real motive.

NOURISHING THE MIND   Exposing ourselves to the right sort of stimulation is at least as important as avoiding exposure to the wrong sort of stimulation! The mind is always on the look-out for stimulation, and, up to a point, it's a genuine need. Like a child who will stuff itself with sweets and junk food unless its mother provides regular nourishing meals, our mind will become interested in any old rubbish unless we provide it with intake of some quality.

Cultivate whatever tends to put you in an inspired, positive mood. There are probably people who inspire you, and with whom you could profitably spend more time. If you also spend more time looking at paintings, reading poetry, listening to beautiful music, or out of doors among greenery and flowers, your meditation practice is very likely to improve. A lot of people find that they are happier if they have a certain amount of physical exercise every day. All these activities make a very good counterbalance to the often dull, tense, and noisy city environment where the majority of us must live and try to meditate.

As well as being discriminating about the *quality* of what you take in, you   can also usefully reduce the *quantity*. Otherwise you can become so saturated with experiences that you get overstimulated. This is particularly likely in the city. Some symptoms of overstimulation are a continual feeling of restlessness, and a 'hangover' of dullness.

To simplify your experience you could perhaps avoid looking distractedly here, there, and everywhere as you walk to work, and instead try to remain mindful of your body, feelings, emotions, and thoughts. You could also seek enjoyment in simple pastimes, rather than complex activities that only dissipate energy. Most people living busy lives will know how easy it is to lose sensitivity and interest when there are too many events, too many experiences, jostling for attention. If you mindfully observe your sense-experience, however, you will become more sensitive to what is affecting you. And as you get to understand your needs better, you will become less enslaved by the pressure of external things.

ON SOLITARY RETREAT

I went to the woods because I wished to live deliberately[37]
   Henry David Thoreau

The value of meditation retreats in general has already been referred to several times. Getting away from it all occasionally is really an indispensable aspect of meditation practice. It is a good way of reviving your meditation when it has become a little run down. Going on retreat is a way to give yourself good meditation conditions. It provides a wider context, and allows you to forge deeper links both with your practice and with other meditators.

Once a regular meditation practice has been established, say over a year, this idea of 'getting away from it all' can be taken even further. At some point you may also find it extremely valuable to spend some time completely alone.

The most important experience a solitary retreat provides is *an undiluted experience of yourself*. This can be even more useful than the opportunity it gives for meditation. How often in your life have you spent time completely on your own, without seeing anyone at all? Even to the extent that you have, it probably wasn't by choice. It seems fairly natural that many people avoid solitude, associating it with loneliness. Yet loneliness can sometimes stem from a negative state of dependence on others—we are developing insights, through our meditation, that can free us from such dependence.

Imagine arriving at some isolated cottage and experiencing the thrill of knowing that you are going to be entirely alone—for a week, a fortnight, a month, or perhaps even longer. You are completely free to do what you like, to think what you like, without ever having to take others' needs into account. Whatever you choose to do with your time, you can count on never being interrupted by other people—even your thoughts will be uninterrupted. What a rare and precious opportunity this is in our crowded, timetabled society! It's a time for reflection, readjustment of perspectives, and meditation.

THE PLACE

The third external condition that one must possess if one is to hope for success in the practice of dhyana, relates to shelter. A retreat ... to be satisfactory must be quiet and free from annoyances and troubles of any kind. [These kinds of places] are suitable for dhyana practice: a hermitage in the high and inaccessible mountains, [or] a shack such as would serve a beggar or a homeless monk. These should be at least a mile and a half from a village where even the voice of a cowboy would not reach and where trouble and turmoil would not find it.[38]
Chi-I

The place you choose for your period of solitude—which could be a cottage, a caravan, a camping site, or even (if you're keen) a mountain cave—could make a considerable difference to the extent to which you can concentrate. First of all, the retreat place needs to be quiet—ideally somewhere completely silent. The fewer disturbances there are, the easier it will be to become concentrated. The two main distractions to avoid are traffic noise and people nearby (who may be talking, working, playing radios, etc.).

The need to be undistracted means that you must go as far away from other human beings as possible. For a solitary retreat, it is ideal if you don't even see anyone else. This obviously means that your place of retreat has to be in the country. When choosing a site for a solitary retreat you should make sure you are happy with its atmosphere. You should find the place attractive, and feel inspired by the thought of staying there. This is quite important because, once you settle into your meditation, you will become more than usually sensitive to your surroundings. So if possible it's best to inspect a place personally before committing yourself, especially if you are planning a long retreat—it could eventually become a source of strain if you find, say, the interior furnishing of the house jarring, or the local countryside unattractive.

MATERIAL NEEDS

Nowadays there are places where all the facilities for solitary retreats, including food, are provided. Otherwise, if you are completely on your own, the availability of supplies is an important consideration. Walking several miles to get food may be acceptable to some, but once you have established a meditation practice you might prefer to remain undisturbed for the whole of the retreat. It is a pity to have to break a good retreat just because you have run out of some basic necessity. Meditative states can rely on a delicate balance of factors, and once those factors are disturbed it can take days to restore the balance. If you plan carefully, you should be able to avoid leaving your place of retreat.

Once these basic needs are provided for, you need to ensure that you really do have the freedom to concentrate. If there is any unfinished business left over from your life outside the retreat, it will plague you whenever you try to meditate. It is therefore important that you deliberately tie up all such loose ends before you go away, and if necessary ask others to manage your affairs during your retreat. You can take similar steps to avoid letters arriving that might distract you. In fact, it might be best not to tell too many people where you are!

FREEDOM TO ENGAGE

Another factor that affects one's ability to engage with a solitary retreat is the state of one's communication. Away from people, you will become more sensitive to your relationships with others. It is wise to patch up any quarrels or misunderstandings before you go, because any unresolved tension will play on your mind and could possibly obstruct your practice. You may also feel sensitive to anyone who lives in the neighbourhood of your retreat place—it's a good idea to create some basis of communication with them at the beginning of your stay. Speculation could be running rife in the locality—'what can she be getting up to, all on her own?'—or (more to the point) you may *imagine* that it is. You could introduce yourself and let someone know roughly what you are doing. In my experience, most people seem well-disposed towards Buddhists, and may even offer to help now and again with provisions.

COMMUNICATION

INTERNAL CONDITIONS

Now you have set up all the external conditions. You are prepared for meditation. You've been trying to act more ethically, found a quiet, isolated, inspiring place for meditation, sorted out your material needs, made sure you are on good terms with people, and taken a break from your life outside the retreat.

So next comes the actual meditation practice. Now that you are here, you need to pay attention to conditions that will encourage the dhyanas to arise. These 'internal' conditions mainly consist of methods of working in meditation, such as those introduced in Chapter Three (and explored in detail in Chapter Eight). But also included as 'internal' conditions are those subtler aspects of preparation which can only be fully created on retreat.

On retreat you are able to meditate several times a day; you're never far away from a period of meditation, so you need to be continually prepared for it. It is especially important to be mindful of your actions between sessions of meditation. Sometimes this is called 'in-between practice'.

If you maintain your preparation, then you will retain what you gain during each session of meditation. Your concentration will steadily accumulate, so that instead of taking a whole meditation session to get into a state of preliminary concentration—only to run out of energy as soon as you get there—you may be able to begin most of your meditation sessions already in a concentrated state.

You'll probably find that your awareness of what you need to do in preparation for meditation is especially keen on a solitary retreat. When you have been on your own for some days (the change may not show itself at first, since it takes time to adjust and relax) you are likely to find yourself in a very different realm of experience. You may notice how rich and alive everything seems. This is because your life is simpler; you have created a space in which you have no responsibilities other than being yourself and thinking your own thoughts. You may be less preoccupied by distractions, and the workings of your inner life may show themselves far more than usual. You may find it easy to maintain mindfulness continually—you'll probably experience all your feelings, thoughts, and inner motivations quite clearly.

Life in this realm of 'being yourself' is a kind of meditative state in itself. You'll want to maintain this state, and to do so there are two factors which need to be regulated. There are factors which tend to dullness (a sleepy mind), and factors which tend to excitement (a disturbed mind). As we'll see in a later chapter, finding ways to transcend these two extremes is the principal method of working in meditation.

On retreat (it's also the case outside, but on retreat you experience it more clearly) you will find some conditions dulling your mind and others exciting it. When you find yourself going to one extreme you need to learn how to get yourself moving in the opposite direction. As an aid to reflection, here are some typical causes of dullness and excitement which were compiled by the late C.M. Chen. Mr Chen was a renowned Ch'an Buddhist hermit who practised for many years in Kalimpong, West Bengal.

Condition	Sleepy mind (sloth, sinking)	Disturbed mind (restlessness, drifting)
Food	A lot	A little
	Earth element (potatoes, etc.)	Fire element (chilli, pungent food)
	Much meat	Just vegetables
Drink	Milk	Coffee, tea
Weather	Hot	Cold
	Rain	Strong sun
Season (Chinese)	Spring, autumn	Summer, winter
Light level	Low, or darkness	Very bright
Clothes	Too many	Too few
Colour	Green, blue, black	Red, orange, yellow
Eyes	Closed	Open wide
Circulation	Quietly	Excitedly
Mode of action	Tired	Wide awake
Mental poison	Ignorance	Greed, hatred
Body	Fat	Thin

List of factors leading to dullness or excitement in meditation (C.M. Chen)[39]

One or two of Mr Chen's correspondences may seem odd at first glance, but you'll probably get the idea. At least you can see from the table the sheer variety of factors that can affect your mental state under retreat conditions. You might find it worthwhile to draw up such a list for yourself. You could add, for example:

Sleep	Too much	Too little
Exercise	Too little	Too much

Take a look now at some of the main internal conditions. The most important areas which will need your attention on retreat are **speech, food, rest, exercise**, and **information**.

SPEECH

Unless you often talk to yourself, you aren't likely to find *speech* upsetting the balance on your solitary retreat! But on retreats generally—and many of these tips are just as useful on a group retreat—you may be surprised to discover how powerfully speech affects your practice.

A really good communication may have an inspiring effect which strengthens your ability to meditate, while a disharmonious exchange can disturb you and prevent you from settling down and concentrating. So if you pay attention to what you say, how you say it, and the effects of your speech on your mental state, you can maintain your inspiration and prevent unsettling disturbances.

Because words have so much influence over our consciousness, many meditation retreats incorporate an hour or more of verbal silence into their daily programme—often it's much more. Verbal silence is something most people hardly ever experience. Yet it can be deeply relaxing—and even a profound relief after the continual chatter which our minds so often have to cope with. One's thoughts become clearer when they are not subject to interruptions, and so it becomes possible to experience oneself more deeply and continuously.

Deliberately refraining from speech can be a very beneficial preparation for meditation, as well as a way of absorbing its effects. This can be useful for your practice at home too. For example when you get up in the morning it can help to be silent before you meditate; a very good way of preparing is to dress and wash silently, with awareness, perhaps sitting by a window for a few minutes. A quiet period afterwards also helps. Silence before meditation helps to prepare your mind for concentration, and the silence afterwards helps you absorb its effects.

FOOD

Food is an important consideration; both the type and quantity of food will affect your sensitive mental state on retreat. The type of food you choose depends on what you like, your constitution, and the climate. As a general rule it is best to avoid heavy, fatty foods, while making sure you have food that you can enjoy. There is no need to make life difficult by enforcing an ascetic diet on yourself. Sometimes people place retreats in the same 'purificatory' category as health cures and giving up smoking, and so go in for fasting and special diets. This can be all right, even a good idea, if you know yourself well. Just remember that on retreat you will find yourself becoming generally rather sensitive, and that details like food may have quite an influence on your mood. And when you discover you need something, the shops may be miles away! Regarding quantity, it is best to avoid eating too much or too little. If you eat too much, your meditation is likely to suffer from dullness and drowsiness. If you eat too little, you'll be faint, low in energy, and restless.

REST AND EXERCISE

Rest and exercise is another basic area for attention. You need to take sufficient rest, and also to maintain a certain level of fitness.

Once you have recovered from the upheaval of getting away and travelling to your retreat, you will probably need an hour or so less sleep than usual (though needs vary). Once you have settled into the retreat it is necessary to establish a sleeping pattern. If you are on your own it can be tempting to stay up unduly late, or over-indulge in sleep. As a general rule, you should not sleep too much or too little. Too little sleep results in sleepiness and dullness, and perhaps also tension. Too much sleep results in sleepiness and dullness too, as well as wasted time.

That said, sleep and dreaming are necessary and valuable activities. On retreat you are likely to experience deeper levels of your mind in dreams, some of which may be very intense and colourful. This kind of dreaming often reflects inner changes caused by your efforts in meditation, so you'll probably need to experiment to see what 'too much' and 'too little' really means for you.

You need some physical exercise on retreat. As there isn't usually much practical work to be done, you can easily become inert and sluggish. This will eventually cause the energy that is available for meditation to run down. Most people need some specific kind of exercise, though a daily walk may be all you need. But beware of spoiling your meditation through overdoing exercises to the extent that the mind becomes restless and the senses coarse. For some reason it seems easy to go to extremes with one's physical energy. Many people take no exercise at all for a week, by which time they are so sluggish that they are forced to do something about it. Then they go to the opposite extreme with an intense physical work-out which is so stimulating that they lose their sensitivity in meditation. No doubt the best answer is to have a little exercise every day.

INFORMATION

We are living in the middle of an information explosion. We have become so used to the media giving us scores of new facts to digest every day that it's really no surprise if we end up a little addicted to information.

After a few days on retreat, you will probably find that you have a lot of extra energy available—and since the mind always wants something to occupy it, you may find yourself on the look-out for interesting objects of distraction. In such a mood it is very easy indeed to pick up a magazine or a book, or even an old newspaper which happens to be lying around, and become engrossed in it for hours on end. The trouble is that this kind of reading squanders the energy which you could otherwise be putting into your meditation.

New information always has to be assimilated, and the assimilation process seems to use a surprisingly large amount of energy—more than you might think. So if you take in too much new information it can temporarily interfere with your ability to concentrate. Your mind may get 'tied up' in a process of assimilation—either consciously reflecting on some reading matter, or unconsciously digesting it.

This will mean that the mind is not free to be deeply involved in meditation; instead, there is just a certain amount of restlessness or dullness. If there is a constant surfeit of information, you may find yourself spending entire sessions just getting to a point where you can concentrate, never able to go deeper. So once you are on a retreat, experiment with the quantity of your information intake—try stopping reading for a while, and see if there is any difference in the quality of your meditation.

These remarks especially apply if you are trying to develop the dhyanas. Of course, there may be other reasons for going on retreat. Even on a meditation retreat you may need to focus on study or reading for a while. A small quantity of inspiring reading material can really help. So it isn't simply a matter of 'no reading', it is a matter of applying the principle of guarding the gates of the senses. Only you can judge how much, and when, to read.

SELF-DISCOVERY

But it needs to be pointed out that people's reading habits can sometimes be a little neurotic. We can pick up the old newspaper and start reading mainly to stave off some unwanted emotion, not because we want to find out about something written in it.

This serves to introduce a very important point about retreats. We have already seen that meditation brings about increasing self-awareness, a discovery of new feelings, emotions, and motivations—new sources of happiness, and also new knowledge about your weaknesses and limitations. Sometimes it is rather a surprise to discover that you are not the person you thought you were.

On a retreat when you are doing more meditation than usual, this process of discovery can happen very quickly. Your previous image of yourself may be uprooted and turned upside down—and your immediate response may be to want to stop all this meditation, abandon the retreat, and go home! Don't do it. Resist the temptation. Just as omelettes cannot be made without breaking eggs, you cannot make progress without readjusting your self-image from time to time. This is actually *a crucially important realization*. It is a realization that you can congratulate yourself on, and even (on reflection) take comfort from. Even though you may feel exposed, and find your ideas about yourself turned upside down, this is the beginning of the possibility of real development. Without true self-knowledge there can never be self-transformation: you can embark on the spiritual path only if you first acknowledge yourself as you truly are. Anyway, other people have probably known that you are like this for years! Nothing is to be gained by running away from yourself. You would do best to let go your doubts, take heart, and be pleased that something so promising is happening.

ACTIVITY

If you are spending a lot of time on your own with little to do—when normally you have plenty to do—the obvious temptation is to fill your time with activities. Your energies will be looking for an outlet. You may start to notice that several little jobs need doing around the cottage you are in; you may remember several letters that you meant to write, you may start several writing or study projects, you may spend hours creating elaborate meals for yourself out of a cookery book. But this is probably a cover-up; most of these activities are probably unnecessary, and wasting this precious time.

If you usually live a fairly active life, you are likely to discover that to some extent you are attached to activity for its own sake. You may not be used to doing nothing, and may, in fact, find it mildly threatening simply to experience yourself. You will therefore need to beware of your activity becoming a substitute for experience, a way of covering up or hiding from a new depth of awareness.

You may not be quite ready to do *absolutely* nothing. Of course, it could be beneficial, even therapeutic, to do a little simple work like housework or gardening—but you will benefit greatly by spending at least an hour or so every day doing nothing but experiencing yourself. If you refrain from unnecessary activity, you can break through to a deeper level of mindfulness. Instead of doing this or that, you should simply sit in a comfortable armchair and relax, watching your mind. It is right here, in 'doing nothing' and simply experiencing yourself here and now, that some of the most important fruits of meditation may be realized. Your mind can become very clear and rich in these circumstances, like a treasure house full of jewels. You will find out what an enormous amount can happen when you are 'doing nothing', and see how much significance there can be in small, everyday things. Your thoughts, over the weeks, will become stronger and more productive. It can be useful to keep a diary of your experiences—your thoughts, dreams, and meditation experiences.

SLOWING DOWN

The 'inner' conditions you set up while on retreat—monitoring your speech, food, rest, exercise, and reading—are a way to 'tune yourself in' with the higher states of consciousness that you are developing. By regulating your behaviour and attitudes in all these areas, you will not waste the energy you need for meditation, or go to such extremes as too much or too little sleep. You'll be able to maintain a balanced, clear, and often joyful state of mind.

Maintaining the best internal conditions for meditation involves all the foundations of spiritual practice which have been mentioned in the preceding chapters. You need awareness, positivity, and purpose to accomplish this 'fine tuning', this continual state of readiness for meditation. You need, above all, to be mindful. To establish yourself in mindfulness it is a good practice—especially during the early days of your retreat—to do everything at a deliberately unhurried pace.

Chapter Seven

MEDITATION POSTURE

THERE IS A GOOD CHANCE that you have had the experience of trying to meditate whilst being distracted by aches and pains in the back or in the legs. To a certain extent you can try to ignore these complaints, treating them as just another hindrance to concentration. This approach can work if you are able to get into the dhyanas, because then minor physical discomforts will recede into the background and cease to matter! But usually these physical discomforts will demand your attention long before you are able to get properly concentrated. Unless you can do something about them, they will nag at you until you are unable to carry on with your practice.

In an introductory meditation class there is rarely enough time to talk about posture in anything but a rudimentary, generalized fashion. If you are not taught how best to sit when you start, you are likely to develop bad postural habits. It is very easy, for example, to adopt a sitting position which gives temporary support, but which may be harmful in the longer term. The problems that arise out of such habits can sometimes be quite difficult to correct. This chapter offers advice to those new to meditation to help them avoid serious problems, and also serves as a 'trouble-shooting guide' for more experienced meditators.

GOOD MEDITATION POSTURE

The body's role in meditation is to support the mind and allow it to concentrate. So the ideal posture is one in which you are completely still and relaxed, yet alert, for as long as you wish.

Since the mind needs to be alert, it is best if the body is upright—if you are lying down, you might become drowsy. So, we are looking for a position in which the body can function with a minimum expenditure of energy, in which the heart can be at its quietest, and the lungs unrestricted, so that the intake and outflow of air is correspondingly quiet and natural.

Generally, if you sit in any posture which minimizes strain, and in which you can also be alert, this will create a sense of vitality which makes it much easier to concentrate. This progression—relaxation and alertness leading to vitality and concentration—is the basic principle of working with meditation posture.

If need be, meditation can be practised in almost any position. An invalid may have no choice but to lie in bed, for example, and, of course, there is walking meditation. There is no reason why you should not meditate standing up. But usually some form of sitting position works best for deep concentration.

If you can sit with the weight of your trunk balanced vertically above your seat, then a minimum of muscular effort will be required to support it. If each arm and leg is symmetrically balanced with its partner, there will be a minimum of distracting physical tension in the body.

PRINCIPLES OF MEDITATION POSTURE

Let's look briefly at some principles of good posture.

SKELETAL SUPPORT AND POSTURAL AWARENESS

Good posture employs the balance and alignment of the skeleton—not the muscles—of the body. Think about it in terms of managing the force of gravity in your body, rather than sitting in a certain position.

Good sitting posture is not a matter of taking up a rigid position and then holding it indefinitely. You need to maintain mindfulness of the body, and understand the principles of meditation posture. You will need to make adjustments, at least occasionally.

PELVIC BALANCE AND WEIGHT DISTRIBUTION

When you sit, the pelvis is the main support for the whole body structure. To enable the pelvis to take the full weight of the upper part of the body without imbalance, it is important that the lower back neither slumps nor over-arches. More details of these postural faults will be given shortly.

The whole weight of the upper body bears down on your pelvic sitting bones—the two bony projections that you can feel pressing against your cushion or seat. The weight must be *equally* distributed over both these sitting bones so that the muscles on either side of your back and neck are not overworked.

HOW PROBLEMS ARISE

The problem that arises most often when you sit in one position for long periods of time is physical discomfort. Sooner or later your knees may start aching, or your back or neck may develop a twinge.

At first, these may have something to do with lack of practice—you may simply not be used to sitting still on the floor. But most aches and pains are caused by muscular tension due to poor posture.

Sometimes strain develops when we form an unconscious habit of using more muscular effort than is necessary, or when muscles remain contracted even when not in use. Sometimes the cause is emotional. But whatever the reason, tension habits frequently become chronic and cause muscular pain, restricted movement, and sometimes fatigue.

Poor sitting posture outside meditation is often responsible for the development of chronic levels of muscular tension, and neck, shoulder, and back discomfort. People often have to sit in poorly designed chairs, which is stressful for the body. If your occupation requires you to spend much of the day sitting down, your posture should be one of your principal health concerns.

Another cause of physical strain may be unacknowledged emotional instability. For example, consider someone who is round-shouldered and closed-chested. This physical stance may have an emotional cause: perhaps the person has a poor self-image and lacks confidence. Moreover, the habit of holding the body in this constricting position may have confirmed the emotion even more, dulling energy, and making the person 'in-turned', over-subjective. So poor posture can be both result and cause of negative emotions.

Generally, if you can develop more awareness of the way you carry yourself, you will naturally find yourself standing more upright, tending to hunch less in the shoulders and being more relaxed in the head and neck. The overall result will almost certainly be an improved mental state.

But there can also be straightforward physical reasons for bad posture. If there is a weakness in one part of your body, it will cause extra strain elsewhere. Either that strain will weaken the affected part, or you will develop extra muscles to cope with it. If extra muscle does develop in compensation, the original weakness may be confirmed, and further degeneration may take place. In this way a pattern of tension and compensatory reaction is repeated throughout the body, and thus begins a gradual process of uneven development. For example, a person with one leg slightly shorter than the other (which is more common than you might think) will have to work the back muscles on one side more than the other. In compensation, one shoulder may be held higher than the other—to adjust for which the neck and head will have to be held over to one side. A slight deformity such as this could go unnoticed for many years—until it comes to sitting still for thirty or forty minutes! Very often it is not until people start practising meditation that their ingrained physical imbalances and difficulties begin to reveal themselves.

The relationship between body and mind—between emotion and posture—has many positive applications. A joyful emotional state naturally reflects itself in the way you sit, stand, and move. In meditation, a bright meditative state naturally gives rise to an improved sitting posture. As you meditate, your relatively chaotic mental states gradually clarify. As they do so, the body begins to feel lighter and more relaxed, and the distracting, niggling discomforts gradually lessen. Then you find that your back begins to straighten, your chest to open, and your shoulders and arms to relax. At the very least, you become aware of the extent to which your present position is restrictive: a straighter back and an open chest will begin to feel more natural, and you may start to acquire an intuitive understanding of what good meditation posture can be.

POSTURE AS A MEDITATION METHOD

As well as serving as an important basis for physical health and meditation practice, posture can be approached as a meditation method in its own right. Postural awareness, on its own, can help counteract hindrances to meditation. Sometimes just a subtle movement of the angle of the pelvis, or the alignment of the head on the neck, can suddenly make energy available and concentration easier.

It is worth experimenting. Sometimes either your mind or your body, or both, are dull and sleepy, uninterested in meditation. At such times you are unlikely to engage with a proper meditation practice; in fact you are probably set to drift away into day-dreams. As an antidote, you could decide to spend the meditation session trying to maintain a good posture. Even if your mind is unable to grasp a more subtle meditation object, you can at least make an effort to remain awake and sit correctly. If you persist in bringing your attention back to your body, checking for arching in your back or slumping—and other points which will be explained later—the hindrance is likely to disperse before the end of the session, and you should be able to move on to a definite meditation technique. But even if sloth and torpor is extremely strong (as it sometimes can be), and you are not able to meditate properly even after half an hour or forty minutes, nevertheless, you will have weakened its power over you just by holding

Fig.1
Full lotus

it at bay. And you will probably notice an improvement in subsequent meditation sessions.

You can also do something about the opposite mental extreme, the hindrance of restlessness and anxiety, through concentration on posture. A method of counteracting both the mental and physical agitation is quite simply to determine to sit absolutely still. Your mind cannot be made to be still, but your body can—if you definitely decide that it is going to be! By taking the stillness of your body as the main object of your meditation

Fig.2
Full lotus, side view

Fig.3
Half lotus

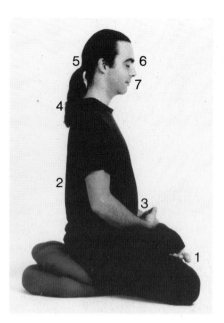

practice, your restless mind will eventually calm down and be at peace. If the agitation is very strong, this process will probably take some time. But if, without forcing your mind, you persist in patiently stilling the body, you will be successful in the end.

Fig.4
One foot on calf

Fig.5
One leg in front

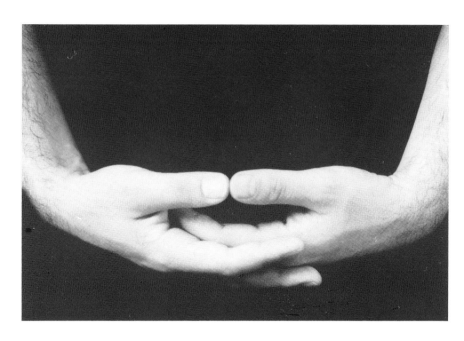

Fig.6
Hand position
(dhyana mudra)

THE IDEAL MEDITATION POSTURE

Now that we have outlined the principles and seen the causes of some of
our problems, let's explore ways of sitting in more detail.

Cross-legged postures are not the only options available when sitting
for meditation. You can use an upright chair, or kneel on a meditation
stool. But if your hips are supple enough to allow you to sit cross-legged,

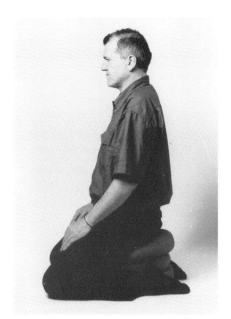

Fig.7
Kneeling with cushions

Fig.8
Kneeling on a stool

Fig.9
Sitting on a chair

Fig.10
Sitting with back
against a wall

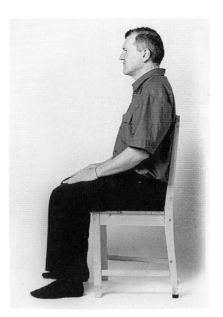

you should try that posture first of all.

The meditation posture that affords the best quality of relaxation and alertness is the well known 'full lotus' position (see illustration). Unfortunately most of us are too restricted in the hips and thighs to sit like this comfortably, or even cross our legs in this way at all. Even those who *can* do so should avoid long periods of sitting in full lotus until (through exercises like fig.25) their hips have loosened and the posture has become fairly easy. This is important, because otherwise the knee joints will be under too much tension—damage could result. Meditators need to take care of their knees.

The full lotus posture consists of seven aspects (see fig.2):

(1) The legs are crossed with each foot placed, sole uppermost, upon the thigh of the other leg.

(2) The spine is upright, neither arching backwards nor slumping forwards.

(3) The hands are held in the lap, two or three inches below the navel. The palms both face upwards, one over the other so that the thumb-tips lightly touch (fig.6).

(4) The shoulders are relaxed and rolled somewhat back, to keep the chest open.

(5) The head is balanced evenly on the spine.

(6) The eyes are directed downwards, either lightly closed or half open.

(7) The mouth is relaxed, teeth unclenched, lips held lightly together. The tongue just touches the palate behind the teeth.

It must be stressed that this is an *ideal* posture. Points 2 to 7 may present little difficulty for many people, but few will find the full lotus leg position easy, at least to begin with. Luckily, it is not essential to have your legs folded like this, since there are a number of variations which are almost as good. Many people can manage a half lotus, which is very similar. If you look at the preceding photographs, you should be able to find a position which suits you for the time being.

POSTURE SETTING UP ROUTINE

It is useful to learn this routine for setting up your posture. If you do it every time you sit to meditate, you will have a systematic way of assessing your posture. After some practice the routine will become second nature. It might take no longer than a second or two; at other times you may need to spend more time on it.

Stage 1 Choose a cushion (or stool, or whatever you use) which seems the right height, and sit, arranging your legs in one of the ways shown (figs.7, 8, 9, 10).

There is no need to be concerned for the moment if both of your knees don't reach the ground. Once your posture is set up your legs will need to be lower than your hips—otherwise the back will slump—but the main thing at this stage is getting whatever you are sitting on to be at the right height. Even a variation of an inch can make a vital difference. At a certain height you will feel the correct balance of your body, and this awareness will then make it easier to adjust your legs and back.

Two common sitting faults, caused by incorrect cushion height, affect the way you hold yourself. These are arching backwards and slumping forwards in the back.

Arching—or perhaps we should say *over*-arching, since the spine naturally arches inwards to some extent—often occurs when the seat is too high. The extra height causes the upper pelvis to move forwards and the tail-bone backwards, so that the buttocks protrude behind. This creates a general tendency for the body weight to fall forwards, so the upper back arches up and backwards to compensate. This strains the lower back so that you begin to feel pain there.

The remedy for over-arching, if slight, is to relax in the lower back, letting the spine return to a natural position. Otherwise, you can experiment with a lower seat.

Slumping may occur when your seat is too low. In this case the opposite happens: the upper pelvis tends backwards and the tail-bone tucks under. You then collapse in the lower back and the weight of your body

Fig.11
Over-arching backwards

Fig.12
Slumping forwards

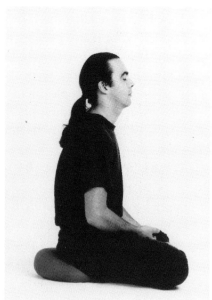

falls backwards. To stop yourself from falling backwards you tend to slump forwards, closing in your chest at the same time. Painful tension is caused in your neck and shoulders by this awkward positioning.

The remedy for slumping, if slight, is simply to remind yourself to sit up straight (not rigidly straight like a broom handle, but with a natural curve). Otherwise, you can experiment with a higher seat.

Stage 2 Become aware of the weight of your body as it presses the two 'sitting bones' in the buttocks down on to your seat. Maintaining this awareness as your base, and keeping your weight evenly distributed between left and right, allow your spinal column to lift lightly and straighten, avoiding rigidity.

Stage 3 Take a deep breath or two, and allow the chest and rib-cage to open. Experience your shoulders and arms lifting slightly on the inward breath, and on the outward breath allow them to roll back slightly, and then relax down so that the chest stays open.

Stage 4 You can then adjust your hands in your lap so that they are not working against the relaxed-back position of your shoulders and arms. It can be helpful to place a small 'hand-pad' in your lap—this will provide a flat surface for your hands, which can then relax more easily. This too will help your shoulders to relax. One hand can be placed over the other.

Stage 5 You can now adjust the position of your head. It is important that you allow your head to be supported by your spine, and not by the muscles of your neck. There should be no sense of rigidity—it's worth checking this from time to time during meditation. The neck muscles

Fig.13
'Direction' of spine,
chest, shoulders, and
arms

Fig.14
Position of head

should be completely relaxed, so that your head can move freely.

So adjust by becoming aware of your neck as an extension of your spine—it may help to roll your head gently backwards and forwards until it feels balanced. Experience the point where your skull balances on your spinal column, and let it tilt forwards very slightly, so that your gaze is upon the floor a few feet in front of you. Lastly, relax your face, jaw, tongue, and throat.

Stage 6 Now check your posture as a whole, especially noting the alignment of your trunk from side to side and back to front. You can rock gently each way from your pelvis, if it helps, until you feel yourself to be in equilibrium. Now you are in a position to check more thoroughly for the basic sitting faults of slumping forward or arching backwards, and make any adjustments necessary.

'FEELING RIGHT' MAY NOT MEAN THAT IT *IS* RIGHT

The entire sitting position needs to be as balanced and symmetrical as possible. Ideally each part of the body is balanced by another, so that there is a minimum amount of strain on the system. Setting up your posture in the systematic way outlined earlier helps achieve this symmetry and balance.

But there is one important problem: you cannot simply rely on whether or not your posture feels right. Very often, what feels 'right' is merely what you are accustomed to. So when you are placed—by a friend or teacher—in a better posture, it will probably be unfamiliar and may even feel awkward and crooked at first. Your tendency will probably be to move gradually back to the familiar (but incorrect and harmful) posture.

So even if you have practised meditation for a long time you should not simply accept a feeling of 'rightness' or 'wrongness' in your posture as the only guide-line, but try to get an objective assessment sometimes. As with many things in life, it is not so easy to see, let alone change, your bad habits! You need personal attention and feedback, so from time to time you should ask your friends to take a critical look at your meditation posture, as well as attending an occasional meditation class or retreat where posture instruction is available.

PAIN

One obvious indication of incorrect posture is pain. Certainly there are some aches and pains which are best ignored—minor discomforts which soon pass, feelings of awkwardness, itches, and other irritations. There can be no end to these, and you will never be able to settle down unless you consciously decide to put up with a few of them.

As we have already seen, these discomforts are often linked with inner restlessness, an unsettled mind fastening on to, and becoming obsessed by, a relatively minor irritation. By indulging such restlessness, you will not connect with your meditation, and other people meditating with you will also be disturbed. If this is all that is happening, try to recognize the fact, and try to put your attention elsewhere.

But it's important to be sensitive in assessing your pain, for some pains may well be danger signals. Pins and needles, or numbness, for example, should not be ignored; it is certainly not good for limbs to become completely numb. Neither should sharp pains, for they invariably suggest that something is wrong. If you are in any doubt about the significance of what you are feeling, talk to someone with more experience. Some people seem to think that meditation practice necessarily involves a little discomfort, but if this means ignoring danger signals, you run the risk of damaging yourself.

Buddhist tradition reminds us that the human body is exceedingly precious and hard to obtain; since it serves as the basis from which you can meditate, gain insight, and even attain Enlightenment, it should be treated with kindness and respect.

Fig.15
Soft floor covering to
protect knees and
ankles

Fig.16
Padding supporting
raised knee

WAYS TO MAKE SITTING PRACTICE EASIER

The long-term solution to posture difficulties is to learn some kind of physical training which will give the body more flexibility and strength, and instil some postural awareness. We will soon be looking at a few helpful exercises. In the short term, however, there are a number of ways to make sitting easier.

Unless the weather is really hot, it is generally helpful to keep your legs and hips warm. Warmth takes the edge off those temporary, inconsequential aches and pains mentioned in the last section. Beneath your legs, whether you are kneeling or cross-legged, you should place a doubled blanket or a foam-rubber pad (though if the foam-rubber extends under the cushion it may make your seat unsteady). This not only insulates the legs but protects your knees. For people who are kneeling it also takes the pressure off their ankles and upper parts of the feet.

In fact, cushions and pads are generally good for alleviating pressure. Some people find a small pad, or perhaps a roll of material, helpful to cushion an ankle which is pressing into a thigh. If one knee (or both) will not touch the ground, a small cushion can be placed there for support.

Uncomfortable hands can be a source of distraction. It is therefore very helpful to have some padding beneath them, a flat surface on which they can be be placed evenly. The position of this hand pad should be high enough to relieve the weight of your arms from your shoulders, so that the shoulders can more easily relax down the back, allowing the chest to open more freely (fig.17).

**Fig.17
Padding supporting
hands**

**Fig.18
Blanket for warmth**

EXERCISES

MOVING 'UP' TO A BETTER POSTURE

It is important to remember that there is no point in trying to force yourself into an ideal position that you cannot sustain. The correct posture is
the one which enables *you* to be as relaxed and as alert as possible within
your physical limitations. You need to be sensitive, not forcing your body
but caring for it, working as best you can with what you have.

However, in terms of the principles outlined earlier, some sitting positions are definitely better for concentration. For example, the cross-legged
full lotus posture gives the best skeletal balance. On the whole, it allows
more access to subtle physical energies than other postures, and it is also
(if you are used to it) the most comfortable position for long periods of sitting. The next best is some other form of cross-legged posture, for example the half lotus, or a variation of it (fig.3). Then come, in order of
preference, kneeling on a stool or cushions, and sitting on a chair. All
these positions can be very good for meditation, but though you can
meditate effectively in any of them, you should always aim for the position which affords the most relaxation and alertness.

HOW EXERCISE CAN HELP

Of course, the trouble with such advice is that our stiff joints and weak
muscles are not used to it; they are going to hold us back. Can anything be
done?

Whatever your age—and however stiff you are—it is possible, over time, to make some progress in loosening your joints and giving your muscles more strength and tone by taking a little regular exercise. There are many systems of exercise, and within each system there are many exercises. I have collated here a small selection which can be used to work on the parts of the body most affected by meditation practice.

A warning is required before you read about—or try—these exercises. The problem with learning exercises from a book is that without a teacher you may do them incorrectly and damage yourself. If you do not fully understand how to work in a particular exercise, you may become over-confident, push yourself a little too hard, and overdo it. At worst, you could put your back or knees askew, painfully and even permanently. So, while the exercises which follow can certainly be experimented with, you must be very gentle with yourself. If you decide to take them up seriously, find someone who can help you to do them correctly.

BE GENTLE WITH EXERCISE

FOUR TYPES OF EXERCISE
Of all the many different types of exercise, four stand out as being particularly valuable, though each is quite distinct from the others.

Firstly, there is the approach of standard Western 'PT' (physical training), which usually involves the vigorous movement of selected parts of the body. There are many kinds of PT—some very specific, like weight-lifting, others more general. With PT there is less emphasis on bodily awareness, but some very effective methods for stretching and strengthening particular muscles have been developed. PT is good for keeping basically fit.

Then come two Eastern disciplines, t'ai chi and hatha yoga. T'ai chi involves the whole body in a very fluid, dance-like movement. Practised consistently, t'ai chi develops physical stamina and 'grounded' body awareness, and combines this with awareness of body movements. Yoga seems at first sight more static since it involves special postures (or *asanas* in Sanskrit) rather than moving exercises, but within each posture there is a complex of inner stretches, movements, and relaxations. Yoga is perhaps the most exact of the physical disciplines, combining training in bodily awareness with specific, directed exercise.

Another kind of 'exercise', the Alexander Technique, does not involve exercise, as such, at all. Like t'ai chi and yoga, it trains the student in awareness of the body and its movements. But it is unique in that it does so in the context of ordinary, everyday movement. Practitioners learn how best to use their body—how to re-train the bad postural habits they have

Fig.19
Walking on the outside
edges of the feet to
open and strengthen the
ankles

Fig.20
Gentle exercise for the
knees

acquired over years. I have not included any Alexander Technique methods here (apart from the relaxation at the end) but some people may find it well worth looking into.[40]

These four types of exercise have been chosen to demonstrate some of the basic approaches. Obviously other methods are widely practised, for example 'martial arts' such as karate or aikido. From the exercise point of view, these combine different elements of the four types. Teachers of all four methods are widely available these days. You could consider either learning one, or a little of each. Perhaps the ideal approach would be to get a thorough grounding in one physical discipline, and then learn a little of one or two others.

PT
ANKLES

For strengthening and stretching ankles, you can try the 'duck walk'. Walk about the room—in curves, not straight lines—on the outside edges of your feet (fig.19), keeping the feet straight. You can also try lifting your toes and walking at the same time.

KNEES

Knees can be gently exercised by standing against a wall and supporting one thigh at a right angle from the wall with clasped hands. Relax both the ankle and knee, and then swing the lower leg (fig.20). It is important to relax the hip on the supported side and really 'give' the leg to the supporting hands.

You should rotate the lower leg only very gently and slowly, with just a very little sideways movement—swing mainly to and fro. The knee joint

Fig.21
Exercise for thighs

Fig.22
Skiing exercise for
thighs

has very little sideways flexibility, and stretching it sideways too much, or too sharply, will damage it. It may be easier to do this exercise sitting on a table, dangling both lower legs (i.e. knees, calves, ankles) and swinging them from the knee.

(1)   For thighs, you can stand on one leg near a wall (close enough so that **THIGHS** you can reach out and regain your balance if necessary), holding one ankle with the leg bent back behind you (fig.21).

The hip on the supported side needs to be relaxed so that it drops to the same level as the other hip. The top of the pelvis should tilt backwards with the tail-bone tucked under; the spine and chest should gently lift. Try to relax and release the thigh muscles as you stretch the thigh.

Then repeat the exercise for the other leg.

(2)   Here is a skiing exercise which is good for thighs. Stand at an arm's length, sideways, from a wall, with your feet together. With your hand on the wall for support, keeping the feet flat on the floor, trunk upright, knees together, and hips at right angles to the wall, lean towards the wall, bending your knees and arm as you go down (fig.22). Then repeat on the other side.

The hips and pelvis are often stiff and in need of opening up. These exer- **HIPS AND PELVIS** cises especially help improve cross-legged positions.

(1)   You can try kneeling on all fours, with knees wide apart and toes together. Then with your buttocks kept low, you take your chest and arms

forward on the floor (fig.23).

(2) Or kneel with one bent knee forwards, the other leg bending straight back along the floor behind you, the foot in line with your leg. You support yourself with straight arms, palms against the floor on either side of your trunk. Then turn in your waist towards your kneeling leg (fig.24).

(3) Again, try sitting cross-legged on the floor and cradle one leg in your arms, holding your knee and the sole of your foot between your elbows. Then swing the leg gently from side to side or in a figure of eight. This is good for knees and thighs (fig.25).

KNEES AND THIGHS

(1) Lie on your back with your legs out straight, gently bending one knee and bringing it close to your body by clasping it with your hands. At the same time, keep your other straight knee on the ground (fig.26).

(2) Or squat down on the floor with your feet apart, holding the knees inside your elbows and clasped hands (fig.27).

T'AI CHI

There are a number of very useful general exercise movements in t'ai chi which are good for loosening and relaxing—as well as strengthening—the whole bodily framework. Here is one.

Stand with your legs a little apart, feet facing forwards. You should not stand up straight and erect, but bend slightly at the knees, letting the lower pelvis tuck forward. Let the shoulders relax and the arms hang loose. Become aware of your breathing, at the same time becoming particularly aware of the stomach area.

Then, keeping your feet where they are for the time being, rotate your whole body—from head to ankles—gently from side to side, letting your arms swing freely. Let the arms lift out and swing away from the body as the rhythm of the rotation gets under way. Swing round to the left, round to the right, turning the abdomen, chest, neck, and head, all together in one fluid motion. As your momentum builds up, let the shoulders relax

Fig.23
Opening up the hips
and pelvis

Fig.24
Stretching thighs
and hips

Fig.25
Opening the hip joints.
Gentle exercise for
knees and thighs

Fig.27
Exercise for knees
and thighs

as the arms swing; let your loose arms fall naturally against your trunk, if need be, each time you turn. You shouldn't turn violently, but gently and evenly.

Get more and more involved in the movement. As you swing to the left, let the weight of your body move onto your right foot. As you swing right, feel the weight on your left foot. Keep the knees bent—they can be well bent now—and the lower pelvis tucked under. When you are performing the movement easily you should feel that the momentum comes only from your abdomen.

After a while, move your feet too; turn each foot on the heel when your body turns, so that when you are three-quarters of the way to the right the right foot comes round on its heel to follow the swing of your body. As you turn back to the front, turn your toes to the front. As you go round to

Fig.26
Exercise for knees and
thighs

Figs.28 & 29
Swinging from side to side, loosening and strengthening the whole framework of the body

the left, turn on the heel to the left in the same way (figs.28, 29).

In spite of such a long description, this is a very simple, relaxing, and enjoyable exercise! Give it time—it may take five minutes at least to get into the feeling of it. This exercises and tones your whole body. It is especially good for the shoulders, hips, and abdomen.

HATHA YOGA

Yoga is probably the most thorough of all the physical disciplines. There are hundreds of specific *asanas* for developing every part of the body, only a few of which can be included here. The emphasis in yoga is on being aware of, and deliberately working, every part of the body in each pose. Inner relaxation and subtle movement is consciously 'directed' through close attention to what is happening in the body, but (as in the Alexander Technique training which follows) these subtleties can only be appreciated fully through communication with a qualified teacher.

First, here are two simple leg stretches which increase the suppleness of the leg muscles, strengthen the knees, and loosen the hip joints (figs.30, 31). (These are not in fact traditional yoga exercises but are often taught in yoga classes as a 'warm-up'):

FRONT LEG STRETCH

Stand upright, with your feet together, in front of a raised ledge that is a little below waist height (the height can be adjusted according to how supple you are). Draw in the muscles of the thighs and knees so that the kneecaps lift up. Then, raising one leg, place one heel on the ledge, so that your leg reaches out in front of you (keeping the knee straight). The ledge

Fig.30
Developing flexibility in the knees and backs of thighs

Fig.31
Sideways leg stretch

should be at a height that allows you to do this bearably, but with a good stretch.

Stand erect with both feet pointing forwards, arms relaxed at your sides. Concentrate on what is happening in your body, encouraging your chest to open and your shoulders to relax back as in meditation posture. Continue to lift your leg muscles.

After a while, change legs.

This, and the next exercise, will develop the flexibility of your knees and the backs of your thighs.

The sideways leg stretch is good for the hips. You use the same ledge as before—or a lower one if it is difficult—this time standing sideways to it.

SIDEWAYS LEG STRETCH

Lift one leg and place your heel on the ledge with both legs and your knees straight as before. Have your toes pointing upwards, and your trunk in line with your standing leg, placing your hands on your hips.

Triangle pose pose is performed in definite stages, and each stage should be regarded as part of the pose, so that your awareness is not scattered.

TRIANGLE POSE (*TRIKONASANA*)

(1) First stand upright with your feet together, knees and thighs lifting, hands loose at your sides. The coccyx or tail-bone is slightly tucked under and forward. Relax mentally, concentrating and increasing awareness of the body.

(2) Now take your feet about a metre apart, feet facing forwards. Then turn your right foot out ninety degrees to the right, and point your left

Fig.32
Triangle pose
(1) Stand erect

Fig.33
Triangle pose
(2) Legs apart,
feet to side

foot just a little to the right. Raise both arms to shoulder height, keeping your head facing in front. Next, leading with your right arm, extend the trunk sideways over the right thigh, without bending your knee, and keeping your legs, hips, waist, and shoulders all in a straight line. Hold the calf as low down as you can while keeping that straight line. The head is still facing forwards, neck relaxed, knees and thighs still lifting.

(3) Next extend your left arm—wrist, hand, and fingers too—upwards to the ceiling, and turn your head, looking upwards. Remain in the pose for a few breaths, trying all the time to make it more steady. (If you can keep your awareness in your feet and legs it will be easier to do that, and the pose will generally feel more satisfactory.)

(4) Then, keeping your knees straight, come up to the centre (on an in-halation, ideally—generally, try to be aware of your breathing) with arms outstretched and feet facing the front.

Turn your feet to face the front, and do the same pose on the other side. Turn your left foot out to the left, your right foot slightly in, and (on an ex-halation) extend over to the left as before. It can help to do this with your back against a wall to keep your trunk and legs in a straight line.

Triangle pose is an excellent all-round pose. It develops flexibility and strength in your legs, knees, hips, and lower back. Take it slowly, and don't strain. Do the pose twice or three times on both sides.

COBBLER'S POSE
(BADDHAKONASANA)

Cobbler's pose is good for loosening at the hips, and regular practice of this pose will make it easier to sit cross-legged.

Fig.34
Triangle pose
(3) Extend over

Fig.35
Triangle pose
(4) Raise arm
and look up

Sit on the floor and bring your heels together near your body, catching your feet with your hands. Sit upright with an open chest (it might be helpful to have your back against a wall). Then concentrate on the groin and thigh muscles and try to relax in the groins. As you do this your knees will move down towards the floor.

Two people can help one another in this pose if, as you sit against a wall, your partner kneels so that their knees hold your heels close to your

Fig.36
Cobbler's pose
loosening the hips

Fig.37
A partner can help you
relax in this exercise

body. Then your partner gently places their hands upon your knees without applying pressure. Now you relax in your thighs and groins; the weight of their arm will help stretch your thigh muscles slightly and give you some tension to relax against.

RELAXATION

It is beneficial to lie down and relax, maintaining awareness, after any session of exercise, and this is especially recommended after yoga practice. The Alexander Technique form of relaxation which follows (figs.38, 39) can be used.

ALEXANDER TECHNIQUE

There are no specific exercises in the Alexander Technique—it works through developing awareness of how we use the body in everyday activities like sitting, standing, and walking. But Alexander teachers do recommend the following.

GENERAL RELAXATION

Sit down on the floor with a small pile of paperback books—say one or two inches high—two to three feet behind you. Bending your knees, allow your feet to rest flat on the ground at the same width apart as your shoulders (fig.38).

Now roll your back down on to the floor, supporting yourself with your elbows and lower arms, until you are lying on the ground with the back of your head resting on the books. Using your hands, adjust the position of the books if necessary, so that the bony back of your head is resting on the books without their touching your neck.

You may need to adjust the height of the pile so that your head is neither dropping back and down towards the floor, nor raised up to the point where your chin presses down on your throat, causing discomfort.

**Figs.38 & 39
Alexander semi-supine position
(1) Sitting down for the relaxation
(2) Final position**

Have the pile too high rather then too low. Generally, your forehead should be slightly higher than your chin.

Then bring your feet a little closer to your buttocks, so that your knees

balance easily as they point towards the ceiling. You may need to take your feet a little further apart or closer together to achieve this balance. A certain amount of muscle tension may be necessary to maintain this position, but it should be as little as possible so that there is no gripping on your hip joints or your toes, and no straining in your leg muscles.

Slide your elbows out to the side and place your open hands on your abdomen or your hips; let the floor support your weight.

If the above relaxation is combined with Alexander 'directions' to your body, it will bring about a lengthening of your spine, a widening of the whole of your back, and a release and lengthening through the musculature of your legs and arms. Giving 'directions' is a process of 'thinking into the body', and is best conveyed by a teacher. Wilful attempts to make this process happen might lead to your muscles contracting further, instead of the release and integration which directing should bring about.

ALEXANDER 'DIRECTIONS'

The directions consist in thinking of the neck muscles releasing, so that the head can move away from the shoulders in the direction shown by the arrow (in fig.39), and in thinking of your back lengthening and widening, and of your knees releasing 'upwards' towards the ceiling away from the hip joints and ankle joints.

After you have been lying down for some time, you should never get up abruptly. Instead, roll over on to one side first, letting your eyes lead the movement. Then you can get up gently.

Practised daily for 15–20 minutes, this develops greater poise, and a noticeably improved awareness of bodily movements.

Chapter Eight

WORKING IN MEDITATION

ONCE YOUR MEDITATION PRACTICE is established, you need to keep taking it deeper. An established practice is like a plant that has managed to put down roots. To some extent it can be left to look after itself, but it still needs regular attention if it is to remain alive and growing. Sometimes it may need extensive pruning, weeding, and even transplanting!

If you can approach your meditation creatively and systematically, you will find it easy to retain your present interest in it. The initial novelty may wear off, but your meditation will acquire its own direction and inner life, so that it never becomes routine.

ACTIVITY AND PASSIVITY

Perhaps the idea of *working* in meditation conjures up an image of hard exertion and knotted brows. Yet meditation needs to be viewed as creative work, work that we can feel joyful about doing. We need to think in terms of making a definite effort, because we are dealing *directly* with strong habitual tendencies. If we see our practice merely in terms of relaxation, as some people do, we may just reinforce these habits. Sometimes people refer to meditation as though it were something 'passive'. It's certainly true that we are trying to become more receptively aware in meditation. But this receptivity in meditation is an attitude which is very deliberately cultivated—it's hardly passive.

In meditation we are trying to combine both activity and receptivity together in a stream of mindful action. We are *receptively* aware of the mental states which arise, and we *actively* respond to these states by cultivating the factors of dhyana and counteracting the hindrances.

P	Posture	Body position allows energy to flow	Receptively experiencing
I	Introspection	Awareness of present state of mind	
P	Purpose	Strategy for this session of meditation	Actively responding
E	Enthusiasm	Engaging with motivation	
R	Resolve	Unification of all factors—total engagement	

A SETTING UP ROUTINE

There is a useful way of beginning your meditation which can help establish creative working habits. It involves five stages which you can go through at the start of every session of practice. (Each stage is also a principle which applies to meditation generally.)

The five stages are: **(1) Posture, (2) Introspection, (3) Purpose, (4) Enthusiasm**, and **(5) Resolve**. We'll go through these briefly first, then in detail.

(1) Working in meditation starts with your sitting, your **posture**.

(2) Once your bodily awareness is established, you need to **introspect**—in other words, try to experience what is going on in yourself.

(3) It is only then, when you know what is happening, that you can decide on how best to approach this particular session of meditation. The approach or strategy that you choose is your **purpose**.

(4) Yet it is not enough just to know what your strategy is. To commit yourself to it, you need to feel motivated and enthusiastic. This emotional aspect of your purpose is **enthusiasm**.

(5) Resolve is the sum of the previous elements, and more. Only when you have created those four factors—physical and mental self-awareness (i.e. posture and introspection), together with conscious and well-motivated direction (i.e. purpose and enthusiasm)—can you truly start to meditate. The self-awareness and the directedness, the active and receptive elements, work together on the meditation object in one unified process called resolve. The combination of all the factors makes up a resolution to engage fully in the practice.

You can use this routine as a foundation for a session of meditation. Checking your posture, introspection, purpose, enthusiasm, and resolve can help you to recall the main principles of working in meditation right from the start. And once you have established them, you can more easily maintain awareness of them while you are meditating.

The five principles can easily be remembered using the acronym PIPER, made up from their initial letters.

This method makes a good general *introduction* to working in meditation. Once it has been assimilated, you may not consciously employ it very often.

In a way, it's rather like learning to drive. The instructor insists that you hold the steering wheel in a particular way, look in the mirrors, and signal very deliberately. At first you need to employ the various elements of driving technique quite formally, but later, when experience comes, and you evolve your own driving style, you no longer need consciously to employ formal techniques. The techniques have served their purpose, which is to implant a complex set of habits at an unconscious level, so that your whole body 'knows' how to drive safely.

PIPER is this kind of method. The initial discipline of identifying and using these factors in your practice will eventually give you a more intuitive 'feel' for approaching meditation.

Here is a more detailed description of the stages of PIPER.

POSTURE

The first thing is to find the best possible sitting position. You could use the information in Chapter Seven to establish a posture in which you feel alert and able to develop concentration. It can sometimes be beneficial to pay attention to your posture for an extended period, say for the first ten minutes or more of the meditation session, checking the body's inner balance and relaxing any tension.

Postural awareness can be used as a method of working in meditation in its own right. In some forms of Buddhism, such as Zen, there is a considerable emphasis on correct sitting. Awareness of subtle bodily energies is also a factor in the development of higher states of consciousness, as we shall see shortly.

At a more basic level, postural awareness can be used to counteract certain hindrances. One specific use, which we saw in the last chapter, is as an antidote to the hindrance of sloth and torpor. Trying to sit well provides a certain physical stimulation, so if you are sleepy the most effective counter-measure may be to spend the meditation session just maintaining a good posture. The 'opposite' hindrance, restlessness and anxiety, can also be counteracted by postural awareness. Concentrating on your body—a part of you that is at least relatively stable—has a calming, grounding effect.

As a general rule, you should periodically check your posture in order to see whether it is still helping your practice. Make sure that you are not slumping or arching, and verify that you are still correctly aligned, still relaxed, and that your vitality is flowing. We shall be going into some of these details shortly.

INTROSPECTION

Introspection means checking and assessing your state of mind as you meditate. It's important that you notice when you become distracted, and the specific ways in which you get distracted. Unless you check out what is happening, you will have no way of assessing what kind of effort to make.

Introspection is an art which requires practice. It isn't simply an analysis, or a distanced observation of your experience. You'll need to use intuition as well as hard reasoning—but acquiring some theoretical understanding of the principles of meditation will be useful. If you can give names to your experiences, you'll be able to get a better grasp on what is happening in you.

Introspection can be both receptive and active. You can be *receptive* by simply being open to your experience, letting whatever is there reveal itself. You can be *active* by questioning and checking yourself—checking perhaps for hindrances to concentration, or latent dhyana factors.

What *exactly* you look for will depend on your temperament, your experience, and what is going on at the time. Perhaps you could look for laziness or restlessness, or ask whether your thoughts are directed or wandering. The basic question is 'What's happening?'

Once you have made it a habit, checking like this can give a quick general picture of your present state of mind. It is a faculty which to some extent develops in its own time, and the time you actually spend doing it may be long or short, depending on the strength of your self-awareness and the general momentum of your practice. At the beginning of a session you may only be able to muster a vague, fuzzy awareness of the state you are in, so in that situation you may benefit by giving more time to introspection. But you may find, with experience, that such an emphasis is unnecessary: just making a little effort to introspect will often set going a momentum of clarity which will sharpen more and more as you continue.

It is important, however, to establish that initial effort. Mental states can change rapidly, and you will need to check frequently throughout the session. At first, such checking may seem artificial. If you are not accustomed to it, introspection will probably feel like an obstruction to concentration. But when it has become more familiar, you will appreciate the edge that it gives.

PURPOSE

Purpose means having some kind of strategy for this session of meditation. Now you know the state of your mind, you can decide on your approach, formulating aims and goals. There are two aspects to this: specific and general purpose.

Your *specific* purpose is the immediate direction which you decide to take in *this* session of practice. It is not a rigid aim, but a provisional line of action which you are prepared to adapt to meet changing conditions. For example, at first you might notice the presence of sloth and torpor, and in response decide to put extra energy into the practice. Later on you might need to reverse that decision. You might need to start calming down if over-application of that approach arouses too much energy.

Here, both the arousing and the calming of your energy would be applications of specific purpose. Specific purpose is the intention to use a particular strategic working method. Deciding on the right approach need not involve a lot of thought, though in particular mental states it may sometimes be necessary to spend extra time considering exactly what is needed. At other times you may be able to act quickly and intuitively, without thinking about it much at all. Both are valid ways of determining your specific purpose.

General purpose is the overall intention to apply principles of working in meditation. You have a certain general knowledge of methods and principles—an understanding of the need to introspect, recognize hindrances, and so on—which you have built up in the course of your practice. Over a period of time you'll learn how best to approach the particular configurations of hindrances that you experience most often. You will find certain hindrances continually cropping up and, through continually trying to work with them, you develop a strategic sense. This sense of strategy will continue from one meditation to the next, so that rather than taking each meditation 'as it comes', you base the approach for your next sitting on what happened in the previous one.

This strategic awareness is most likely to build up on retreat, when there is little to distract you. Otherwise, you may be able to maintain more of a continuity of awareness by keeping a simple meditation notebook. If you maintain this sense of strategy you'll need to spend less time in constantly re-discovering the needs of the situation. This will make more energy available for actual meditation.

ENTHUSIASM

It is important to have a clear strategy, but only emotion can actually move us into action. Our approach to meditation cannot just be cool and rational—it also needs some spark that will fire our efforts. The stage of enthusiasm is rather like saying—'Yes, I *really* want to do this.' Purpose has to do with forming intentions; enthusiasm is our emotional engagement with those intentions.

In order to arouse enthusiasm for working in your meditation, you'll need to awaken—or re-awaken—some of the positive associations you have with it. You could try reflecting on why you were drawn to meditation in the first place. You probably have a strong personal feeling for your growth and development. Try to re-kindle it, if you can. You might have been inspired by the example of the Buddha—or perhaps you would just like to become more aware and concentrated, more friendly and helpful, better organized, wiser, more insightful. Ask yourself what results you hope for from spiritual practice. These considerations will arouse your motivation and give you the courage, the confidence, and the enthusiasm that will be needed for you to involve yourself wholeheartedly in meditation.

RESOLVE

Resolve is a fully integrated approach to the task in hand, combining all the previous factors—posture, introspection, purpose, and enthusiasm—and bringing them to bear on the meditation object. It is the full weight of one's physical, rational, and emotional being.

Resolve is what you actually meditate *with*. The word 'resolve' implies a resolution which you make, even a vow to achieve something. You have now marshalled all the forces at your disposal and are in a position to make a very effective effort. Resolve really comes into its own when you are quite clear in your mind that you actually want to meditate.

Resolve is an especially important quality in the spiritual life generally. You need to constantly clarify and re-clarify the motives that you have for practising. Re-clarification will often be necessary because, until you are irreversibly established on the Path, new doubts—new levels and degrees of doubting—will keep arising. In the long term, resolve will unify your entire life; it is the dynamic centre around which the whole process of integration takes place.

WORKING IN MEDITATION—A REVIEW

Now we are going to explore ways of working in meditation in more depth. But in accordance with that principle of 'working from the ground up' let's go back, briefly, to our mental states outside meditation.

MINDFULNESS OF THE HINDRANCES OUTSIDE MEDITATION

Just now I mentioned looking for the five hindrances in meditation. But it is a good practice to look for them outside meditation too. They will almost certainly be there—much of the content of our ordinary consciousness is usually coloured by these mental states.

It's natural, for example, for your attention to be centred around pleasurable sense experience (this is the *kama-loka*, after all!). It may be useful for you to monitor how your intake of sense experiences affects your ability to concentrate. Other hindrances may not be far away: under pressure, it's easy to become irritated or angry; often we either cannot relax because of restlessness, or we become sluggish and dull. At times we are indecisive and lacking in confidence. If you establish the habit of recognizing these hindrances outside meditation, you'll be in a far better position to notice them as you meditate.

Much the same principle applies to the five factors of dhyana. It will help the delicate art of coaxing positive mental states into being if you maintain awareness of the 'seeds' of the dhyana factors that are present in your everyday consciousness.

ENCOURAGING THE SEEDS OF MEDITATION

Let's take the first two factors, initial and sustained thought, as an example. Thinking, of course, is much less clear in ordinary consciousness than in dhyana, but if you try to be mindful of your thoughts you'll be more generally tuned in to the thinking faculty. Then, when you meditate, your thoughts will tend to be clearer—they'll be closer to being dhyana factors.

Maintaining a consistent base of mindfulness may also, in the same way, tune you in to the potential of the other dhyana factors, like rapture and bliss. Rapture is 'potential' in enjoyment of ordinary sense pleasures, like the enjoyment of visual beauty, lovely sounds and forms—they do not have quite the same quality of experience, but it's as though the higher state is reflected in the lower, or suggested by it. By acknowledging such pleasant sense experiences, and enjoying them in an aesthetic way, you will be cultivating the 'seeds' of the dhyana factor. You'll be making a connection with the *possibility* of rapture and bliss, even though on a more ordinary level. You may find it generally helpful to cultivate your sense experience outside meditation, to enjoy more actively what you find pleasurable. This does not mean being over-indulgent, in a way which might increase a tendency towards craving—it's more to do with awakening the imagination. One-pointedness of mind, the fifth dhyana factor, can also be seen reflected in ordinary consciousness. Take more interest in the phenomenon of concentration. Be curious about what you find yourself concentrating on in each moment. Albeit on a lower level, you'll be learning to familiarize yourself with the quality that leads the way into the dhyanas.

MORE ABOUT WORKING PRINCIPLES

Continuing to work from the ground up, let's just remind ourselves of the four working principles that were introduced at the end of Chapter Three. These were **acknowledgement, faith in one's potential, working from the ground up,** and **the creative use of antidotes**. At this stage we can say a little more about each of them, and the procedure will serve as a good introduction to working in meditation, our main theme.

But first a word about principles generally. Meditation is an art which can only be learned through practical experience. This needs to be borne very firmly in mind when exploring all these principles of meditation. There are probably as many different ways of applying a particular principle as there are meditators, but the principles themselves are indispensable. PIPER is just one particular way of expressing a few vital principles. The principles can be expressed in many ways—but without something like PIPER, no one is going to be able to concentrate their minds. Without some awareness in these areas, they will be distracted by (1) their body, (2) their lack of self-awareness, (3) lack of direction, and (4) lack of emotional involvement. With this in mind, we are going to re-visit each of the four working principles.

ACKNOWLEDGEMENT AND FAITH IN ONE'S POTENTIAL (RE-VISITED)

At this stage, more light may be shed on possible reasons why people *don't* acknowledge what happens in their meditation. It may sometimes have to do with their poor self-image.

It appears that the principles of **acknowledgement** and **faith in one's potential** are very closely linked. No one can work in meditation without taking responsibility for their mental states. But it is very common for meditators to refuse to accept that a negative state is there, or at least to view it as an alien intrusion into their consciousness. Those for whom this rejection is a habit usually attempt rigidly to 'meditate', regardless of what is actually happening in their mind. Unfortunately this approach can only increase their mental rigidity.

As already suggested, *acknowledgement of what arises is the essence of meditation*. To some extent we all tend to avoid 'what is'. 'Human kind', said T.S. Eliot, 'cannot bear very much reality'.[41] One common reason why we cannot bear it is a negative self-view. Nowadays there are many people who suffer from irrational guilt feelings. They are convinced that they shouldn't feel this or that emotion, and they have an attitude of condemnation towards their 'lower nature'. They don't like to admit the possibility that negative emotions could exist in their mind—often because they really think, underneath it all, that they are 'a bad person'. But people are always both 'good' *and* 'bad', in varying proportions. We need to understand that hatred and craving are normal in human beings. Negative emotions obviously shouldn't be encouraged, or their consequences condoned, but the habit of viewing them as 'bad' or 'sinful' may actually prevent us transcending them. It is better to think of the hindrances as immature parts of ourselves that need developing, rather than as evils to be rejected and destroyed.

Buddhism has always seen this problem quite clearly. It puts negative emotions in perspective by suggesting positive correspondencies to them. Buddhaghosha, for example, says:

> *Understanding is strong when profitable [action] occurs in one of hating temperament, owing to its special qualities being near to those of hate. For, in an unprofitable way, hate is disaffected and does not hold to its object, and so, in a profitable way, is understanding. Hate seeks out only unreal faults, while understanding seeks out only real faults. And hate occurs in the mode of condemning living beings, while understanding occurs in the mode of condemning formations [i.e. cyclic tendencies].*[42]

Hatred, because it rejects and discriminates, is said to have a certain correspondence with intelligence and wisdom; it may even be transformed into them. The sharp, cutting energy that we invest in hatred can be 're-channelled' into keenness of intelligence. The negative quality of craving, which wants to draw desirable things and beings exclusively to itself, also has a certain correspondence with compassion, which wishes to nurture and help all beings. The desire that at present manifests as craving could one day (if systematically re-channelled through spiritual practices like the Metta Bhavana) manifest as a genuine desire for the well-being of all. The very idea that such problematic emotions can be *transformed*—as opposed to needing to be destroyed—may help to break down this damaging attitude of self-condemnation.

As we saw earlier on, the principle of 'working from the ground up' has to do with establishing the necessary groundwork for concentration. Sometimes people pitch into their meditation in a very driving, ambitious manner. But the basis for their concentration is often too weak, narrow, and intense, and their fire can dissipate itself very quickly, like a red-hot stone being dropped into a tub of cold water. To develop a stronger basis to sustain the concentration, it is necessary to proceed from a *general* awareness of *all* aspects of yourself before investing your energy in the *particular* intense awareness of the meditation object. 'Working from the ground up' could also be called 'working from the general to the

WORKING FROM THE GROUND UP (RE-VISITED)

Balancing focus and breadth in meditation

Breadth Receptivity to one's groundbase of mindfulness	Focus Active attention to the object of practice
• Body • Feelings • Emotions • Thoughts	• The meditation object

particular'. This principle underlies the emphasis on frequent self-checking in PIPER.

FOCUS AND BREADTH   Here's a useful way of applying this principle to meditation practice. We could refer to the ground—the more broad, generalized awareness of ourselves—as our 'breadth', and to the object of meditation as our 'focus'.

Now think of your ability to focus as being *supported* by the breadth. It's like the way the topmost peak of a great mountain—a very small piece of ground—stands on such a huge volume of rock as its base. Perhaps this is where the idea of 'sitting like a mountain' in meditation comes from. You focus on the breathing process, or the development of metta, but if this focusing is going to lead to full concentration, it has to be supported by a broad base of experience.

When you *don't* have a balance of focus and breadth the concentration will 'fall over'. If your focus on the object isn't well grounded, then concentration will feel tight, as though you have to grit your teeth to hold it all together. Proper focusing should be relaxed, carrying your breadth of experience along with your concentration. It should not be forced. Forced focusing feels narrow, tight, and greedy. It demands extra effort and is impossible to keep up for long—hence the quick dissipation of attention.

If it takes into account the breadth of your experience, your focus can be more relaxed and kept up indefinitely. Your 'breadth' is how you are as a whole, taking into account your body and its vitality, your feelings and emotions, and your thoughts and mental images. If you allow these other elements a place in the background of your consciousness, your focus will be relaxed and, most importantly, there will be more energy available for the concentration.

When contacting breadth, the idea is not to get involved with these broad elements of your experience but simply to acknowledge their existence. If you are *over*-involved with breadth, you will become distracted. But if breadth is balanced with focus, there is no such danger.

In terms of PIPER, breadth, like acknowledgement, is an aspect of introspection (it's receptive introspection), and a relaxed, properly directed focus is equivalent to resolve.

In Chapter Three we mentioned several traditional antidotes to the hindrances, but didn't say much about their *creative* use.

It is important that you use antidotes to hindrances creatively and sensitively. You need to be aware of the effect a particular approach is having and be ready to change it if it seems appropriate. Using antidotes creatively means having an open-minded attitude to the possibilities of your practice, rather than applying a ready-made remedy and expecting automatic results. The mind is constantly changing, so you may need to experiment with different methods before you know which works best for you at any particular time.

Efforts to concentrate can be wrongly and inappropriately directed. It is possible to bend and force your attention, through impatience and lack of sensitivity, without properly experiencing your actual state of mind. For example, you could persist in going through each of the stages of a meditation when it would be more realistic, and helpful, to stay with just one stage until you experience yourself fully in that stage. (Or you might do the opposite—insist rigidly on the method of staying in one stage 'until something happens', when it might be more helpful to move on through the usual sequence of stages and allow yourself to be buoyed up by their momentum.)

This tendency to inappropriate effort is similar to that of ignoring your breadth. You are under the influence of a somewhat acquisitive and insensitive attitude, too concerned with *results*. If the dominating idea is to get results, there is no time to stop and consider what you are actually experiencing. It is not wrong to want successful results, but it is unhelpful to have a rigid idea of what results you want, and how you are to get them. A result-oriented approach may stem from a pleasant memory of some past meditation experience. It is natural to want to get back to that experience. However, trying to recapture meditation experiences is not really possible. It is best to start completely afresh every time.

The typical result of inappropriate or wilful effort is pain and frustration. When you force yourself to concentrate, you may create physical pain—headache, digestion problems, and stiff shoulder muscles are very common. Your mental state may also be affected; agitation, anxiety, or dull, blocked states—or a generally 'spaced out' condition—can be expected. Obviously this could affect your overall ability to meditate, and also your attitude to meditation. It may, for example, confirm a tendency towards rigid-mindedness—you may resist even more the idea of creative working in meditation, and try even harder to 'get on with the meditation' in an unrealistic, tunnel-visioned, sort of way.

A more general effect of applying inappropriate methods in meditation

Acknowledgement	• Acknowledging mental states that are present
	• 'Owning'—taking responsibility for—hindrances
Faith in one's potential	• Self-confidence
	• Self metta
Focus supported by breadth	• 'Background' mindfulness of oneself
Appropriate effort	• Maintaining an open attitude to one's approach
	• Not just 'going through the motions' in daily practice

could be acquiring the habit of 'going through the motions' in your daily practice. Some meditators sit 'religiously' to meditate every morning. They do it in exactly the same way every time they sit—year in, year out. They put themselves through a set sequence of mental actions with no regard for their actual mental state. This is not meditation! Such people may admit that they do not particularly enjoy their practice, yet still cling to this way of doing it. It's always hard to change ingrained habits.

If you ever think that your meditation is becoming wilful, simply stop for a moment—stop 'trying to meditate', and instead try to tune in to what is actually happening, try to get back to a real experience of yourself. This might take some time, but however long such a readjustment in your practice may take—hours, days, perhaps even weeks—it will be worth it. You may learn to develop a much needed relaxation in your approach, both in your practice and outside it. It could change your whole life.

The issues raised in connection with the last two working principles, breadth of focus and creativity, may imply that you could do with a little more richness and colour in your life. It is a question of inspiration: some more imaginative ingredient must be allowed to enter your practice. You may be able to introduce this by reading literature, looking at paintings, playing or listening to music, meeting people, spending time alone—whatever keeps the well-springs of inspiration flowing for you. You could also try reflecting on the pleasures and value of meditation, and in that way develop a more positive attitude—an attitude which generally regards spiritual practice as something enjoyable and accessible.

SUMMARY

Above, in tabular form, is a summary of the four principles of working in meditation—some with new names to reflect our enhanced under-standing of them. Working in meditation must involve these four general principles. Though meditation is primarily a matter of appreciating the meditation object more and more deeply, at the deepest level that object is not different from 'you', the subject. (Where does 'it' end, and 'you' begin?) So the subject must always be taken into account during the act of concentration. To experience the meditation object effectively, you need to

Meditation worksheet

Practice		Date		Time	
Gross hindrance	✓	**Subtle hindrance**	✓	**Dhyana factor**	✓
Desire for sense experience		Stray thoughts		One-pointedness	
Ill will		Sinking		Initial thought	
Sloth and torpor		Drifting		Applied thought	
Restlessness and anxiety				Rapture	
Doubt and indecision				Bliss	
PIPER	✓	**Working principles**	✓		
Posture					
Introspection		Acknowledgement		Breadth	
Purpose				Appropriate effort	
Enthusiasm					
Resolve				Focus	
Other notes					
Preparation					
Special conditions					
Current 'issues'					
Dream life					

acknowledge whatever mental states are present in your mind, maintaining a positive self-view; there must be some sense of breadth going on simultaneously with your concentration, and when you work to deepen that concentration, it must be done both creatively and appropriately.

TAKING NOTES

Mental states can change very rapidly. It may sometimes help to get more of a grasp of what is happening in your practice if you keep a record. A meditation notebook provides a means of monitoring your practice—it can be a simple log or a systematic analysis, just as you like. At times when you are practising meditation more intensively, or when you want to look at your daily practice more closely, some form of meditation diary can be a very useful aid.

Here are two suggested ways that you can record information—an analytical record and a journal.

This can be in the form of a check-list which you complete after every meditation session. You record what actually happened, and how you approached each session—and anything else you like—in terms of definite categories. By doing this over a few days you will build up a systematic picture of mental states that regularly arise. You can look back, see patterns, and decide on new modes of strategy.

THE ANALYTICAL RECORD

To start, you first of all decide on the areas of experience you wish to monitor. The 'worksheet' table above gives a few suggestions. (Note that some of the terms on it, like the subtle hindrances of 'sinking' and 'drifting', will be introduced later on.)

Immediately after each session of meditation (otherwise it is easy to forget) take out your notebook and tick the factors which were present—or perhaps you could give them a mark out of ten, or write a few words of description. You can work out your own categories and tables. It might be possible to design a table which shows patterns emerging over several days or even weeks, which would be useful.

After the check-list you can add any comments, such as 'good but patchy', 'preparation could have been better', 'couldn't stop thinking about work', or whatever.

Every few days—once a week is about right—it's a good idea to look at the implications of the information you have gathered, and on that basis decide on a definite approach to your practice over the next few days. It may be very useful to go over the contents of your notebook with a friend who meditates—discussion always arouses interest in meditation, and your friend will often see aspects of your practice that you miss. On some retreats there may be an opportunity for daily 'interviews' with a teacher. These can be invaluable.

Most people find this type of diary unsuitable for keeping up indefinitely. Sometimes the process of analysis itself feels restricting, and for a while it seems better to take your practice more day by day. To a degree, these fiddling details are unimportant—compared, for instance, to your basic commitment to the path of development. But there are always times when some extra objectivity is needed, times when your meditation seems to be going nowhere. If you are in the mood to take things deeper, an analytical record could stimulate new energy and creativity.

JOURNAL TYPE DIARY

A second way of making notes about your meditation is simply to keep a journal. This is a more descriptive, personal approach. In this journal you just write down any reflections that you have about each meditation session, in whatever way you like. You could just describe what happened, or speculate on the significance of the experience. You could include some information about hindrances and dhyana factors too. This format may not be so useful for getting an overview later, but it will probably help you contact your practice more deeply. It can also be more satisfying: making a record of your inner life can connect you with your meditation in a new way, and even become a focus for your life generally.

If you record the happenings in your meditation you'll find yourself reflecting more about them—which is in itself a very good support for your meditation. The records you make can be an important reminder—like dreams, meditation experiences are often subtle and easily forgotten.

WORKING IN DHYANA

A SESSION OF MEDITATION

Just to get a more tangible sense of what it is like to work in meditation, here's an imaginary example of you practising the Mindfulness of Breathing meditation.

Let's say you have been on retreat for a week, there is another week to go, you are enjoying yourself and your mind feels quite concentrated. It's mid-morning and you have already been meditating today. You did a good session each of the Metta Bhavana and the Mindfulness of Breathing before breakfast, and now you are about to sit again. In these circumstances you have planned to dispense with the support of the counting stages of the Mindfulness of Breathing practice—you're going to start straight away with the third stage, simply experiencing each breath as it arises.

But before you begin, you do a preliminary run-through of PIPER. Your posture seems OK now—two days ago there was a lot of pain in the knees, but that seems to have righted itself after some discussion with one of the members of the retreat team. An extra inch of cushion height, some support for your hands, and a chunk of foam rubber just under your left ankle, seems to have done the trick! You start checking your mental state, tuning in to feelings and emotions.

In fact you had a very good meditation a couple of hours ago, and what with the overall build-up of concentration over a week of regular meditation, you're very happy, energized—even a little excited. Because of the excitement you know what your strategy has to be—you know that you need to develop calm and tranquillity in the meditation, and you've some idea how to approach it.

You have no lack of enthusiasm for this. Some time ago you saw clearly how meditation could change you—you are inspired by the possibility of gaining insight and compassion. Moreover, your practice has been going quite well so far this week, and you anticipate making some progress.

So—with such a good momentum already behind you, your preparation can be quite short. In less than a minute you have assessed the situation, know what you are about to do, and have your energies gathered. All this adds up to a good overall resolve to practise.

You begin. For a few minutes the quality of your awareness of the breathing is quite good. You enjoy the practice. As you had originally decided, you are trying to find calm and tranquillity in the meditation, looking for those particular qualities.

At first it seems to be working quite well, but after a while you are forced to acknowledge that you don't seem to have the energy you thought you had. In fact you are starting to feel a little bit dull. This state of affairs drags on for a while: it takes several minutes for you to take in the changed situation.

This is the opposite of what you had expected. You had envisaged relaxing into a deep calm, but—it just isn't happening like that. You are very unwilling to acknowledge that your strategy is not working—you can't believe that it isn't, and you keep on doggedly trying to concentrate with the calming, tranquillizing approach that you originally wanted. But the dullness just gets worse. As long as you persist with the planned approach of calming down, you sink further and further into the dullness. Finally, after about a quarter of an hour, you decide that you must somehow pull yourself out of this nose-dive.

You manage to rouse yourself, and formulate a strategy for throwing off the sloth and torpor. You are going to be especially aware of your body— its posture, its stillness, its internal energies—and you're going to check very frequently that your mind is actually on the breath.

This helps, but certainly not dramatically. The postural awareness at least keeps you awake. You feel alert to a degree, but your mind still remains foggy. You realize that in spite of your intention to check, the awareness of the breath remains vague. It lacks intensity.

To counteract this lack of intensity you decide to make your breathing a little more definite. (This method is called 'intentional breathing'. You allow the breath to come and go slightly more strongly for a while, without controlling—just so that you very clearly know that it is there. It's quite a good method for this kind of situation.)

It seems that you need to keep this up for quite a long time. Using intentional breathing, you become much more clearly aware of each breath— but whenever you decide to stop using the intentional breathing, you lose your concentration. So you keep it up. You keep on keeping on.... After half an hour or more by the clock—it seems like an age—the feeling of heaviness and lack of energy begins to lift. It is as though you have just started to wake up.

Something has happened—there is a new, lighter element in your consciousness. Where previously it felt awkward, your whole body begins to feel settled and calm, and you feel perfectly happy to sit there and keep up the meditation. You're in access concentration, or at least the beginnings of it.

You now decide that a different approach to the concentration is needed to adjust to the change. What to do? Well—perhaps it's time, you think, to go on to the next stage of the practice. You had been working so intently, and for so long, that you had completely forgotten that there is a further stage. So now you relax the intentional breathing and finely direct your attention on the sensation of your breath as it enters your body, just below your nose.

This has the instant effect of calming your mind still further. So you know that you were right to relax your efforts slightly. At the same time, you can sense that it would be inappropriate to relax completely. Somewhere, you can tell, there is still the possibility of sinking; it still feels necessary to keep quite a close eye on the breath, and to experience it intensely, even though you seem now to be getting established at a more refined level of concentration.

So along with the concentration on the sensation of the breath, you formulate a commitment to following the whole of each breath, without a single gap in awareness. You try to note the points at which your awareness of the breath seems weak, paying special attention to the beginning and end of each breath and the spaces between the breaths. In this way you establish a very close contact indeed with the breathing process. Concentration deepens further.

However, you start to notice that you are frowning! How long this has been going on is impossible to say—but your forehead is, or has become, somewhat tense. You wonder whether this tension may not be masking some emotion that is hindering further concentration. To find out, you don't immediately try to relax, but you broaden your focus on the breath. You allow yourself to feel every aspect of the tension by degrees—you experience the pleasure/pain of it, experience it in your body, experience it emotionally. As you do this, you become aware of a deep release of feeling and emotion, which comes as a pleasurable relief.

And within a few minutes, the whole nature of the meditation is changed—at once it becomes very easy indeed to keep interested in the breath. A flutter of rapture spreads from your stomach to your heart. Your heart seems to vibrate, and you find your shoulders relaxing (you didn't even know they were tense). As you incorporate more feeling into the concentration, you realize that you are well established in access concentration.

After a while you also notice that with all this pleasurable sensation, you are tending to get carried away. At the same time you remember that this is where you got to in your last meditation, just a few hours ago, but you got distracted at that point. You resolve that this time you will keep the concentration going by counteracting the tendency to drift.

To do this, you decide to change the object of your concentration slightly. For a while you were paying attention to the whole of each breath as it brushed past the point of sensation. Now you pay less attention to the breath. Instead, you focus on just the sensation itself.

As you begin to concentrate on that tiny point of touch, it is as though that point becomes much bigger, as though it had been magnified. You experience the sensation that the breath causes in remarkable detail, and it gets extremely interesting. It feels like an enormous piece of smooth woollen fabric which is being stroked, very smoothly and evenly, with a feather. At the beginning and end of each breath there is a change in the sensation; at the beginning it is rougher, and at the end it is as though it is melting.

After a while, as you watch the sensation more and more continuously, your breath calms down until it seems to disappear altogether. You are not sure what to do now because you cannot find the object of meditation! There is a danger that you will flounder and lose your concentration altogether. However, you decide that you don't have to waver like this—the breath must be somewhere, so you can look deeper for it.

You look deeper, in a way that isn't easily describable in words. But whatever it is that you do, it works. You find the breath. And you now find the character of the meditation changing again, becoming even more stable and even more finely enjoyable. You realize that you have arrived at the first dhyana level, and can taste all the special characteristics of the higher state of consciousness.

GETTING ESTABLISHED IN DHYANA

We saw earlier that as we work on the ordinary hindrances, there eventually comes a point when meditation begins to get easier. We arrive at access concentration—the 'neighbourhood' (as it is sometimes called) of the first dhyana. But even though meditation is somewhat easier, we are still not fully concentrated. There are still subtle obstacles which prevent us from actually entering dhyana.

For example, something which often holds us back is our own excitement. This is quite understandable, since something is happening in our meditation at last!—but it's still a stumbling-block. It is fairly common for meditators to experience a few moments of access concentration, but then at once to become excited and, unable to sustain it, fall back once again into the hindrances.

This is partly due to uncertainty. So when access first begins to crop up in your meditation, it is worth spending some extra time on your practice if possible, gaining experience of this state and finding ways of encouraging it.

One thing that you may already have found from experience is that those times when you do break through to a new level of concentration are frequently followed by a period of *less* concentrated sessions of meditation. This can be confusing and disappointing—if you don't know that it is quite normal. It is not a bad sign at all—it seems that breaking through into a completely new level of integration is rather a shock to your system, and you need to allow a certain amount of meditation time simply to absorb its impact. You should certainly not be discouraged from your meditation by this, but take heart, recognize the significance of what is happening, and persevere through the 'slump'. Then, if you continue sitting regularly, you will eventually find your way back to access concentration more and more easily, accustoming yourself to it so that you become able to sustain it for longer periods.

In establishing access concentration—and the dhyana levels too—you'll still need to use the principles of PIPER and the others which have been mentioned. But there is no longer any need to concern yourself with the ordinary five hindrances. You have passed beyond these (somewhat extreme) states of mind and entered a more subtle, balanced state. Now you need to establish this balanced state more firmly by counteracting the *subtle* hindrances. Think of the subtle hindrances as tendencies for the mind to lose its balance.

We can lose balance in two ways, either through a subtle form of dullness (called *sinking*), or a subtle form of restlessness (called *drifting*). Being in access concentration is such a vast improvement on our usual state of mind that we can rest in a false sense of security, and then these hindrances can creep up on us unawares and topple our stability.

Unless sinking and drifting are counteracted as soon as you notice them—and they are both there, as tendencies, all the time—they will become stronger and eventually turn into the gross hindrance of either sloth and torpor or restlessness and anxiety.

A good general method of working in these more subtle states of concentration is to use the three key points of body, breath, and mind. Your physical posture, breathing process, and mental states are three principal 'viewpoints' from which you can at least maintain access concentration, and develop it further on that basis. These three points now provide your breadth of awareness. Being mindful of them provides a more thorough 'coverage' of the quality of attention, and within this closer awareness you are more likely to notice the subtle hindrances as they arise.

You need:

(1) to maintain your **body** in the best possible posture, so that your vital energy is flowing;

(2) to maintain smooth and calm **breathing**;

(3) to maintain a balanced absorption by adjusting your **mental state** whenever you notice it becoming slightly dull (sinking) or slightly excited (drifting).

BODY

You can view your body both in terms of its structure and its energy. You feel:

- its physical **structure** of bones, muscles and sinews.
- the **energy** and vitality that pervades it.

You can use both these points of view to deepen your meditation, so that your concentration comes, as it were, from your body as well as your mind.

STRUCTURE

From the viewpoint of structure, you will probably find that in access concentration you are already in a fairly good meditation posture. An enhanced sense of one's bodily shape and form is a natural part of this mental state. From the position of the sitting bones on your cushion, you can feel the natural curve of your spine extending through the centre of your shoulders and up to your head. Your legs and hips feel stable and 'triangular', and you feel your shoulders and arms encircling the vertical line of your trunk.

If you maintain a clear sense of your physical structure and position, this will lend stability and continuity to your concentration. Awareness of structure will also help you to contact the vitality and sense of physical aliveness which is the second, 'energy' aspect of bodily awareness. Simply being aware of your physical vitality will bring energy, enthusiasm, and inspiration into your meditation. And because the experience of pleasure is so much concerned with bodily energies, this awareness is an indispensable basis for developing the pleasurable dhyana factors of *piti*, *sukha*, and eventually even *upekkha*.

ENERGY

But we are not always in touch with our energy. Our awareness of it can sometimes be dull and obscure, and this is usually either because of tiredness or physical tension. Tiredness can be cured by resting, but tension is more complex.

Physical tension can be due to physical causes—simply the result of imbalances in the sitting position—but more often it is emotional. Tension in the face, neck, shoulder, or stomach muscles, for example, is often triggered by emotions which have not been acknowledged. In principle if you can relax tension, however caused, then blocked energy is freed; this new energy enriches your consciousness, enabling you to take more of an interest in the meditation and so achieve deeper concentration.

However, if tension is emotionally based, physical relaxation alone cannot resolve it. It is necessary to tackle its underlying *emotional* cause. For example, if you are tense because you are angry about something, you need to acknowledge that emotion before it will be possible to relax the tension. Without that acknowledgement, any attempted relaxation will be superficial and even forced—in fact at first, rather than relaxing, you may need to allow yourself to experience the tension and feel the emotion behind it. If you do not allow for the presence of underlying emotions you will experience a feeling of dullness, and not the enhanced vitality you are looking for.

A good way of 'tuning in', and working with both the structure and energy aspects of your body, is to try to sit very still and receptively, making a definite decision not to move despite any resistance. Such a decision can create a very deep stillness in both your body and mind—generally speaking, the less one moves, the more concentrated one tends to become.

This tuning in will also reveal subtle imbalances in your posture and energy. Of course, you will need to move to adjust for these, but you should preserve the stillness of your posture as much as possible by being economical with the adjustments—you should take time to decide what is needed, and move only when you are sure exactly what you need to change. Such economical use of energy will deepen your focus on the meditation object still further.

BREATH

By audible breathing is meant that when sitting we can hear a faint sound of the breath as it passes through the nose. If we were standing or working we would not notice it, but in our practice it is enough to distract the mind. By silent breathing is meant that there is no sound, no compression, no force, simply the slightest feeling of the tranquillity of our breathing, which does not disturb the mind but rather gives to the mind a pleasant feeling of security and peace. Blowing disturbs concentration, panting gives it heaviness, audible breathing wearies it. We can attain samadhi only with silent breathing.[43]
Chi-I

There is a correspondence between breath and mind: when the mind is calm, the breath is silent with a very smooth, subtle feeling; when we are mentally disturbed or excited, it is audible and rough. There is also a correspondence between the breath and our body: physical stimulation has a considerable effect on the breathing, so that after we exert ourselves physically, our breathing may sometimes remain coarse for an hour or more. We might notice, on the other hand, that when we are doing some very detailed task, such as painting a picture or threading a needle, we may breathe very lightly, sometimes even holding our breath in order to concentrate. So in fact our breath is very intimately involved with both our body and our mind, and the state of our breathing corresponds to our physical and mental state.

Awareness of the breath can therefore be used as a key in meditation: by noting the quality of our breathing we can maintain a very sensitive awareness of both body and mind, and so focus extra sensitively on the meditation object.

Since the quality of our breathing is such an influence on our mental state, it is not surprising to learn that full dhyana is only attainable with fine breathing. Although fine breathing is an ideal to aim for, we should not force our breath to calm down—any such efforts would be a strain on our nervous system, and could even be damaging if taken to an extreme. Nevertheless, if we are patient, our breathing can be gently allowed to quieten naturally.

Access concentration is a state of mind which is highly responsive to any attitude we bring to it, and simply maintaining awareness of the *quality* of the breath may be sufficient to keep us balanced there. However, awareness of the breath is also the basis for a number of active methods of counteracting the subtle hindrances.

For a dull state of mind (e.g. sinking), for example, you can stimulate more energy by imagining that your breath is coming into your body from your toes, up through your body, to your head; or you could simply focus on your breath high in your body, perhaps at the nose. For excitement (or drifting), you can imagine your breath flowing down your body from your head to your toes—which has a calming, quietening effect—or focusing on your breath low in your body. It is possible to experience your breath as though it was coming into your body at almost any point you choose.

Generally, if you feel you are too much 'in your head' (full of thoughts, perhaps dreamy, without much awareness of your body), then it may help if you gradually try to transfer your awareness of yourself, with the aid of your breath, away from your head and down into your body. You could do this by concentrating on the experience of your breath lower down—at the point where it touches your abdomen, for example—or perhaps you could pay attention to the external sensation of your abdomen rising and falling with your breath. Alternatively you could take your attention, and awareness of your breath, straight to your heart area. You could also take it down your body in stages: from your head to your throat, then to your heart and lungs, then to your diaphragm and abdomen, etc. You may need to spend a fair amount of time, perhaps twenty minutes or more, doing this—but if you cannot otherwise engage with your meditation, it will be time well spent.

Now we come to the subtle hindrances of **sinking** and **drifting** (as well as a third, less problematic, subtle hindrance known as **stray thought**). From the viewpoint of mind, working in access involves maintaining a constant awareness of the possibility of one of these subtle hindrances arising, and making appropriate adjustments when it does.

**MIND
THE SUBTLE
HINDRANCES**

All three subtle hindrances are characterized by a lack of strong emotional content—in contrast to the five gross hindrances which are all highly flavoured with greed, hatred, and confusion. These three hindrances are subtle tendencies which will not develop enough power to take hold if only we can stay aware of what we are trying to do.

To recognize these subtle hindrances it may help if we understand more about the way our mental energies work in higher states of consciousness. The meditative state of dhyana is a 'middle way' which brings the positive aspects of two sides of our nature into a higher harmony. If we understand the different aspects of our mind, we can cultivate this harmony more directly.

**TRANSCENDING
POLAR OPPOSITIONS
IN DHYANA**

Each of us has both a receptive side and a dynamic side. Both are very different—rather like the positive and negative poles of an electric current. But each 'pole' needs the support of the other, otherwise it will go to an extreme: receptivity on its own can become dull; dynamism on its own can become hard or over-excited.

At the 'receptive' pole of our experience, for example, we are calm, openly aware, patient, and still. Usually, however, we can only maintain calm and stillness for a certain length of time, unless there is also present, within that state of calm, an element of inspiration. Inspiration is part of the 'dynamic' energy pole. If our mind is *merely* calm and still, without any energy, we will gradually become dull, lazy, or gloomy, and eventually—in terms of the hindrances—fall into sloth and torpor. It is only when the receptive pole is united with the dynamic pole that we can maintain a balanced state of concentration.

At the 'dynamic' pole of our experience, we apply ourselves energetically and enthusiastically, and we are able to penetrate and investigate. On

Transcending polarities in access and dhyana

Receptive pole →			← Dynamic pole
Extreme negative aspect (hindrance)	Balanced positive aspect (dhyana)		Extreme negative aspect (hindrance)
Sinking			**Drifting**
Sloth and torpor	Calm	Energy	Restlessness and anxiety
	Receptive	Active	
	Grounded	Inspired	
Dullness			Distraction
Laziness			Over-exertion
Depression ← Gloom		Enthusiasm → Hysteria	

its own, however, this mental state is unbalanced. It needs to be 'grounded' or 'anchored' in receptivity and calm, otherwise its inherent excitability will lead towards extreme distraction and restlessness. You may know people who tend towards this kind of one-sidedness. In terms of the hindrances this tends towards restlessness and anxiety.

If we can bring both energy poles together in meditation, we will move towards dhyana.

Some other aspects of the polarity are shown in the table above, with the different extremes at either side and the balanced qualities of dhyana at the centre.

In our normal, relatively unaware state of mind, we usually tend towards one of these poles, and become either too dull or too excited. Often we oscillate between one and the other (perhaps dull in the morning, excited in the evening). However, in meditation we can learn to develop a balanced state which contains *both* heightened vigour *and* heightened calm.

You can learn to generate this state by developing the positive qualities of the *opposite* pole to the one that you seem to be moving towards. In other words, if you are feeling energetic (but moving towards distraction), you need to allow an element of receptivity to enter your practice; if you are calm (but tending to be a little dull), you need to cultivate more inspired, active energy.

Now that we have this overview, let's look at the subtle hindrances themselves. As we have seen, there are two main ones—sinking and drifting—plus a third, stray thoughts.

SINKING

'Sinking' describes a state of mind which, though very concentrated, is becoming dull. In terms of our subjective state, we are just beginning to lose our 'edge' of intensity of focus. In terms of the way we may experience the object of meditation, there is less vibrancy and aliveness in it—

Stages of sinking		Subjective experience	Experience of object
Subtle hindrance	1 Subtle sinking	Intensity of concentration fades	Object remains clear
	2 Gross sinking	Intensity of concentration fades further	Clarity of object fades
Gross hindrance	3 Sloth and torpor	• Dull concentration • Heavy feeling • Very little interest in object	Little or no awareness of object

perhaps the breath is a little less interesting, our metta is a shade uninspired, or our visualization has slightly lost its immediacy.

Sinking is caused by some *slight* neglect or lack of awareness—at some point you don't register the need for a change in the quality of your effort, and the character of the concentration changes without your knowing it. You're in access concentration—at least—so you still have a stable concentration on the meditation object: the object is quite clear and the concentration quite pleasant. But something is missing. You have started to lose a little of the 'dynamic', energizing, inspiring aspect of concentration. The concentration has become a little *too* stable—the mind is starting to become fixed and wooden. This is happening gradually, but the longer you delay, the more the sinking will increase.

There are two stages of sinking: first the intensity of the concentration fades, while the object remains clear; then that clarity also starts to fade. Sinking is akin to the gross hindrance of sloth and torpor, though much subtler. If your mind is allowed to sink further, this will degenerate into the gross hindrance and you will then fall away from the dhyana state (or from access) completely.

DRIFTING

Drifting is also part of a very concentrated state of mind, but we are just starting to get distracted by thoughts and by our senses. Drifting is caused by *slight* over-excitement, which in turn is usually caused by making a little too much effort. Perhaps a few minutes ago you were sinking, and made a counteracting effort, but the effort you made was a little too strong and overstimulated your mind. Or perhaps your introspection wasn't quite clear enough, and you kept applying that counteracting effort when it was no longer appropriate.

When you 'drift', the meditation object is in the forefront of your attention. It may be very clear and stable. But your attention has started, very subtly, to include objects other than the meditation object.

For the time being, your concentration may remain strong enough to include both the meditation object and these slight distractions. But if the slight excitement remains unchecked, your mind will drift further and further away from its grounding in the receptive mental pole—so far *that* has been keeping your attention on the meditation object. Eventually the gross hindrance of restlessness and anxiety will interpose itself and you will fall away from absorption.

STRAY THOUGHTS Sinking and drifting are the main obstacles to look out for as you work to maintain a balanced concentration. However, a third factor, the phenomenon of 'stray thoughts', may also arise in access concentration and dhyana.

Stray thoughts are the flotsam and jetsam of the mind. They consist of thoughts and other mental phenomena, but nothing that we are especially attracted towards. Since they do not arise out of any desire for distraction, stray thoughts are not distractions in the usual sense. Stray thoughts are simply present in our general state of consciousness, 'in parallel', as it were, to the meditation practice. They can be compared to radio interference: we can clearly hear the music on the radio, but we can tell there's another programme going on somewhere in the background.

The content of these stray thoughts can be almost anything. Disconnected ideas, in which you have no special interest, may simply arise and present themselves. You might remember an old acquaintance, who suddenly appears in your thoughts. Other disconnected mental elements such as old pop tunes, nagging physical discomfort, sounds from outside, etc., can also be of this type.

Remember that you are very concentrated. These phenomena are not actively distracting you—they just remain on the edge of your concentration as *potential* distractions. They could eventually become a source of active distraction if you let them do so, but otherwise they are relatively harmless.

Nevertheless, since they are a potential danger, it may be worth doing something to counteract stray thoughts. You may feel them as a 'pressure' to become distracted, and that nagging pressure could eventually sap your interest in the meditation.

The basic antidote is to recognize them for what they are—as merely stray thoughts on the edge of your mind rather than actual distractions. If you put them in perspective like this, you may then be able simply to ignore them. It is useful to see stray thoughts in perspective, for that will give you the confidence to abandon them and focus more strongly on the object.

You could also apply some more vipassana-type reflection to them: remind yourself, perhaps, that they are conditioned phenomena which, having arisen, are eventually going to disappear. This may put them in a deeper perspective, which may have the effect of dissolving any power they have over you.

Now that we know about the subtle hindrances, we can work with the mind to retain a balanced concentration on the meditation object.

The sooner you can recognize that sinking or drifting has started, the better you will be able to maintain a smooth, continuous concentration. You need to be constantly looking for the signs of sinking or drifting.

Broadly, the method is to recognize what is happening, then provide what is missing—dynamic vigour in the case of sinking, calm receptivity in the case of drifting. As soon as you spot the 'loss of edge' which is the sign of sinking, you need to make a little more effort to intensify the experience of the object. This could be done in the Mindfulness of Breathing, for example, by breathing slightly more fully, or experiencing the breath higher in the body. You could perhaps intensify your Metta Bhavana by trying to create an extremely clear image of your good friend.

However, you have to be a little careful that you do not make too strong an effort here: remember sinking is a *subtle* hindrance. You are balanced in access concentration (or perhaps dhyana), and very strong stimulation could take you 'over the top' into drifting or even restlessness.

Indeed, something of this kind is almost inevitable at this stage. You will tend to oscillate between sinking and drifting, applying now a stimulating antidote, now a calming antidote, at subtler and subtler levels until, as you progress, meditation becomes completely effortless.

The general antidote to **sinking**, then, is to introduce a more dynamic quality. Concentrate more strongly on the object, grasping it more tightly, perceiving it more intensely. Sometimes the necessary intensity is there, but nevertheless you may be feeling somehow withdrawn. In such a situation you can enlarge the 'scope' of the object in a number of ways, and widen the feeling of the practice out. If you are doing the Mindfulness of Breathing, you can imagine that the breath is entering through all the pores of body. In the case of the Metta Bhavana, you could concentrate on sending the metta outwards to all sentient beings. If you are doing a visualization practice, you could concentrate on perceiving the details, or brightening the image.

The chief antidote to **drifting** is receptivity. Slacken off the intensity of your concentration slightly—but not too much, otherwise you may start sinking. The usual cause of drifting is an over-application of effort. At this point you can relax a little and be somewhat more receptive to your experience. Enjoyment, emotion generally, and enthusiasm (as in PIPER), are important aspects of working towards balanced concentration. As always, you need to check that feeling and emotional response exist in your concentration. To the extent that feeling is not there, you are likely to be sinking, so you'll need to recover the feeling. Drifting, on the other hand, has a recognizable feeling tone—perhaps a slightly greedy excitement—which, if acknowledged, can then be 'pacified'.

After prolonged application and experience with this stage of meditation, you may begin to alternate between sinking and drifting only very subtly. Eventually, the simple recognition of whether sinking or drifting is arising will suffice to reset the equilibrium of the mental state.

TAKING DHYANA FURTHER

You should now have quite a good idea of how to work from access concentration towards full absorption. As the oscillations between sinking and drifting become increasingly smooth, the dhyana factors will begin to arise in their fullness. You will then be in the first dhyana.

MOVING THROUGH THE FOUR DHYANAS

Generally, working from the first towards the second dhyana, and from the second to the third and beyond, involves the same technique of balancing; sinking and drifting keep occurring at subtler levels and with varying time spans.

We saw earlier the way in which the mind can ascend from the first into the second dhyana, as the absorption factors of initial and applied thought are left behind. With a little experience it is possible to encourage this to happen. When you know how the process of moving into the second dhyana feels, you can recollect how much more calm, clear, and enjoyable the second dhyana is, and in that way transcend the thinking mind.

You can move from the second to the third dhyana in a similar way, recollecting that bliss is a far calmer and more deeply concentrating experience than rapture, and so on.

> On emerging from the now familiar first dhyana, he can regard the flaws in it in this way: 'This attainment is threatened by the nearness of the hindrances, and its factors are weakened by the grossness of the applied and sustained thought.' He can bring the second dhyana to mind as quieter, and so end his attachment to the first dhyana and set about doing what is needed for attaining the second.
>
> When he has emerged from the first dhyana, applied and sustained thought appear gross to him as he reviews the dhyana factors with mindfulness and full

*awareness, while happiness and bliss and unification of mind appear peaceful.
Then, as he brings [the meditation object] to mind ... again and again, with
the purpose of abandoning the gross factors and obtaining the peaceful factors,
(knowing) 'now the second dhyana will arise' ...*

*'With the stilling of applied and sustained thought he enters upon and
dwells in the second dhyana, which has internal confidence and singleness of
mind without applied thought, without sustained thought, with happiness and
bliss born of concentration.*[44]

Buddhaghosha

SOME SPECIAL CHARACTERISTICS OF DHYANA

Dhyana is characterized by tranquillity or *passaddhi*. We saw earlier that
this means the whole process of calming down, relaxing and releasing unresolved energy.

With this release of energy comes a general **agility** of mind (*lahuta*)[45]—
we become increasingly buoyant, light, quick-witted. No concerns are
weighing us down, and this freedom gives us the capacity to turn our
mind quickly to any object we choose. With this agility, positive emotions
such as faith or understanding arise very quickly, and we can work very
clearly and quickly in the meditation.

There is also a quality of emotional freedom. There is no rigidity or
hardness. On the contrary, we feel receptive and adaptable in spirit. We
have a willingness to learn and also—just as important—to re-learn from
experience. This is sometimes called **pliancy** (*muduta*).

Though the mind feels soft and pliant, that doesn't mean that it is weak.
This softness implies a kind of strength—because there is no brittleness,
no tendency to fragment, the mind can really work. So another characteristic of higher consciousness is its **workability** (*kammannata*)—it feels
tempered, like a finely made tool. Because of this workability we can easily keep pace with the subtle changes of sinking and drifting.

There is another kind of strength which is the self-assurance and confidence which the experience of dhyana gives us. We have a certain
proficiency (*pagunnata*) in working in meditation. We feel competent, in
control.

There is also an ethical dimension to the experience. We feel quite pure
in our motivation—there is no sense of crookedness or craftiness in us.
We're **upright** (*ujjukata*), straightforward. Our intention is completely un-
ambiguous.

Since it is partly a matter of confidence born from experience, it may take
us some time to penetrate into higher dhyana levels. Much also depends

**DHYANA INVOLVES
MORE THAN
TECHNIQUE**

on the conditions under which you meditate and the time you are able to devote to your practice.

You should bear in mind that getting into dhyana, remaining in it, and moving 'up' into higher dhyanas, is not only a matter of manipulating techniques like recognizing sinking and drifting. The dhyana state is best not regarded as something you 'get into'—it is more like something that you *are*. You become the dhyana, and it reflects your whole life, all your actions and thoughts. It is the outcome of the inner integration of a multitude of unresolved emotions and ideas, and—as we've seen—the process of integration never follows a smooth, logical course.

The process of integration often comes to a head in a temporary resolution—a dhyana experience—the clarity of which may immediately reveal the presence of new unresolved material! You will then find it necessary to work with that, which will probably involve re-experiencing the five hindrances. The experience of dhyana is never a permanent attainment, though it indicates important inner changes. You may not be able to concentrate so well for a while, but if you are working, good progress will be taking place under the surface.

So meditation can never be just a matter of technique. Many of the factors governing the arising of higher states of consciousness are happening in the unconscious mind, and are therefore outside your direct control. You can only provide the best possible conditions by living a life as conducive to meditation as you can, and by working systematically in meditation to the best of your ability.

SAMATHA AND VIPASSANA IN DAILY PRACTICE

Dhyana is not the end point of meditation, as we saw in the chapter on samatha and vipassana; it is an excellent *basis* for meditation on ultimate reality, and it is only through insight into ultimate reality that permanent progress can be made. If you wish to practise vipassana regularly, at least a good general level of samatha needs to be maintained. If you have had experience of access concentration and dhyana, you can sustain such a level if you meditate regularly. For this degree of practice you need to meditate at the very least once a day, preferably two or three times. This means maintaining good supportive conditions for meditation too, not just 'putting in the hours' on the cushion. If you practise in this way, then a certain level of dhyana, and a certain amount of vipassana reflection, may be sustained even in a city environment.

Chapter Nine

REFLECTION

All I want is the truth[46]
  John Lennon

HUNGRY FOR THE TRUTH

Everything that we have learned about meditation comes together in reflection.

As we've seen, the method of insight meditation is 'reflection within tranquillity'. We first gain access to a good state of concentration, and then use the dhyana factors of initial and applied thought to *reflect* on some aspect of ultimate reality.

In order to reflect *undistractedly*, our thought must be supported by the two basic qualities of concentration and positive emotion. This also means, of course, that it needs the support of the conditions which make them possible: we must have a life-style that is conducive to meditation, a regular meditation practice, a continual concern for the development of awareness, and plenty of practical experience in engaging with the heights and depths of our mind. Above all, we must really want to know—we need to feel a kind of hunger for the truth.

When hearing the Dharma you must be like deer listening to the sound of music; when thinking about it, like a man from the north shearing sheep; when making it a living experience, like a man getting drunk; when establishing its validity, like a yak eating grass hungrily; and when you come to possess its fruition you must be free from clouds like the sun.[47]
  Gampopa

THE NATURE OF THOUGHT

We also need some specific *ideas* on which to reflect. We need a modicum of basic understanding—at an intellectual level—of the nature of reality. These, broadly, are the conditions for reflection. If we are well grounded in the conditions for samatha, and have some knowledge of the Dharma, then our reflection will bear mature fruit.

As background information, it may also be useful to understand something about the nature of thought, how we can develop the capacity to reflect, the different levels of reflection, and the way these levels can work together in a deepening process of insight.

KINDS OF THOUGHT

ASSOCIATIVE THINKING

Mindfulness of thoughts (the fourth of the Foundations of Mindfulness—touched on in Chapter Three) can be an interesting practice. It is especially interesting to see the way one thought leads out of another. You have to be quite sharply concentrated to catch the changes, but sometimes you can trace the stages of your thinking from *this* thought, now, right back to its source.

It is rather like the way some conversations go. You start off talking with a close friend about something that happened to you last week, and by the time ten minutes have gone by you are both sounding off on what appears to be a completely disassociated topic. After this has gone on for another ten minutes, one of you wonders 'Now, how did we ever get on to talking about *that*?'—and you may not be able to remember.

The same thing is constantly happening in the mind. Perhaps you are sitting in meditation, not really very concentratedly, and you gradually become aware that you are thinking about how to make a particular kind of sandwich. In your imagination, you've been in the kitchen, making that sandwich—thinking about the *best way* to make that kind of sandwich—for at least five minutes! Where did that thought come from?

You think back, and try to see the chain of connections that produced that line of thought, and you remember that some time ago—in fact it was quite soon after you sat down for the meditation session—you heard the late-afternoon chimes from one of the local ice cream vans. You know this one well—it repeats, *ad nauseam*, a single phrase from 'Eine Kleine Nachtmusik'. Sometimes you find this profoundly irritating. But you didn't this time—and it also seems that ice cream wasn't the immediate occasion for you to start thinking about food. But it *was* the chimes that set your chain of distracted thoughts going. So what were the thoughts?

Yes—of course—it's spring now, and this is the *first time* you have heard the chimes this year. You remember now—your thoughts were ranging far, far away. You went back to a former springtime, years ago when you were very young indeed, and you had afternoon tea with one of your aunts. What a strange old lady *she* was! Anyway … you thought about that for quite a long time, and it was only *then* you started mentally making the sandwich.

Chaotic? Well, the degree of chaos may vary from person to person, but this 'associative' style of thinking is the way our minds seem to work quite a lot of the time. Often, of course, we form our ideas quite deliberately. But the majority of ideas come into our mind unbidden, and usually through some kind of association. This happens all the time, not only when we are day-dreaming.

It is natural for the mind to chase mental objects, and to associate one mental object with another. The associations of ideas that we make are often very interesting from a psychological point of view. Very often the most creative and original ideas arise through this kind of associative thought—it's how Einstein conceived his theory of relativity, for example.

The other kind of thinking is what we usually mean by the word 'thought'—it's the kind that we deliberately create and direct, as when we are planning our day, or working out some problem. We have a more or less definite purpose in mind—we are trying to keep our mind on a particular subject and are looking for a conclusion. Or we may be looking for the implications or ramifications of a certain idea—asking ourselves what something *means*. In all this deliberation we employ logic (often it's our own personal kind of logic). We may or may not jump to premature conclusions, make rash generalizations, or avoid obvious truths. We may succeed, or fail, in thinking an issue through towards its most satisfactory solution.

DIRECTED THINKING

Most of us spend a relatively small proportion of our thinking time in directing our thoughts. And even when we do, our directed thinking is often strongly influenced by associative thoughts—we often just direct our attention to a certain topic, and from there our thinking method is one of associating ideas; we simply bring our attention back to the main issues from time to time.

Generally, this seems a fairly healthy way of proceeding, since it acknowledges the place of unconscious 'lateral' thought processes. But the conclusions to which we come do matter. The clarity of our reasoning is a certain measure of our development—we must be alert to the dangers of vague, woolly thinking.

Ideas are important. From where we are at the moment, what we have is a *notion* of spiritual development. It's mostly an idea, and only partly a reality. We need to transform abstract ideas like this into concretely experienced realities. This is why so much spiritual practice is concerned with deepening one's experience, becoming mindful of what one is actually doing, what is actually happening. That's the *practice*—but there's also our *view*. We always have views—of some kind—about what we are doing, and like everything else in us, our views need periodic reassessment and change. The ideas, the 'operational concepts' of Buddhism, provide an essential framework for our practice. They give guidelines as to *why* we do what we do.

REFLECTION

Wisdom is a butterfly and not a gloomy bird of prey
W.B. Yeats

Reflection is the process of increasing clarification of views—particularly, in this context, views that relate to the path of liberation. We may reflect on any topic that catches our mental eye, and different revisions of the same idea may continue to turn over in our minds for weeks, and perhaps many years, afterwards. But there is always some reference to 'the nature of things'—to the great unsolved mysteries of existence.

Such deeper references may be subconscious, a part of the associative nature of the mind. It may be that we don't really know why a certain topic interests us. But one day, maybe years later, we may see that it is deeply connected to the fundamentals of our existence.

For example we may find ourselves often thinking about the phenomenon of violence. We may be inclined to be fascinated by the military posturings of the different world powers, perhaps both excited and appalled by the media reports of conflicts and wars. Our reflection topic here is 'War and Peace'—as Tolstoy's must also have been for many years before he compiled his great collage of human experience. With a certain amount of self-knowledge, we may wonder what possibilities there are for peace in a world made up of immature, confused beings more or less like ourselves. Turning to our immediate experience, we may marvel at the multitude of conditions for both peace *and* war that we set up in our own attitudes towards others, and that they set up towards us. Or we may simply reflect on peace, and on the possibilities of human potential.

There is an ocean of such topics, issues that can never be brought to easy 'conclusions'—they will always be rich topics for reflection, to be turned over and over again in the mind.

There is a 'musing' type of reflection that is a close relative of the associative type of thought. It's as though we are sitting by a warm fireside on a frosty winter's night, gazing into the flickering coals of our thoughts and ideas. Or it's like looking out of the window on a long train journey, our eyes taking in both the changing scenery and the reflections in the glass, our mind elsewhere. The window is just a medium—it's just somewhere to rest the eyes, something to keep the senses occupied while the thinking mind engages in deeper concerns. Our inner eye wants to observe the ideas as they arise of themselves, and as they disclose previously unseen layers of meaning.

MUSING ON THE FLICKERING COALS

It may be a good idea to work some of these spontaneously arising ideas into some kind of shape. In other words, reflection may usefully be employed in a directed way too—we may deliberately choose some object of contemplation and think it through. Deliberate thinking may be very calm and cool, like a surgeon's scalpel. But sometimes we may need to seize on our ideas hawk-like, challenging them and testing them. Sometimes we may even need to force ourselves, reluctantly, to face obvious conclusions.

DELIBERATION

It is essential to do this—though the slow, musing, butterfly-like aspect also needs to be allowed space in our reflections. To live up to its name, reflection must include both activity *and* receptivity, musing *and* deliberation. Indeed, the word *reflection* implies a two-way relationship between subject and object.

LEVELS OF INSIGHT

Reflection thus involves listening to our thoughts—gazing into the fire, or at the reflections in the window—as well as directing them with clarity and purpose. Reflection, as a method of gaining insight into deeper truths, seems itself to possess a many-sided nature.

Buddhist teaching distinguishes three separate phases of deepening of insight. There is a **listening** phase when we take in information, a **reflection** phase when we digest the implications of that information, and a **meditation** phase when we take the process deeper towards full realization.

(1) LISTENING

We do not always realize the extent to which our ability to learn is dependent on attitude. A traditional Buddhist model for 'listening'—taking in new information—is to be like a clean, empty receptacle, ready and waiting for some important spiritual teaching.

Not to listen is the defect of a pot turned upside down; not to bear in mind what you have heard is that of a pot with a leaky bottom; to be affected by [negative emotion] is that of a poisonous pot.

…When you listen to the explanation of the Dharma, you must listen to the voice of him who explains it without the perceiving faculty of your ears straying to some other sound. When you do not listen in this way, it is as if juice is poured on a pot with its opening down, for, though your body is present in the teaching room, you do not hear a single word of the Dharma.

…When you do not bear in mind the Dharma … though the words have reached the perceiving and hearing faculties, it is as if juice is poured into a pot with a leaky bottom—however much you may pour, nothing will remain there; and however much of the Dharma you may have heard, you do not know how to instil it into your mind and how to take it to heart.

…When you hear the explanation of the Dharma, but listen to it with … thoughts affected by the five [mental] poisons[48] … not only will the Dharma not become beneficial to your mind, it will even turn into its very opposite, and this is like healthy juice poured into a poisonous pot.[49]

Gampopa

'Listening' here may refer to any medium of communication—for example reading counts as 'listening'. In fact, books are likely to be a major source of information.

Perhaps a more accurate expression, then, is 'absorbing information'. If we want to absorb some new information, it helps if we take an active interest in it—if we *actively* listen. The verse quoted shows that the traditional expectation for listening to, or 'hearing', spiritual teaching (*suta-maya panna*) is more than just having one's aural sense functioning at the same time and place as the teaching is delivered.

The same considerations can apply in the realm of learning. If we are to learn, it's important that we are prepared to put aside our immediate emotional reactions to new material—for listening really means understanding the material, not merely as we 'hear' it, but *as it is actually taught*. In order not to be a 'poisonous vessel', it is necessary to be mindful of emotional responses—otherwise what we understand to have been said may be quite different from what was actually intended. It is easy to filter what a speaker or writer is saying through our own immediate reactions. If we don't like the sound of a particular example or turn of phrase, it can distort the meaning for us. So if the writer's meaning is unclear to us, we should ask what he or she was *intending* to say.

(2) REFLECTION

Sometimes, when we have absorbed a new idea, it gets under our skin and just won't let us go. We keep thinking about it, and the more we think and consider and reflect, the more clearly we understand it.

This is reflection proper (*cinta-maya panna*). This stage of insight is about deepening our understanding of ideas that we have already heard. A good way of expressing it is *making ideas your own*—it's the art of digesting received ideas into the body of your own thinking.

To a certain extent, reflection goes on in us naturally, because often we cannot help thinking about the implications of certain ideas. However, if we leave reflection up to our natural impulses, we will only consider those topics which naturally occur to us, and possibly miss important topics. We may also be too uncritical in our thinking.

So deliberate reflection is also important. The principal method of doing this is to recall a topic and simply turn it over in the mind. You can do this at any odd moment, but it's a good idea to put aside time specifically for reflection.

PUTTING TIME ASIDE

When you have some free time—half an hour or even twenty minutes may sometimes be sufficient—don't automatically reach for a book. Resolve to use this time solely for reflection. Put everything else aside, sit in a comfortable chair, and relax. Tune in to your thoughts.

Thoughts go through our minds all the time, so we may consider that there is no need to stop doing other things in order to think. But though it is possible to do two, three or even four things at a time, it is not always the most effective way of conducting ourself. Certainly our thought will benefit greatly from being given some time to itself. Often the reason we waste so much of our meditation time in thinking is because we don't provide any other mental space for it.

So don't hesitate to spend time in this way. It isn't a waste of time or an indulgence—giving a little time to the activity of thinking could make a huge difference, not only to the quality of your life, but also to your relationships with others.

To some extent reflection is a human need—it's a faculty that wants, as it were, to be exercised. It may be that many emotional problems are made worse—or even caused—by lack of reflection. If you always squeeze your thinking in between other external activities of life, or last thing at night before you fall asleep, you may be fostering a keen inner sense of frustration (not to mention insomnia).

Don't feel that it's pretentious to put time aside for thinking, just because you're no great intellectual. Reflection is not about self-importantly 'thinking great thoughts'; it's about using a human faculty—thought—to deepen your awareness of what it means to be a human being. It's something every human being has deep in his or her nature.

Think about what is going on in your life and the lives of others, think about your spiritual development, think about issues that have arisen recently. Try to work out more clearly what you think about them—and also, think about the world situation. Think about life and death, love and will. Think about potential, about actions and consequences.

The Tibetan Buddhist tradition lists a number of 'preliminary foundations'—topics of reflection that are very effective in galvanizing an interest in spiritual growth.

For example, there is **our potential for Enlightenment**.[50] The historical Buddha and many other practitioners of his teachings all gained a state of complete spiritual freedom. Anyone can do this by making an appropriate effort. Then there is **the preciousness of human life**. Sometimes human existence may be difficult and frustrating, but we are also uniquely free, especially if we have all our physical and mental faculties available. We are even more fortunate if we are living in a part of the world where we have not only heard about Buddhism but have the political freedom to practise it openly. There are many situations in the world where there is very little freedom of choice, where the main consideration has to be finding very basic necessities. Do we really understand how lucky we are? Then there is the fact that we live in a universe characterized by **impermanence**. Nothing can last very long, not even our own bodies. From this it seems clear that life is basically **unsatisfactory**. It certainly isn't possible to find any lasting satisfaction, though there may be temporary compensations—which don't really *compensate* for the unsatisfactory nature of things, but keep us happily(?) distracted from reality. This is the situation we are all in, and—like impermanence—it's a fruitful topic for reflection. The fact that **actions have consequences** is a very profound and mysterious theme indeed, one that seems bottomless in its depth of potential for reflection. Then there is **the need for spiritual friends**—think of all the people who have helped you gain your present perspectives on life. Where would you be without their influence? And where would others be without *your* influence? It's worth reflecting on **the benefits of liberation**—the sheer value of growth and development. The more you think about the possibilities for growth, the more appreciative and positive will be your response towards it. **Positive emotion** itself is a valuable topic for reflection, together with what is perhaps the supreme positive emotion, **the motivation towards Enlightenment for the sake of all beings**, or

Bodhichitta. It is on the basis of the stirrings of *Bodhichitta* (literally, 'enlightenment-mind') that one conceives the desire to commit oneself to the Buddhist Path, and grow towards the state of Buddhahood.

All these topics will bear almost endless reflection. You may relate to them easily or with difficulty—difficult emotional responses are par for the course, since the implications of all these topics are so vast—but nevertheless the deepening process of reflection will benefit your mind to an immeasurable extent.

Introspective reflection is not the only way of bringing to maturity the ideas we have taken in—interaction with others can also have a ripening effect. Discussing a topic such as one of these 'preliminary foundations' with a friend can often have far more of a galvanizing effect than thinking it through quietly at home. It's interesting to see how much it is possible to *disagree* on such themes—and discussion might often reveal levels of much-cherished unclear or wishful thinking that we would probably never see on our own. *Then* we can go home and think about it all, again! Thus discussion makes a very good support for reflection—it can lead our thinking on from reflection to further reflection. Spontaneous discussions after dinner, or over the washing up, can sometimes be very useful. But more formal discussion groups, or study groups, may be even more valuable if they are arranged on a regular basis. Perhaps you could organize a weekly get-together with some like-minded friends, either using your own choice of material, or agreeing on a more experienced study leader whom all of you respect.

OUR REFLECTIONS GET REFLECTED BACK TO US

Sometimes it is said that we only learn deeply about something when we start teaching it. If we know a topic well, teaching can be an excellent support for our reflection. Teaching is a way of *intensifying* our understanding, because when we teach, we have to account for our ideas. For example, if we have been studying Buddhism for some years it may be useful to start assisting with—or leading—study groups, or giving short talks. The feedback we get from these efforts will show us the gaps in our understanding. We'll see more clearly the extent to which we have *really* made the teaching our own, and to what extent it is still just theory.

Reflection sooner or later yields its own crop of ideas, and these fruits of our intellectual labours will, in turn, seed further ideas. We'll return again and again to these 'seed' ideas in our further reflection.

SOWING DHARMA SEEDS

Seeds like this are the ideal object of reflection in the vipassana sense. It is not enough merely to have a bare, undigested idea of a topic like 'impermanence' or 'shunyata'. We need a *Dharma seed*—an idea that has developed numerous facets of meaning for us. The more we reflect on the Dharma, the more Dharma seeds will emerge for us, and the more genuine topics we shall have for vipassana meditation.

(3) MEDITATION

The third level of insight is *bhavana-maya panna*—or vipassana meditation, as explored to some extent in Chapter Five. However, some other aspects of its nature may be clearer now that we have gone into its basis in thinking and reflection—now that we have seen the way that thinking and reflection are just as necessary, as *preliminaries* to insight meditation, as samatha meditation.

THE VARIETIES OF DHARMA SEEDS

There are other kinds of Dharma seeds in addition to conceptual ideas like impermanence. Many forms of vipassana meditation employ symbols, mantras, and 'seed-syllables'. In the same way as a meaningful concept, this more symbolic type of Dharma seed contains a great deal of previous reflection.

This aspect of Buddhist meditation apparently remains something of a mystery to some meditators. For example mantras like *om mani padme hum* have become widely known in the West. But since mantras are often repeated many times in meditational and devotional practices, they are sometimes wrongly seen as embodying a merely mechanical approach to spiritual development. The point of repetition, however, is the same as that of repeated reflection—the meaning of the mantra needs to penetrate beneath the surface of the conscious mind before deep transformation can take place. Of course, there will always be people who practise in a mechanical way—we probably do it ourselves from time to time—but properly speaking a mantra becomes a Dharma seed in the same way as a concept. For example the mantra just quoted may encapsulate, symbolically, a great deal of reflection on the Enlightened qualities of friendliness and kindness. It is the mantra of Avalokiteshvara, the Bodhisattva of Compassion.

GERMINATING DHARMA SEEDS

An experienced practitioner of Buddhist meditation, one who seriously reflects on the Dharma, will have many Dharma ideas, ideas regarding the ultimate nature of things, growing in his or her mind. Since it has no defined conceptual meaning, apart from general associations such as compassion, a mantra is a very useful peg upon which to hang a particular family of ideas, understandings, and mini-insights. The same principle also applies to all the many kinds of symbolic representation found in most traditions of Buddhist meditation—the visualized Buddhas and

Bodhisattvas, for example. For the practitioner they can come to represent the potential living reality of Enlightened wisdom and compassion in a way that mere words cannot.

All these symbols are Dharma seeds that are continually maturing in significance within the meditator's mind. For someone who is practising vipassana meditation regularly, reflection feeds into insight meditation, the results of which feed back into further reflection, initiating a spiral process of continually growing insight into reality. **DEEPENING INSIGHT**

We can now see how the system of the three levels of insight (Pali *panna*, Sanskrit *prajna*) works together as a whole. Reflection is its central core, absorbing whatever information it has 'listened' to by continually winding round the idea, turning it upside down and inside out in a quest for its inner meaning, then from time to time it tackles that inner meaning— at a word-transcending level—in meditation. Finally it allows the fruits of that work to nourish even deeper reflections. **THE PROCESS OF INSIGHT**

CREATING CONDITIONS FOR INSIGHT

Like meditation itself, all three levels of insight require certain conditions in order to be fully effective. Most of these have already been alluded to, but it's worth collecting them all together.

Perhaps the most important condition is our sense of motivation, the 'hunger for truth' that was mentioned at the start of this chapter. Unless we *strongly* want to gain insight, it won't happen.

Then there is discussion and debate with like-minded friends. This will focus your mind on the issues involved. In discussion, it is important to try to understand what another person is *trying* to say as well as what they seem, to you, to be saying. It is also important, for you, to express your own ideas.

It is important to exercise the intellect and nourish it with good quality material. Remember the analogy of the child who if not fed properly will just eat junk food—the mind naturally wants to take in ideas, so use discrimination in what you choose to give it. Reading is a precious gift—contact with great minds, through literature, is invaluable. Use the opportunities that you have to read whatever good literature, ancient and modern, takes your interest. Study some Dharma on your own as well as in study or discussion groups.

Read the books you find most valuable again and again. What was said just now about mechanical repetition was not meant as a suggestion that repetition has to be mechanical. On the contrary, repetition is vital. Reading and re-reading the works you love—in a receptive way, with an attitude of desiring to learn—will take understanding deeper. As a general principle, when we encounter anything for the first time we do so at a relatively superficial level. We rarely fully understand every aspect of an idea the first moment we encounter it.

The condition that will tie all these conditions together—and enable us to focus our energies in one-pointed reflection—is the practice of mindfulness. Mindfulness acts as a support to the development of insight in the same way as it supports concentration in meditation. If we continually maintain a **breadth** of awareness—of body, feelings, emotions, and thoughts—we may then more easily **focus** on our most important thoughts in deep reflection, and so form the Dharma seeds that may flower, later, into fully matured insights.

SOLITUDE

Everything that was suggested earlier as a condition for meditation will also aid the whole process of listening, reflecting, and meditating. But there is one very immediate condition that we also need to provide. Taking our thoughts deep requires a certain measure of inner solitude.

My own teacher once wrote the following advice to a young poet. To produce meaningful poetry, a writer needs to spend long periods of time in reflection. After stressing the importance of mindful preparation for writing poetry—in terms of awareness of the external world, your own inner feelings and responses, and sensitivity towards other people—Sangharakshita compares reflection to the fire in which one smelts the gold ore of the unrefined poem (or, as we can also say, the unrefined insight). This crude gold ore is to be melted, he says, in the crucible of *solitude*.

> *Without some degree of solitude reflection is impossible, and without prolonged reflection no great work of art was ever brought forth. The poet needs solitude as the lungs need air.*
>
> *By solitude is meant not so much physical loneliness as inner isolation, for the time being at least, from all that does not directly concern the process of poetic creation.*
>
> *Physical withdrawal from normal human activities and interests can be included in the definition of solitude only to the extent that the latter is dependent on it. In the urbanized and industrialized societies of the present age this is with increasing frequency the case. Without withdrawing externally*

from the hurry and bustle of modern life the poet may not be able to find the internal solitude necessary for the progress and perfection of his work.[51]
   Sangharakshita

Reflection provides a context for our practice of Buddhism. If we reflect often, our understanding will remain in touch with the 'flavour' of Dharmic ideas, and will always be ready to take them further. All our experience will be seen in the light of the Dharma, and so, when the meaning of the Dharma is with us all the time, we will obviously tend to put the Dharma more into practice.

Just as, monks, the mighty ocean is of one flavour, the flavour of salt, even so, monks, this Dhamma [i.e. Dharma] is of one flavour, the flavour of release.[52]
   Gautama Buddha

Chapter Ten

TYPES OF MEDITATION PRACTICES

BUDDHIST MEDITATION is a living tradition with a very long and fertile history. The principles of samatha and vipassana have been developed through an enormous variety of meditation practices, all of which can lead, eventually, to insight and Enlightenment.

THE FIVE BASIC METHODS

The Five Basic Methods are a traditional set of meditations, each one an antidote to one of the five principal obstructions to Enlightenment. These five mental 'poisons', as they are called, are *distraction, hatred, craving, conceit*, and *ignorance*.

No doubt you can recognize most of these from your own practice. *Distraction* is an obstruction which can be overcome by developing concentration in the **Mindfulness of Breathing** meditation. The energy we invest in *hatred* may be transformed into loving-kindness through the **Metta Bhavana** (and the other *Brahma-vihara Bhavana* practices to be described shortly). The other three poisons are best tackled through insight meditation: *craving* is displaced by inner peace and freedom through the **Contemplation of Impermanence**, our tendency towards *conceit* is transformed into clarity regarding the nature of selfhood through another vipassana method known as the **Six Element Practice**, and *spiritual ignorance* is transformed, through the **Contemplation of Conditionality**, into wisdom and compassion.

All Buddhist meditation practices can be traced back to one or more of these five principles. We shall be going into the nature of each of these practices in turn. Later we'll explore three further examples: visualization, just sitting meditation, and walking meditation.

The five poisons
counteracted by the
five basic practices

Meditation type	Meditation method	Counteracts poison	Develops
Samatha	1 **Mindfulness of Breathing**	Distraction	Concentration
	2 **Metta Bhavana** **(and Brahma-viharas)**	Hatred	Love
Vipassana	3 **Contemplation of impermanence**	Craving	Inner peace, freedom
	4 **Six element practice**	Conceit	Clarity regarding nature of self
	5 **Contemplation of conditionality**	Ignorance	Wisdom, compassion

SAMATHA

1 MINDFULNESS OF BREATHING

The Mindfulness of Breathing and the Metta Bhavana practices, the fundamental samatha meditations, were introduced at the beginning of the book.

2 METTA BHAVANA AND THE FOUR BRAHMA-VIHARAS

However, considerably more can be said about **Metta Bhavana**. On the basis of the loving-kindness that may be developed through Metta Bhavana, we can develop three further positive emotions. These are **compassion, sympathetic joy,** and **equanimity**.

The four meditation practices connected with these qualities are known as the *Brahma-viharas*. The word means 'the dwelling-places of Brahma', or 'the Sublime Abodes'. The Four Brahma-viharas are:

(a) The Development of love—*Metta Bhavana*
(b) The Development of compassion—*Karuna Bhavana*
(c) The Development of sympathetic joy—*Mudita Bhavana*
(d) The Development of equanimity—*Upekkha Bhavana*

DIFFICULTIES WITH WORDS

It's usually the case that translations of specialized Buddhist terms rarely convey the full meaning of the original. There are usually no direct equivalents for these terms. Metta is particularly hard to translate—it is a pity that the obvious English word, 'love', may include emotions like sexual desire, greed, or sentimentality. The word 'love' rarely conveys simple regard for someone's welfare and happiness. We use the word in many contexts— we love people, clothing, food, ideas—so that our 'love' for another person can sometimes be no different from our 'love' for a fashionable item of clothing, or from the way we 'love' some favourite food. Moreover, our 'love' for another person may be confused with sexual desire, neurotic craving, and fear of loneliness. Since the meaning of the word metta is free from these problems (see the definition below) it seems best to leave it untranslated in the hope that it will eventually pass into the language.

So long as we steer clear of the English word 'pity', which can sound patronizing, there is no problem translating *karuna* with the more familiar 'compassion', which seems a very good word for it. But there is no direct translation for *mudita*, which can only be rendered into English through a compound like 'sympathetic joy' and then explained. For *upekkha*, too, we have no word—the only one available, 'equanimity', can easily suggest a cool, neutral attitude rather than anything truly positive.

Since their names do not give us much idea of how to practise them, we'll need to reflect closely on each of these Brahma-viharas. As we explore the practices, try to evoke each quality in your mind and compare it to your experience in life. Then practise the meditations themselves when you have an opportunity.

NEAR AND FAR ENEMIES

You may be able to evoke each quality in experience by contrasting it with its 'enemy'—that is, its opposite. Each quality has, traditionally, both a 'near enemy' and a 'far enemy'. The **near enemy** is a negative quality which we tend to mistake for the true quality, as when we mistake pity for compassion. The **far enemy** is the more obvious negative opposite of the Brahma-vihara: the far enemy of compassion, for example, is cruelty.

As we go through each of the Brahma-vihara meditations, we'll begin by outlining each particular quality. Then we'll go over the practical details of each meditation practice (except the Metta Bhavana—we've already covered that), and finally explore the special qualities of the Brahma-vihara by contrasting it with its 'enemies'.

The quality of metta is a heartfelt concern for another person's happiness: we just want someone to be happy. And we want them to be happy on their *own* terms—we don't assume that we necessarily know what they need in order to be happy. We ourselves have no vested interest in their happiness—we simply want them to be happy, whether we personally get something out of it or not. Metta shows in our care about someone's welfare, and kindness in our relations with them.

(A) METTA
THE QUALITY OF METTA

There is an explanation of the stages of the Metta Bhavana in Chapter Two.

THE METTA BHAVANA MEDITATION

Hatred, the desire to harm another person, is—fairly obviously—the far enemy of metta. We can view the metta practice as a way of overcoming the tendency towards hatred.

Hatred is a fault that each of us has to varying degrees. Broadly speaking, hatred arises when our desires are frustrated. Since other people

THE FAR ENEMY OF METTA—HATRED

frequently get in the way of our achieving our desires, we are often tempted to indulge in it. In each of us there is usually some residue of unconscious resentment, irritation, and anger—all of which are forms of hatred—which can build up until we find some unfortunate person on whom we can 'unload' our feelings. But this residue very much affects our happiness; hatred is a very painful, and damaging, emotion.

Reflect of the benefits of metta

If we are prone to the different forms of hatred, it might be more helpful to reflect on the benefits of kindness and friendliness, rather than the disadvantages of hatred. Traditionally, the development of metta has these benefits:[53]

(1) Good sleep—we fall asleep and wake up happily, and don't have nightmares!

(2) Love and appreciation from other living beings.

(3) Protection from violence.

(4) Swift concentration of mind.

(5) Good looks!

(6) At death, freedom from confusion.

(7) If there is no attainment of insight in this lifetime, rebirth in a happy state of existence.

THE NEAR ENEMY OF METTA—SENTIMENTAL ATTACHMENT

The near enemy of metta—that is, the emotion we are in danger of mistakenly interpreting as genuine friendliness—is sentimental attachment or *pema*. Pema is an emotional attachment to another person, our craving of some kind of experience from them.

This attachment may be very subtle or very obvious. It can range from a slight tendency to sentimentalize or idealize someone to strong sexual desire. It's quite easy to confuse pema with metta: it is common for people to consider that they are experiencing purely altruistic feelings towards someone, when in fact they simply 'fancy' them.

An example of the same kind of misunderstanding can occur on the part of parents towards their children—genuine desire for the child's well-being may be mixed with ideas that he or she must grow up according to the parent's own personal wants. This confusion is not restricted to parents—it is an attitude that can form in the mind of any more experienced person with regard to a less experienced person. And from the opposite point of view, examples of pema can arise in our relationships with older people—we can regard them, unknowingly, as being like a father or mother, and perhaps have expectations that they will protect or look after us.

However, don't become over-concerned about your metta being 'adulterated' with pema. Remember that the idea is to mature emotionally, rather than get rid of 'sins'. Think mostly in terms of *developing* the positive quality of metta—whilst being aware of the likelihood that pema still remains in your attitude somewhere. Your development of Metta Bhavana will inevitably have elements of attachment mixed in with it. But as with unrefined gold, such elements may be 'panned out' through regularly cultivating the quality of metta, until just the real thing remains.

Growing out of
need-based attachment

But the process cannot be hurried. Emotional refinement is essentially a matter of growing up—growing out of your need-based response to others, growing towards the spontaneous desire to give and to help. Such growing up requires insight into the essentially frustrating nature of need-based attachments. This insight cannot be hurried, because need-based attachments are generally very strong! All the Brahma-viharas, especially the Upekkha Bhavana, can help to develop this maturing insight.

The fundamental Brahma-vihara quality is metta—the desire for another's happiness. Each of the other Brahma-viharas is basically metta too—it's the same emotion arising in response to differently 'testing' situations.

(B) KARUNA— COMPASSION

For example *karuna* (compassion) is a 'metta-full' response towards anyone who is suffering. It is *more* than just friendliness. If we are feeling generally friendly towards all, but then perceive that someone is suffering, we'll feel that a deeper response is required of us. We'll no longer be happy simply to remain with that friendly, open, generous response—positive though it is. Nor can we be content just to be aware of their suffering. We'll want to do something to help. If we truly desire the happiness of someone who is suffering we will appreciate their position and we'll want to *relieve* their suffering if we can.

The conflict between our awareness of their unhappiness and our desire for their happiness gives birth to a new emotion—the emotion of compassion. Compassion is the desire to relieve the suffering of another person so that they may be happy.

There are seven stages to the Karuna Bhavana.

THE KARUNA BHAVANA MEDITATION

(1) The practice begins with the development of metta. This can be done either by practising the first or the last stage of the Metta Bhavana meditation, or—if you want a stronger basis than that would give you—by going, perhaps more briefly, through all the stages.

(2) Once you have established a feeling of metta, call to mind someone who is suffering. This person could be someone you know, or perhaps

(1)	Develop metta towards yourself
(2)	Develop metta towards a suffering person, creating compassion
(3)	Develop compassion towards a good friend
(4)	Develop compassion towards a neutral person
(5)	Develop compassion towards an enemy
(6)	Develop equal compassion towards all five persons
(7)	Extend compassion towards all living beings throughout the universe

someone you have heard about. Perhaps their circumstances are miserable—or maybe they are suffering through illness or have acted in an unskilful way which is bound to bring them unhappiness.

It is not necessary to choose someone who is suffering in an *extreme* way. Remember that the object of the exercise is for you *effectively* to develop a positive emotion. Watch out for despondency.

It's worth stressing that in the Karuna Bhavana you do not try to develop compassion!—at least, not directly. Don't assume that you know what compassion is. Remember that the basic emotion is metta. So just as in the Metta Bhavana, simply try to develop loving kindness towards the person. Your awareness of the person should *include* the fact that they are suffering—their suffering shouldn't be the only thing that you see in them. This broader awareness will help to transform that basic attitude of friendliness into compassion.

(3), (4), (5) The progression of stages in the rest of the meditation is similar to the Metta Bhavana. Now develop loving kindness towards a good friend, neutral person, and enemy in turn, with awareness of their suffering.

(6) Finally 'break the barriers' by imagining all five persons together— yourself, the suffering person, your good friend, neutral person, and enemy—and develop this loving kindness equally towards each one, with awareness of their suffering.

(7) Then radiate that equality of positive emotion throughout the entire universe.

Compassion is, on the whole, a more *demanding* emotion than metta. Generally, people seem to find the sufferings of others—even very slight degrees of suffering—very difficult to handle. We may tend to associate suffering with failure. We may not like to admit that such failure can happen. Sometimes even to acknowledge that someone suffers can feel as though we are letting them down. 'Oh, he's OK—there's nothing wrong with him, leave him alone, let him get on with his own life,' we may say, and dismiss the matter from our mind. But this way of thinking may, in some cases, become a way of justifying, to ourselves, a neglect of the needs of others.

This kind of conflict is just one of the 'tests' to which the suffering of others continually subjects us. Whether it is just some momentary feeling that someone is experiencing, or a major tragedy, our awareness of their suffering may pose a problem for us. We may tend to hide from the intensity of knowing that people are all around us, all suffering in different ways. This is where the near enemies may start showing themselves.

Sometimes people try, perhaps unconsciously, to avoid getting involved with other people's suffering. This may lead to cruelty. Cruelty means showing indifference to suffering. (It can also mean actually inflicting it, or taking pleasure in inflicting it.)

THE FAR ENEMY OF COMPASSION— CRUELTY

When the forces of circumstance give us power over those we dislike, we may need to make a conscious effort not to exploit them in this way. Often what we don't like about someone, or feel uncomfortable with, is also a source of suffering for them. But we may not notice this at all, especially if we naïvely tend to think of ourselves as a 'nice person'. We need to make conscious efforts to acknowledge our dislikes, and see that another person does actually suffer.

Cruelty is the 'far enemy' of compassion. Clearly such a response is to be avoided, and if possible we should also avoid the pressures which spark it off. But we should recognize that our own discomfort with the suffering of others can sometimes make us capable of cruelty.

It is difficult to find any kind of solution to the dilemma of human suffering. However, if we are going to be true to our aspirations of personal growth, we need to seek some resolution, at least in our own hearts. The Brahma-vihara meditations are a very good medium for this kind of seeking.

THE NEAR ENEMIES OF COMPASSION

In our own day-to-day experience of these conflicts, we may recognize compassion's two 'near enemies', sentimental pity and horrified anxiety, which are examined below. It is possible to mistake these emotions for compassion, or at least regard them as something vaguely positive. But, in fact, they can have very negative effects. They both stem, in different ways, from our fear of the feelings aroused in ourselves by the suffering person's situation. Perceiving another person's suffering is often painful and confusing. We are often unable to respond warmly and open-heartedly to them because we get preoccupied by our *own* discomfort.

Sentimental pity arises when we shy away from the discomfort and try to cover it up by 'feeling sorry for' the suffering person. We are so confused

Sentimental pity

or afraid that we feel we cannot try to understand or engage with them. Yet we think of this response as positive.

If it is not recognized as an unskilful reaction, sentimental pity easily becomes the basis for 'explaining away' the person's suffering, and may often be subtly combined with contempt and condescension. People often say things like 'Oh, I'm *so* sorry to hear that …' but it isn't genuine. They don't *really* care, even though they may think they do.

We sometimes express sympathy and sorrow for a suffering person, and think we are genuinely being compassionate; but inside we feel afraid or confused. We don't really want to address their *actual* needs. An indication of this is when our communication with a suffering person seems unreal and out of touch. We haven't seen what is really required—and we aren't really interested in finding out what it is. What we are most interested in (though we don't see it ourselves) is getting out of that situation, because it frightens and confuses us. Whether their suffering is great or small, the suffering person will certainly detect this.

The characteristic of true compassion is that we take the trouble actually to get involved with the person concerned. A possible outcome of sentimental pity is coldness and even, eventually, cruelty.

Horrified anxiety

'Horrified anxiety' is another counterfeit form of compassion. This arises in a somewhat different way. We allow ourselves to experience the uncomfortable feeling that the person's suffering arouses in *us*. The problem is that we become so affected by it that we lose our perspective on *them*. Again, we don't really see them at all. We allow ourselves to become so affected by their suffering—or what we see as their suffering—that we stiffen and panic, and so are unable to be of any actual use (though we may busy ourselves in all kinds of 'helpful' ways). Since we are feeling *something* that is apparently concerned with them, we may tell ourselves that this is a kind of compassion.

FEAR OF FEELING

Both of these near enemies can be illustrated by imagining how you might feel if you meet a friend who has recently experienced a terrible tragedy. Perhaps they have lost a child in a traffic accident. The knowledge that such a dreadful thing could happen is very painful indeed to you, too, but how to respond to them? (That is, to the degree that you *have* a choice.)

You may simply not want to feel the shock of your own response, and fall into the trap of sentimental pity. Your mouth says, 'What a terrible thing to happen,' but you can't really relate to your friend in a personal way. Later you may say to someone else, '*poor* old so-and-so, it's *such* a shame'—but you still don't allow yourself to feel anything. Or you may make a great outward fuss of it all—but still not really connect with your friend and their needs. Both reactions are based on a fear of feeling.

An example of horrified anxiety could be that you yourself become depressed on account of the tragedy, out of ersatz compassion—again, this is of no use at all to your friend, who probably just needs to see that you care, that you at least want to understand, and that you wish them well.

This is, perhaps, an extreme example; the principles apply much more broadly. Since suffering is everywhere, you will find less demanding tests of your attitudes towards others cropping up continually. You may see subtler versions of these near enemies influencing you in all your relations to others.

Just as was the case with pema, simply be mindful of the possibility of these near enemies without worrying overmuch about them. There will almost always be a component of one or another near enemy—or both— in your responses to people. They will be there in your meditation too. Whenever you recognize one or the other of these, see it as an opportunity to change. In the case of pity, recognize the need to acknowledge and engage with your actual feelings about someone's suffering. In the case of horror, recognize the anxiety in your mind and see how it prevents you from really sympathizing or being of any use. In meditation, it is simpler and more direct—you can more easily recognize your feelings and work to transform them.

Compared to *karuna*, sympathetic joy (*mudita*) represents a very different kind of emotional 'test'. If we are in a positive emotional state and encounter a happy person—perhaps someone happier or more fortunate than we are—the natural, healthy response is one of mudita. Mudita is a feeling of joy and gladness in the happiness and well-being of others.

(C) MUDITA— SYMPATHETIC JOY

There is a similar Buddhist practice called 'rejoicing in merits' in which we applaud the good qualities of other people. Here we don't just inwardly acknowledge, but actually express, how very generous and kind (or whatever) we find that person to be. Just try telling someone you know how much you appreciate them. You may be surprised by the effect it has on you (and them!).

(1) In the same way as before, begin the practice by developing loving-kindness.

THE MUDITA BHAVANA MEDITATION

(2) Then direct that loving-kindness towards someone whom you think of as being particularly happy and joyful—perhaps they are enjoying

Summary of stages of Mudita Bhavana (meditation on sympathetic joy)

(1)	Develop metta towards yourself
(2)	Develop metta towards a happy person, creating sympathetic joy
(3)	Develop sympathetic joy towards a good friend
(4)	Develop sympathetic joy towards a neutral person
(5)	Develop sympathetic joy towards an enemy
(6)	Develop equal sympathetic joy towards all five persons
(7)	Extend sympathetic joy towards all living beings throughout the universe

good fortune; perhaps they are just happy a lot of the time. Or maybe they are particularly happy at the moment. So inwardly congratulate them on their good fortune and genuinely wish that their happiness continues for a long time. The initial feeling of metta will eventually be transformed into a sympathetic, appreciative joy for them.

(3) (4), (5) Then develop this feeling in turn towards a good friend, a neutral person, and an enemy, this time dwelling particularly on their good qualities and their happiness.

(6) Then comes the stage of 'breaking the barriers': equalize the feeling of sympathetic joy between yourself, the happy person, good friend, neutral person, and enemy. This means that you rejoice in your own merits and appreciate your own good qualities in just the same way that you appreciate those of others.

(7) Then, as with the other Brahma-viharas, radiate the emotion outwards towards the whole universe of sentient beings.

THE FAR ENEMY OF MUDITA—RESENTMENT OR ENVY

The opposite, or 'far enemy', of mudita is resentment or envy, though very often it is not so 'far away' as some of the other far enemies! We can probably recognize that someone else's happiness is something to rejoice in—rationally, we can see that it's a good thing. But inside we can feel very resentful about it! Sometimes our own lack of self-esteem can make us feel inferior and unworthy—especially if we feel our 'inferiority' in contrast to their 'superiority'. So a good way to work with this emotion of resentment—from our subjective point of view—is to see its basis in feelings of inferiority, and then try to dissolve that basis by appreciating our own merits in this meditation.

THE NEAR ENEMY OF MUDITA—VICARIOUS ENJOYMENT

The near enemy of mudita, which we can mistake for a genuine appreciation, is a sentimental kind of satisfaction in someone's happiness: we indulge in a kind of vicarious enjoyment of it, and on that basis think to ourselves that we really appreciate *them*.

This works in a completely different way from resentment. When we are resentful, we really don't want to acknowledge the happiness of the other person at all. With vicarious satisfaction, we welcome their happiness, but inside we are still avoiding any real connection with the person. We may go 'over the top' in our admiration, in an almost idolizing sort of way. But we have no real awareness of them, or even interest in them as they actually are. What we are really after is a certain kind of satisfaction that we get from our *idea* of their happiness. It's easy to see how this can be mistaken for genuine appreciation. To counteract both resentment and sentimental satisfaction, we need to pay closer attention to the person themselves, to try to appreciate what their experience of happiness and good fortune is really like.

All the Brahma-viharas combine together in the Upekkha Bhavana meditation—whatever work has been done with metta, karuna, and mudita provides a foundation for this more complete practice.

(D) UPEKKHA— EQUANIMITY

So this is a good time to remind ourselves that we are talking about a set of meditation practices, as well as a series of positive emotions. We may, for example, wonder what relation these practices bear to the higher states of consciousness and insight.

Tradition[54] says that a meditator may gain access to a considerably higher level of consciousness through this Brahma-vihara as compared to the other three. Metta, Karuna, and Mudita Bhavana are each said to give access only to the third dhyana but no further, whereas Upekkha Bhavana can open the door to all the rest—to the fourth dhyana, as well as the 'formless' dhyanas which arise on the basis of the fourth dhyana.

This makes a partial link with that special dhyana factor, arising only in the fourth dhyana, which is also called upekkha. But upekkha as a Brahma-vihara is different from the dhyana factor of upekkha. It is more powerful. The dhyana factor of upekkha is a product of whatever meditation practice we happen to be doing, experienced in terms of our own, personal, psychic integration; the Brahma-vihara of upekkha arises because we are meditating specifically on the other-regarding quality of equanimity. The other-regarding quality has inspirational qualities that make it, potentially, far stronger.

(1) Once again, start by developing metta.
(2) Then choose a neutral person. Consider, and try to engage emotionally with, their suffering *and* their joy.

THE UPEKKHA BHAVANA MEDITATION

At the same time, bear in mind that they themselves have created their situation. This is a form of vipassana reflection: try to respond *to their conditionedness* with metta.

As you engage with them in this way, you may develop a quality of

Summary of stages of Upekkha Bhavana (meditation on equanimity)

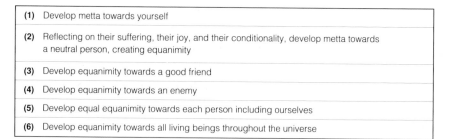

(1)	Develop metta towards yourself
(2)	Reflecting on their suffering, their joy, and their conditionality, develop metta towards a neutral person, creating equanimity
(3)	Develop equanimity towards a good friend
(4)	Develop equanimity towards an enemy
(5)	Develop equal equanimity towards each person including ourselves
(6)	Develop equanimity towards all living beings throughout the universe

patient understanding which is the beginning of equanimity.

(3, 4) Then choose a good friend, then an enemy, and work with them in the same way, trying to deepen the sense of equanimity.

(5) Then 'break the barriers' by applying equanimity equally to each person, including yourself, and then

(6) take that out to all living beings, everywhere, regardless of what sort of person they are or how they may see you.

This raises the sense of equanimity to a universal level: developing upekkha can synthesize our experience of the three other Brahma-viharas to the highest possible degree. It can become all of them interacting without any bias or partiality—with equal love, equal compassion, and equal joy in the joy of others.

THE NEAR AND FAR ENEMIES OF UPEKKHA: NEUTRALITY AND INDIFFERENCE

As well as being a more universal emotion than the other three, upekkha is at the same time more subtle. This subtlety is illustrated by its near and far enemies. Superficially, at least, the near and far enemies appear to be very similar to one another.

The near enemy, which we could perhaps mistake for upekkha itself, is neutrality—a lukewarm, apathetic lack of interest. The far enemy of equanimity is a cold, hardened, fixed indifference.

The distinction is between a passive and an active indifference. Clearly, the far enemy of cold indifference is in total opposition to the all-embracing insightful love that is the full manifestation of upekkha. But in the case of the near enemy, our feelings about a certain person are so weak—we are neither attracted nor repulsed by them—that it seems pointless to take any interest in them at all. Sometimes, if we are rather out of touch emotionally, this may appear to represent a positive, disinterested regard for someone.

No doubt this is why the *neutral* person is the first other person that we contemplate in this practice. We choose a neutral person *because* we have little or no feeling for them. It's a subtle relationship—but subtle though it may be, our relationship or non-relationship to the neutral person may actually be as challenging a test of our emotional maturity as is our relationship to the suffering person in the Karuna Bhavana, or the happy person in the Mudita Bhavana.

As is the case with near enemies like pity or sentimental enjoyment, we are in fact refusing to really experience this person. We cannot be bothered to engage with them—we find them at best neutral and at worst boring and uninteresting. This is, of course, our prejudice: such a feeling about another human being inevitably has something, at least, to do with our own psychological make up.

By providing a medium through which we can work with our response to 'neutral' people, all the Brahma-viharas allow us to extend ourselves far beyond the present limitations of our imagination. The Upekkha Bhavana enables us to do so at a higher level than the other Brahma-viharas, since it is supported by them.

It should by now be clear why Upekkha Bhavana cannot be effectively practised unless some preparatory work has been done with the other Brahma-viharas. Metta is fundamental, but some experience of both Karuna and Mudita Bhavana is also definitely required. It is necessary for us to have experience in *exercising* our appreciation of the suffering of others and enjoyment, which is what these two practices do. This will teach us more about empathizing with others, and we shall be better able to imagine something of how the person that *we* find uninteresting might feel.

At the moment, when we are happy ourselves we feel that that is enough, and if other people are unhappy it is not our problem. When we are unhappy, we just want to get rid of whatever we find unpleasant as soon as possible—we neither remember nor care that others might be unhappy too. This is all delusion. Instead, put others in your place, and put yourself in their place. This is called 'exchanging yourself with others'.

...Even if for the moment we cannot actually help anyone in an external way, we should meditate on love and compassion constantly over the months and years until compassion is knit inseparably into the very fabric of our mind.[55]

Dilgo Khyentse Rimpoche

Through the upekkha meditation we may see how upekkha is not different from karuna or mudita or metta, though it takes each quality to the highest, most universal level.

The Mahayana Buddhist tradition[56] greatly emphasizes a practice called 'exchanging oneself with others'. To be aware of the 'enemy' of indifference in us (whether active or passive) is extremely useful, since most of the people we come into contact with are 'neutral'. Gaining knowledge of our own indifference will help us to engage more fully with feeling, to work with subtler shades of pleasure and pain, and appreciate subtler emotional responses in all our dealings with people.

Essentially, upekkha is the development of *equality* of positive emotion towards all living beings. This doesn't just mean 'equal' positivity (which perhaps could be rather a lukewarm affair), but love which is equally *strongly* felt towards all. This is the highest possible degree of positivity. Equanimity is a very rich, highly developed emotion which can only arise in its fullness when metta, karuna, and mudita have already been cultivated.

Karuna and Mudita Bhavana help us to free ourselves from attachments and aversions. These negative emotions keep us preoccupied with our own subjective needs, and cut us off from any real interest in others. If we are to be truly non-discriminating in our love for others, we must have this particular kind of emotional freedom—we cannot remain dependent on the pleasures they can give us, or averse to the pain they may cause. As we have seen, karuna and mudita arise out of fundamental metta, the 'no strings' desire for the happiness of others: karuna being our metta-full response to pain, mudita our metta-full response to pleasure.

Upekkha, however, is different in that it does not see others in terms of either pleasure or pain. The attitude of upekkha *includes* compassion towards the fact that everyone suffers, and gladness in the fact that everyone can be happy. So it recapitulates, at its own level, the Karuna and Mudita Bhavana. But in addition, this attitude involves the realization that the suffering and joy that all living beings experience arises from self-imposed conditioning—that we all inherit the effects of our previous actions on our present mental states.

Thus upekkha is an extremely positive emotion combined with a powerful element of insight. An understanding of the universality of action and consequence necessarily gives birth to equanimity, since we see that everyone, even if they are not immediately responsible, must take ultimate responsibility for their own happiness. In accepting the way things actually are, we can realize a new kind of connectedness between ourself and others, and a new kind of patience and kindness, which we could call metta at a higher level.

A TRADITIONAL EXTENSION FOR THE FINAL STAGE OF BRAHMA-VIHARA MEDITATIONS

We have already seen that at the end of all the Brahma-viharas comes the final 'consummation' stage of radiation (known in Pali as *pharana*). If the practice is going well—certainly if you are getting into access concentration or dhyana—it is worth spending longer on this stage. In fact, if the previous stages are well developed, you could occasionally go through them more quickly and concentrate mainly on the conclusion.

If you do so, it may help to have a more thorough method of practising radiation. In Chapter Two we outlined the usual method, in which you include ever-widening circles of beings in your metta, moving from everyone meditating in the same room out to all living beings in the universe.

Some traditional methods are more systematic. One of these is to divide every imaginable type of being into various categories, and then direct positive emotion towards each in turn. The quantity of living beings in the universe can be bewilderingly vast (especially if you take a traditional Buddhist perspective!) so perhaps dividing them into categories may help you to get more of an imaginative grasp. These categories may be used in a flexible manner—the ones that are given, as you'll see, overlap quite a bit.

The categories are (1) all females (human or otherwise); (2) all males (human or otherwise); (3) all enlightened beings; (4) all unenlightened beings; (5) all gods; (6) all human beings; (7) all living beings in states of suffering.

The 'ten directions' of space are divided and meditated upon in turn for each of these categories. With ourselves at the centre, we radiate metta towards the four cardinal points, the four intermediate points, the zenith, and the nadir. So we imagine, for example, all females in the north, in the south, etc. And also, in each category, in each direction, four phrases of metta-aspiration are then applied. We wish that (1) they may be free from enmity, (2) they may be free from hatred, (3) they may be free from suffering, and (4) they may remain happy in the future.

Each combination of metta-aspiration, category of person, and direction of space is called an *appana*—a multi-faceted 'object' of concentration which, when focused upon sufficiently intensely, is a potential entry point into dhyana. One such *appana* would go like this (not just in words of course, but in imagination): 'May all the women in the east be free from enmity.' Others could be 'May all the women in the east be free from hatred,'—then 'May they all be free from suffering,' then 'May they all keep themselves happy!' Try to imagine the actual existence of all these people, at this moment, aware of their direction in relation to the place you are sitting. In the next round you could consider the men in the same way, and so on.

After each direction has been completed, you can come back to developing metta (or karuna, or whatever) for yourself, in order to ground your awareness before continuing. If you follow this method strictly, all the

Radiating (final stage of the Brahma-vihara meditations)[57]

May all the	in this direction	be free from
• Females	• east	
• Males	• south-east	
• Enlightened beings	• south	
• Unenlightened beings	• south-west	
• Gods	• west	
• Unhappy beings	• north-west	• enmity
• Humans	• north	• hatred
	• north-east	• suffering
	• zenith	
	• nadir	—and keep happy!

combinations of beings, aspirational phrases, and directions add up to 280 *appanas*—twenty-eight in each of the ten directions—which will, of course, take a long time to go through! But if your meditation is going well (certainly if each *appana* actually takes you into dhyana) you will *feel* like meditating for a long time, and to do so is certainly very beneficial. So long as you are happy in meditation you should extend the time you spend sitting as much as you can: when you are getting easily into dhyana your body starts adjusting so that you may be able—on a good day, perhaps on a retreat—to sit for some hours. In fact this particular method provides a good way of employing the extra energy that one often finds when meditation starts going well.

I have included this as an illustration of how much one can elaborate and embroider certain meditation practices. Feel free to simplify or adapt this method however you like: you could choose fewer types of people, or limit yourself to just four cardinal points, for example. The important thing is to keep the imagination alive and working.

VIPASSANA

3 CONTEMPLATION OF IMPERMANENCE

This particular vipassana practice—or family of vipassana practices, since there are many variations—is designed as an antidote to the mental poison of craving.

ADDICTION AND CREATIVITY

We saw earlier (Chapter Five) that the nagging worry about 'things not lasting' is a root cause of insecurity. Insecurity and craving always go together: craving—whatever it seems to be directed towards—is basically craving for security. Our ego-sense seeks security and yearns for sensations and possessions.

How can we best define the mental poison of craving? Craving is a kind of desire. But it is not the same thing as desire, for we can desire things in a healthy way. We can very usefully cultivate a desire for objectivity, compassion, and even Enlightenment itself. Craving is ignorant, self-centred desire. It is better known as the universal tendency towards addiction—the tendency to cling on to anything that seems to offer security. It is so harmful because no matter how much we indulge craving, we always feel that we must have more.

In this sense, everyone is an addict in certain ways and to certain degrees—unless they are heading irreversibly towards Enlightenment (and even then, they will not have *completely* eradicated the poison of craving). According to the Buddha, craving is the basic human predicament, and the primary cause of all human suffering. Part of the definition of Enlightenment itself is freedom from craving.

Craving for unrealistic, impossible satisfactions is at the root of so many of our tightly held attitudes, habits, hopes, fears, irritations, and passions. Essentially it is our addictive tendencies—the whole complex of clinging to whatever seems to give security—which stand in the way of our freedom and creativity. If we could loosen the knot, even very slightly, we would experience a great deal more happiness.

The only way to untie the knot of craving is to use *vipassana* to look into the basic predicament. We need to look clearly at impermanence, the reality that we are all running away from. If we can deeply acknowledge the impermanent nature of the objects that we crave, we shall eventually realize, in our heart, the possibility of complete freedom from craving.

Craving can go very deep, so strong antidotes may be required to overcome it. The basic form of impermanence meditation is to look it straight in the eye, as it were, and contemplate death—usually the most dreaded form of impermanence. There are other approaches too, as we shall see. There are a number of different ways of reflecting upon death, designed for the needs of different temperaments.

REFLECTING UPON DEATH

The first method is rather radical: it is to contemplate the decomposition of a dead body. This may be done in one's imagination. (Tradition recommends using an actual corpse, which obviously may be difficult to arrange!)

REFLECTING UPON THE IMPERMANENCE OF THE PHYSICAL BODY

People do, of course, die, and if you are present in these circumstances it may be natural and appropriate to spend some time with the body, which may be that of someone you have known. In spite of the fear or loathing that such an idea may arouse—usually as an idea, rather than as a real experience—at such times we may feel a deep sense of clarity and perspective, the very antithesis of craving.

In Eastern Buddhist lands where cremation and burial were not practised, human remains were often simply left in a charnel ground to decompose naturally or to be eaten by wild beasts. A meditator would go to such a place and mindfully observe the bodies lying there in various states of decomposition. Recollecting that his or her own body would go through similar processes after death, they would acknowledge their experience of these things and try to come to terms with whatever emotions might arise. Provided effective preparation had been made in terms of samatha practice, the effect would be the conquest of irrational anxiety through a deep sense of inspiration.

Clearly, anyone wanting to use this method will need to be an emotionally positive and well-balanced individual, and not someone prone to morbid depression. This proviso is particularly necessary in the modern West, which seems to be quite unlike the environment in which these practices arose.

India, in the Buddha's day, seems to have had an emotionally healthy atmosphere. Yet there is a story that even the Buddha misjudged the suitability of this practice for a particular group of monks; returning later, he found that they had all committed suicide, apparently due to depression.

So the 'recollection of impurity', as this meditation is sometimes called, requires a firm basis in metta and mindfulness. If that basis is there, then we'll be able to engage with the universal fact of death with a real interest and inspiration. If the reflection is developed gradually within a balanced and happy frame of mind, it will loosen our small-minded clinging to security and create a tremendous sense of confidence and freedom.

GENERAL REFLECTION UPON DEATH

The second method is less 'confrontational', yet may be just as effective. It is simply to recollect, on the basis of a concentrated state of mind, the fact that we are one day going to die. Of course we all know this theoretically, but it's an extremely difficult fact for us actually to realize and fully accept.

Start the practice with a good session of Metta Bhavana, taking the practice towards dhyana, or at least access concentration. Then turn the fact of death over and over again within your concentrated mind. Traditionally, one repeats inwardly the word 'death', or some phrase that will keep the fact of death in the mind. The main thing is to keep a receptive and peaceful quality of attention upon this phrase, or idea, until the fact of death really does sink in.

As a preparation, you will probably find that metta alone is not enough to contain the power of this practice. Concentration is also important, because the mind may well make attempts to evade the issue, throwing up smoke-screens of distraction and dullness. (These, in fact, are the commonest problems.) If you find these hindrances arising then go back for a while to samatha meditation before returning to the vipassana.

A variant of the 'phrase' approach is to repeat slowly to oneself, from memory, these Root Verses from the *Tibetan Book of the Dead*.[58] Consider the following lines.

REFLECTION ON THE ROOT VERSES FROM THE *TIBETAN BOOK OF THE DEAD*

O now, when the Birthplace Bardo [i.e. the Bardo of Life] upon me is dawning!
Abandoning idleness—there being no idleness in (a devotee's) life—
Entering into the Reality undistractedly, listening, reflecting, and meditating,
Carrying on to the Path (knowledge of the true nature of) appearances and of
*   mind, may the Trikaya[59] be realized:*
Once that the human form has been attained,
May there be no time (or opportunity) in which to idle it away.

O now, when the Dream Bardo upon me is dawning!
Abandoning the inordinate corpse-like sleeping of the sleep of stupidity,
May the consciousness undistractedly be kept in its natural state;
Grasping the (true nature of) dreams, (may I) train (myself) in the Clear Light
*   of Miraculous Transformation:*
Acting not like the brutes in slothfulness,
May the blending of the practising of the sleep (state) and actual (or waking)
*   experience be highly valued by me.*

O now, when the Dhyana Bardo upon me is dawning!
Abandoning the whole mass of distractions and illusions,
May (the mind) be kept in the mood of endless undistracted samadhi,
May firmness both in the visualizing and in the perfected (stages) be obtained:
At this time, when meditating one-pointedly, with (all other) actions put aside,
May I not fall under the power of misleading, stupefying, passions.

O now, when the Bardo of the Moment of Death upon me is dawning!
Abandoning attraction and craving, and weakness for all (worldly things),
May I be undistracted in the space of the bright (enlightening) teachings,
May I (be able to) transfuse myself into the heavenly space of the Unborn:
The hour has come to part with this body, composed of flesh and blood;
May I know the body to be impermanent and illusory.

O now, when the Bardo of Reality upon me is dawning!
Abandoning all awe, fear, and terror of all (phenomena),
May I recognize whatever appears as being my own thought-forms,
May I know them to be apparitions in the intermediate state;
(It has been said), 'There arrives a time when the chief turning-point is reached;
Fear not the bands of the Peaceful and the Wrathful, who are your own
    thought-forms.'

O now, when the Bardo of (taking) Rebirth upon me is dawning!
One-pointedly holding fast to a single wish,
(May I be able to) continue the course of good deeds through repeated efforts;
May the womb-door be closed, and the revulsion recollected:
The hour has come when energy and pure love are needed;
(May I) cast off jealousy and meditate upon the guru, the Father-Mother.

O procrastinating one, who thinks not of the coming of death,
Devoting yourself to the useless doings of this life,
Improvident are you in dissipating your great opportunity;
Mistaken, indeed, will your purpose be now if you return empty-handed (from
    this life):
Since the Holy Dharma is known to be your true need,
Will you not devote (yourself) to the Holy Dharma, even now?

Our lives nowadays would benefit greatly from a more positive view of death. The *Tibetan Book of the Dead*, which is a guide for skilful dying, places the notion of death in a very inspiring context. Death is conceived of as just one of six *bardos* or 'in between states', states of being that come 'in between' other states of being. For example death is a bardo between this life and the next, just as life itself is a bardo between a previous death and the coming one. The dream state is a bardo between last night's and this morning's waking state, and meditation (in the sense of dhyana) is a bardo between states of more ordinary consciousness.

Here death is seen not only as inevitable, but as part of life—with its own positive value. Moreover, not only can spiritual progress be made during life, it can also be made in the bardo after death—provided there has been adequate preparation in the form of mindfulness and meditation.

MEDITATION ON CHANGE

This is another, even more general, way to reflect on impermanence. With this practice we simply reflect on the basic truth of change. Once you are established in a concentrated state of mind, mindfully observe your mental states as they change from moment to moment, always flowing on and on like a river. Observe objects in the outer world as, little by little, they grow old and begin to break up, always turning into something slightly different. Reflect on the fact that things are never solid and fixed, as they appear to be.

The lovely flowers of turquoise-blue
Are destroyed in time by frost—
This shows the illusory nature of all beings,
This proves the transient nature of all things.
Think, then, you will practise Dharma.

The precious jewel that you cherish
Soon will belong to others—
This shows the illusory nature of all beings,
This proves the transient nature of all things.
Think, then, you will practise Dharma.

A precious son is born;
Soon he is lost and gone—
This shows the illusory nature of all beings,
This proves the transient nature of all things.
Think, then, you will practise Dharma.[60]
  Milarepa

This reflection can also be done in conjunction with the walking meditation outlined at the end of this chapter.

4 THE SIX ELEMENT PRACTICE

The next of the Five Basic Methods, the Six Element Practice, is an antidote to the mental poison of conceit.

DISSOLVING HABITUAL SELF-IDENTIFICATION

Conceit is an emotion which arises out of a very strongly held *self-identification*. In this meditation we try to experience what this 'self' really consists of, and we do so in terms of six 'elements'—earth, water, fire, air, space, and consciousness. Everything that we could possibly identify with as a self—whether physical, mental, conscious, or unconscious—is included in the six elements.

In the practice, we dwell upon each element in turn. First of all, we see the way it manifests naturally in the outside world. Then, as we look at the way it also manifests in us, we reflect that we cannot regard this manifestation as truly our own, even though that is how it feels.

In reality, neither our body nor our mind was consciously created by us, and we have almost no control over their continual change. What, then, in our experience, *can* we call 'I'? By questioning in this way, we start to experience ourselves more as we really are: as a continually changing flux of impersonal processes.

THE STAGES OF THE MEDITATION The practice begins, at least ideally, in the first dhyana—certainly we need to be in a state of clear concentration and positive emotion. Then we reflect on each element in turn, as follows.

THE EARTH ELEMENT This represents everything we perceive as solid and resistant, whether it is out in the world or inside our own body. For example, in the world outside ourselves there are houses, cars, roads, trees, and rocks. All these consist of hard, solid matter. We also find this element of 'earth' in the solid parts of our own body, in its bones and sinews, muscles, hairs, skin, etc.

In the meditation practice, we first of all generate samatha. Then we establish a general awareness of the earth element—of the fact that it exists both outside us and inside us, and of its qualities of relative hardness, opacity, and impenetrability.

We then reflect that, although we conventionally regard these relatively solid parts of our body as 'mine', we cannot say that we really possess them. The earth element in our body has naturally formed itself out of the earth element in the outer universe. Our body has been built up and constantly replenished by the solid food we have put into it. We have certainly played no conscious part in its creation: it is as though we had 'borrowed' it for a while. Which means, of course, that one day we shall have to return it. One day—we cannot say when, or predict how—we shall have to die. When that happens, the earth element in our body will once again become a part of the 'outer' universe. But now we can see that both the 'inside' and the 'outside' of us have always been exactly the same in nature, being equally of the nature of earth.

THE WATER ELEMENT This refers to every form of liquid—everything that flows downwards, that drops, that dribbles and splashes, that oozes, drips, or forms into puddles. In the outer world, for example, we have seas, oceans and great lakes, rivers and streams, clouds and raindrops.

In our own body too there are many varieties of fluid, such as tears, joint-lubricant, sweat, urine, blood, mucus, saliva, and digestive juices. Again, all these have been 'borrowed' from outside; and again, in the meditation practice we reflect that all will inevitably have to be 'returned' when the body breaks up and becomes part of the universe at large. Though we may feel a sense of identification—even possessiveness—about it, we nevertheless cannot claim any real ownership over the water element.

This comprises everything to do with *relative* heat and cold—it is the element of temperature. In the outside world there is, above all, the sun. There is hot and cold weather; there are volcanoes, hot springs, frozen seas, glaciers, icebergs. Nearer home, there are man-made fires and heating systems.

THE FIRE ELEMENT

In ourselves, there is body temperature: there is the heat caused by physical exertion and the digestive processes. Heat is involved in the body's processing of food as its fuel, and in the need for clothing to keep our body warm or cool.

But when death comes, our body will gradually lose all its heat. That heat was not really our 'own' heat, in any real sense, for it was entirely dependent on the natural processes involved with maintaining a body. So accepting this fact, coming to terms with it, we let the fire element go back, in our imagination, to its source. Without clinging on to it, without thinking that it is ours, we let the borrowed fire element in our body return to the fire element in the universe.

Air fills the outside world, giving life and breath. In this part of the meditation we imagine the all-pervasiveness of air and its qualities of lightness and transparency, perhaps visualizing the vast movements of air through space, through streets and city buildings, across immense areas of land—mountains, oceans, deserts—sometimes hot, sometimes cold, sometimes moving, sometimes still, carrying with it fumes and fragrances of every kind, coloured by every kind of light and shade.

THE AIR ELEMENT

Air moves inside our body too. In fact we may reflect that life—our life—is dependent on air in a very immediate way: we are either inhaling or exhaling air all the time, and when we come to die, we shall breathe in, and then breathe out—for the last time. This is inevitable, and at this stage of the six element practice we try to accept it.

We also reflect that we cannot own the air, or the process of breathing, in any way. We cannot identify ourselves with the air element any more than earth, water, or fire. It is not ours, it is not us; it is not part of us, and we are not part of it. In spite of the fact that we *feel* that it is ours—feel, above all, that we would be losing something if it stopped!—we try to realize the illusion, and accept the fact that breathing is an impersonal process which goes on regardless of our feelings of ownership.

THE SPACE ELEMENT   Space is that in which all the other elements exist, including even air. Space is infinite: we are surrounded by its inconceivable vastness which includes all living beings and all worlds, out of which our own body occupies a tiny portion.

There is a 'me'-shaped space here, which we identify with. But if we reflect, we will have to acknowledge that this space cannot really be said to be ours, except in a very temporary sense. Like the other elements, it is 'borrowed', just for the time that our body exists. When we die, the earth, water, fire, and air elements dissolve, and the space which was 'me' will simply join with the space which was 'not-me'. So at this point in the meditation we reflect upon all this, accepting the fact that we cannot identify with the space which our body presently occupies.

THE CONSCIOUSNESS ELEMENT   Consciousness, in its conscious and unconscious aspects, is rather complex compared with the physical elements, so it is easiest (at least when we start this meditation) to limit our practice of the sixth stage to the normal consciousness which we experience through our five physical senses and ordinary thinking mind.

We are of course surrounded by other people who also experience this kind of consciousness. We all experience the outer world of earth, water, fire, air, and space, either in immediate sense-experience (i.e. via the senses) or in terms of memories, theories, and ideas (i.e. via the thinking mind).

First of all we contemplate all these aspects of our mind, trying to get a feeling for the *element* of consciousness.

Then we reflect that when our physical body no longer exists, our sense organs—eyes, ears, nose, tongue, and skin (i.e. touch)—will also no longer exist. Without sense organs, the external world will no longer exist either, at least not for us; so then we will no longer have any frame of reference for our experience. We should try to imagine what this could be like—imagine how, without a physical, sensory frame of reference for its ideas and images, the ordinary thinking mind must also cease to exist; or at least, it must surely cease to exist in the way that we currently experience it.

Since this change is beyond our control, even this consciousness cannot be said to be ours. So once again we try to accept the fact that our consciousness is 'borrowed' and will have to be 'returned'. What exists is just consciousness itself. It is neither our consciousness, nor is it something other than consciousness. All that exists is ownerless consciousness.

By the end of the Six Element Practice we have dissolved—in our imagination—our attachment to every part of our experience. We have allowed ourselves to abandon, to a certain extent, the limitations of our idea of a 'self'.

As we saw earlier, self-view is the basis of conceit in the specifically Buddhist sense (*mana*). If no self is found to reside in earth, water, fire, air, or consciousness, where else could it possibly reside? So we sit in meditation experiencing the constantly changing phenomena of our mind, seeing that it is all perfectly ownerless. This may be a very liberating experience. We can see that even our perceiving mind is an impersonal process, and that the whole phenomenon of personal existence, though thoroughly real as an experience, is conditioned by our view of reality.

There is no doer of a deed
Or one who reaps the deed's result;
Phenomena alone flow on—
No other view than this is right....

The kamma [i.e. action] of its fruit is void;
No fruit exists yet in the kamma;
And still the fruit is born from it,
Wholly depending on the kamma.

For here there is no Brahma God,
Creator of the round of births,
Phenomena alone flow on—
Cause and component their condition.[61]
     Quoted by Buddhaghosha

This reflection is very deeply challenging, and has many implications for our life. So if you want this meditation to be effective, you'll need to think through any such implications at times when you are not meditating. Otherwise, when you actually sit down and do the practice, you may waste your energies wrestling with intellectual doubts—which would be using the thinking mind in a way that is not compatible with vipassana. In vipassana you need to be as clear as possible about the conceptual meaning of the particular topic being reflected upon.

RESOLVING INTELLECTUAL DOUBTS

Let's try a common example of a doubt. Do you really see that when your body no longer exists, your present mode of consciousness will likewise no longer exist? If you do, then you will be able simply to dwell upon that idea and to let its implications pervade your inspired, dhyanic consciousness. But if you don't, you'll quickly lose concentration.

Such a concept is like the single irritating speck of grit which eventually causes a pearl to be formed. It needs to be one potent, meaningful idea rather than a bundle of unclear, perhaps conflicting, ideas. You need to be able to trust it, at least provisionally. Otherwise you may start wondering and doubting: 'Well, does consciousness *end* at death then? How can I be sure that it does? I can't actually know that from experience,'—and so on. Doubts are arising here because we have not clearly defined what we mean by consciousness. There is no point in attempting vipassana meditation until we can settle these doubts to some extent; and when new doubts arise in the course of practice, as they will, we should examine and settle them too. This means that a certain amount of intellectual preparation and back-up, in terms of thought and study, is necessary in conjunction with the practice. Some contact with an experienced teacher is also essential.

CLARIFYING UNCERTAINTY ABOUT THE NATURE OF CONSCIOUSNESS

That question about the nature of consciousness often arises during the final stage of the six element practice. If it does so for us, then we have the opportunity of taking our meditation significantly further than the non-selfhood of ordinary waking consciousness. We can now plunge more deeply into this profound truth.

When we ask whether consciousness really ceases when it no longer has the support of a body and physical senses, we are at a point where we can also take into consideration the unconscious mind, and even the collective unconscious. Once we have a clear understanding that we do not 'own' our ordinary consciousness, we are in a position to perceive that we do not own our unconscious mind either, for both the individual unconscious and the collective unconscious are, by definition, out of our conscious control, and we cannot be said to own something outside our control. The individual and the collective unconscious can only be experienced after death, in dreams, and sometimes in meditation—situations in which the superficial, conscious personality is dissolved.

The unconscious mind is such a mysterious thing that we can understand how so many religions identify it in some way with a 'soul'. But after some application, one who contemplates within the Buddhist tradition may begin to see things differently.

Certainly, it is only natural to want to find a 'self'. Indeed, most of us seem to need to develop *more* of a sense of individuality. For the greater part of our development, we definitely need the self–other framework, ultimate illusion though it may be. As we have seen, the fundamental stage of the path of samatha represents a progressive strengthening and refining of the personal ego.

But once a certain foundation of refining and strengthening has taken place, it is time for vipassana meditation to show us the true nature of this ego: that it is impermanent and insubstantial. Even so this does not mean that it is completely non-existent: at least our experience is real, even if our interpretation is mistaken. Yet the practice continually refers us back to the totally insubstantial nature in everything we call ourself. Thus, through the Six Element practice, we can gradually come to an understanding of the profundity, richness, and magic that is inherent in our immediate experience.

5 THE CONTEMPLATION OF CONDITIONALITY

This vipassana meditation is an antidote to the 'poison' of spiritual ignorance. Through it we examine, and try imaginatively to experience, how 'the world' comes into being.

Contemplating conditionality gives us an overview of existence which works upon the mental poison of spiritual ignorance (*avijja*). This ignorance is far more than simply not knowing: it is our deep-seated tendency not to *want* to know about the real nature of things.

HOW THINGS ARISE

[Ananda:] How deep is this causal law, and how deep it seems! And yet do I regard it as quite plain to understand!
[The Buddha:] Say not so, Ananda! Say not so! Deep indeed is this causal law, and deep it appears to be. It is by not knowing, by not understanding, by not penetrating this doctrine, that this world of men has become entangled like a ball of twine, become covered with mildew, become like munja grass and rushes, and unable to pass beyond the doom of the Waste, the Way of Woe, the Fall, and the Ceaseless Round (of rebirth).[62]

As Ananda observes in this quotation, the Buddhist teaching of conditionality is in a way very simple. Yet, as the Buddha insists in reply, its implications are vast beyond imagination. We can summarize these by saying that events and objects arise when the appropriate conditions are present. If certain conditions are present then certain events have the potential to arise, and not others. The Buddha summarized the teaching as 'this being, that becomes'—in other words, if *this* phenomenon arises, then *that* one may arise on the basis of the first. We tend to think that a thing has just one cause, but in fact every object and event we experience is the product of innumerable different conditions, some immediate to the event's arising, others far away in its historical background.

This applies even to the ideas in your mind at this moment. They, too, are conditioned by innumerable factors. You have these ideas not only because you are reading this book, but also because of many other ideas that you have had, and because of many other books you have read—in fact all the ideas that have ever arisen in your mind have played some part in the evolution of your present set of ideas. Yet all that is just one aspect of the situation. The book itself is conditioned by a seemingly infinite number of factors. This book has come about partly because I wanted to write it—no doubt there are many more factors there!—and partly because there is a certain objective need for it. Again, there are many factors involved in that need. There are many historical and cultural factors, and those factors have to do with the actions, thoughts, and emotions of many generations of individual people. And each one of these conditions has its own conditions, also going infinitely back in time. And in all this great web of conditions, the decisions that you are making now will also contribute their effects, both to your own life and to the lives of other people.

Meditate on this. See the conditions that you experience in your life going further and further back, wider and wider. Reflect how all of them have affected your particular experience of the present moment. Consider how the present moment also carries all that richness with it, and even now conditions the infinite future.

THE TWO MODES OF CONDITIONALITY   According to the Buddha, there are two *modes* of conditionality, two ways in which events can arise. These are represented by the 'Wheel of Dependent Origination' and the 'Spiral of Liberation'. These describe sequences of change which inevitably occur in our being and consciousness—in the first case when we do not try to develop towards Enlightenment, and in the second case when we do.

The concepts of the Wheel and the Spiral give us an overview on the whole process of conditioned existence and its relation to the realm of the Unconditioned.

THE WHEEL OF CYCLIC EXISTENCE   The Wheel of Dependent Origination is the closed cycle of conditioning factors within which we normally live—unless we become aware of our situation and make the attempt to break out of it. Summarizing the main conditioning factors, we see that our *ignorance* of the true nature of things has necessarily led to a particular kind of *birth*—which has inevitably led, since we have bodies with *senses* and *feelings*, to the predicament of *craving*. This tends to produce an *addiction* to particular ways of behaving, and over a whole lifetime these habits usually become so entrenched that we never break out of the patterns. The entrenched patterns condition the next life—in which, of course, 'we' tend to repeat the same conditions. This cyclic patterning may happen at different levels—some people enjoy happier lives than others—but the cyclic, repetitive tendency may drag us down to lower levels unless our actions somehow prevent that happening.

The spiral of liberation moves upward, representing the fact that this predicament can be transcended. Merely because we have feelings, we do not have to react with the craving, hatred, and other unskilful emotions that bind us to the Wheel. We can break out by developing a positive series of conditions—faith in ourself, samatha, vipassana, Enlightenment—which support one another to produce more and more happy and insightful states of mind.

THE SPIRAL OF LIBERATION

This is our human situation in a nutshell.

In the meditation on conditionality, we dwell on each of these principal links (*nidanas*), on both the Wheel and the Spiral, having established a good basis of samatha.

THE MEDITATION
THE CYCLIC AND
SPIRAL NIDANAS

Obviously we need to understand roughly what we are doing before we can attempt any useful practice. Ideally, we need to understand the exact meaning of each nidana as well as the relationship *between* the various nidanas. So considerable thought, further reading,[63] and access to people who can help us clarify any questions that may arise, are all necessary. This does not mean that we cannot engage in the meditation until we completely understand—if that were the case we might never start. Indeed, provided there is some basis of prior reflection, the meditation will feed back and nourish our intellectual understanding. But for the 'Dharma seed' to grow, we'll need to acknowledge the incompleteness of our understanding.

As usual, we begin in a good state of concentration and positive emotion. (Ideally we should be in the first dhyana.) We then turn our concentrated attention to the opening nidanas of the Spiral, dwelling upon each one for a while before moving on to the next.

Here is the complete list of both the cyclic and spiral nidanas, with an explanation of each, together with a short description of how both the process of conditioned existence, and the movement towards the unconditioned realm, take place. That explanation will be followed by a simple listing.

(1) and **(2)** In dependence upon **dissatisfaction** (*dukkha*)—here meaning an existential dissatisfaction with cyclic existence, and equivalent to the cyclic nidana of **feeling**—arises **faith** (*saddha*), or confidence in the possibilities of spiritual development.

**THE FIRST SEVEN
'SPIRAL' NIDANAS**

(3) In dependence upon **faith** arises **joy** (*pamojja*)—a feeling of self-respect and good conscience based on the fact that one has now begun to practise the Dharma.

(4) In dependence upon **joy** arises **rapture** (*piti*)—the dhyana factor, described in Chapter Three.

(5) In dependence upon **rapture** arises **calm** (*passaddhi*). This is the process of 'containment' of rapture through bliss—the next nidana—which was also described in Chapter Three.

(6) In dependence upon **calm** arises **bliss** (*sukha*).

(7) In dependence upon **bliss** arises **concentration** (*samadhi*). At this point we enter the full dhyana experience.

(8) In dependence upon **concentration** arises **knowledge and vision of things as they really are** (*yathabhutananadassana*). This is transcendental insight.

Summary

As far as possible, reflecting on these links should evoke each one in experience—stages 1 to 7 comprise the establishment of samatha as a basis for stage 8.

To summarize the ideas, we see that in dependence upon the dhyana factors of joy, rapture, calm, and bliss, arises samadhi—the culmination of the process of samatha. Then, going one stage further, we see how the fullness of samatha creates the possibility of developing vipassana.

In the spiral series, each succeeding link cannot arise automatically—it has to be developed with conscious effort. Moreover, the link cannot arise at all without the previous level of conditions being present: no joy (*pamojja*) can arise without the prior existence of some degree of faith (*saddha*).

THE NIDANAS OF THE WHEEL

Having contemplated the conditions for the arising of insight, we now turn our attention to the cyclic mode of conditionality. In imagination at least, we have recapitulated the process of entering the dhyanas, and now, using the following set of twelve cyclic nidanas as a framework, we turn our fully focused attention on to the nature of all conditioned things.

(1) and (2) In dependence upon **ignorance** (*avijja*) arise **karma-formations** (*sankharas*)—this in a very general way summarizes the whole reactive, cyclic process. Because of the darkness and confusion which is inevitable when we do not know the Truth, influential predispositions, or 'steering forces' are formed, and start wielding a conditioning influence upon consciousness.

(3) In dependence upon **karma-formations** arises **consciousness** (*vinnana*)—this is the initial 'spark' of consciousness which arises at conception.

(4) In dependence upon **consciousness** arises the **psychophysical**

organism (*namarupa*)—in other words, the mind and body (initially evolving in the womb).

(5) In dependence upon the **psychophysical organism** arise the **six sense organs** (*salayatana*)—the body/mind's means of contact with an outside world.

(To summarize the process so far—due to unenlightened predispositions, an unenlightened mentality comes into being, complete with body and senses).

(6) In dependence upon the **six sense organs** arises **contact** (*phassa*)—actual contact between the senses and an outside world.

(7) In dependence upon **contact** arises **feeling** (*vedana*)—when we contact the external world through our senses, there is always a feeling—which may be pleasant or unpleasant. Note that we covered some of this ground in Chapter Two.

(8) In dependence upon **feeling** arises **craving** (*tanha*)—that is, craving tends to arise in the case of a pleasant feeling—it would be hatred or something similarly negative if the feeling was painful.

This is the most crucial area of the inner life, because if we do allow craving, or hatred (which is frustrated craving) to take hold, we then bind ourselves to the links of the Wheel which follow. It is the point at which we have the possibility of choosing to continue round the Wheel, or to cultivate the nidanas of the Spiral Path. This has been the underlying theme of much of our discussion of feeling and emotion. Here we could cultivate the Spiral Path; but unfortunately, the following is what we usually do.

(9) In dependence upon **craving** arises **attachment** (*upadana*)—we become 'hooked' on the experience, repeating it whenever opportunities arise.

(10) In dependence upon **attachment** arises **becoming** (*bhava*)—the habit of repeating the experience becomes so entrenched that we 'become' it—the habit becomes a definitive part of ourselves.

(11) In dependence upon **becoming** arises **birth** (*jati*)—the character of our next life is determined by those entrenched habits.

(12) In dependence upon **birth** arise **old age and death** (*jara-marana*)—this is an overall aspect of cyclic conditioning: since we have been born into an impermanent body, its dissolution is inevitable.

Then, as well as contemplating the arising of our existence, we contemplate how, if the previous conditions were not present, each stage would dissolve.

Mundane spiral nidanas	(1)	In dependence upon **dissatisfaction** arises
Process of integration towards dhyana	(2)	**faith** (*saddha*)
	(3)	In dependence upon faith arises **joy** (*pamojja*)
	(4)	In dependence upon joy arises **rapture** (*piti*)
	(5)	In dependence upon rapture arises **calm** (*passaddhi*)
	(6)	In dependence upon calm arises **bliss** (*sukha*)
	(7)	In dependence upon bliss arises **concentration** (*samadhi*)
First transcendental spiral nidana	(8)	In dependence upon concentration arises **knowledge and vision of things as they really are** (*yathabhutananadassana*)
Cyclic nidanas Phase of arising	(1)	In dependence upon **ignorance** (*avijja*) arise
	(2)	**karma-formations** (*sankharas*)
	(3)	In dependence upon karma-formations arises **consciousness** (*vinnana*)
	(4)	In dependence upon consciousness arises the **psychophysical organism** (*namarupa*)
	(5)	In dependence upon the psychophysical organism arise the **six sense organs** (*salayatana*)
	(6)	In dependence upon the six sense organs arises **contact** (*phassa*)
	(7)	In dependence upon contact arises **feeling** (*vedana*)
	(8)	In dependence upon feeling arises **craving** (*tanha*)
	(9)	In dependence upon craving arises **attachment** (*upadana*)
	(10)	In dependence upon attachment arises **becoming** (*bhava*)
	(11)	In dependence upon becoming arises **birth** (*jati*)
	(12)	In dependence upon birth arise **old age and death** (*jara-marana*)
Phase of dissolution	(12)	Upon the cessation of **birth**, old age and death cease
	(11)	Upon the cessation of **becoming**, birth ceases
	(10)	Upon the cessation of **attachment**, becoming ceases
	(9)	Upon the cessation of **craving**, attachment ceases
	(8)	Upon the cessation of **feeling** , craving ceases
	(7)	Upon the cessation of **contact**, feeling ceases
	(6)	Upon the cessation of the **six sense organs**, contact ceases
	(5)	Upon the cessation of the **psychophysical organism**, the six sense organs cease
	(4)	Upon the cessation of **consciousness**, the psychophysical organism ceases
	(3)	Upon the cessation of **karma-formations**, consciousness ceases
	(2,1)	Upon the cessation of **ignorance**, karma-formations cease
Remaining transcendental spiral nidanas	(9)	In dependence upon knowledge and vision of things as they really are arises **withdrawal** (*nibbida*)
	(10)	In dependence upon withdrawal arises **disentanglement** (*viraga*)
	(11)	In dependence upon disentanglement arises **freedom** (*vimutti*)
	(12)	In dependence upon freedom arises **knowledge of the destruction of the biases** (*asavakkhayanana*)

Cyclical and
transcendental (spiral)
nidanas

Upon the cessation of **birth**, old age and death cease.

Upon the cessation of **becoming**, birth ceases.

Upon the cessation of **attachment**, becoming ceases.

Upon the cessation of **craving**, attachment ceases.

Upon the cessation of **feeling**, craving ceases.

Upon the cessation of **contact**, feeling ceases.

Upon the cessation of **the six sense organs**, contact ceases.

Upon the cessation of **the psychophysical organism**, the six sense organs cease.

Upon the cessation of **consciousness**, the psychophysical organism ceases.

Upon the cessation of **karma-formations**, consciousness ceases.

Upon the cessation of **ignorance**, karma-formations cease.

This completes the contemplation of the cyclic nidanas.

So having fully explored 'things as they really are', we then return to the spiral path and contemplate, at least in imagination, the stages leading from that initial insight towards full Enlightenment.

THE REST OF THE SPIRAL NIDANAS

(9) In dependence upon **knowledge and vision of things as they really are** arises **withdrawal** (*nibbida*)—the grip of attachment is loosened through insight, and it becomes possible to take a broader perspective.

(10) In dependence upon **withdrawal** arises **disentanglement** (*viraga*)—as we dwell in that perspective, it becomes possible for us to remove all the conditions from our life which obstruct the further development of insight.

(11) In dependence upon **disentanglement** arises **freedom** (*vimutti*)—this is the initial Enlightenment experience; we are free.

(12) In dependence upon **freedom** arises **knowledge of the destruction of the biases** (*asavakkhayanana*)—we *know* that we are completely free. We have gained full Enlightenment, or Buddhahood.

OTHER METHODS OF MEDITATION

In the 2,500 years since the days of the Buddha, meditation has been greatly adapted and developed. Many more methods are practised throughout the Buddhist world. Among the most important of these are Visualization, Just Sitting, and Walking Meditation.

VISUALIZATION MEDITATION

In Buddhism a large number of meditation practices use imaginative visualization. Here is a typical visualization practice, the meditation upon Green Tara.

VISUALIZATION OF THE FEMALE BODHISATTVA GREEN TARA

Imagine that in every direction, to infinity, you see nothing but the deepest, most transparent, blue sky. You also experience yourself as void and empty, of exactly the same nature as that infinite blue. That emptiness, and that infinity, invests you with a sense of wonder and profound inspiration. You are experiencing your own mind in its greatest clarity and calmness; at the same time you are contemplating the ultimate voidness that is its true nature.

After a while you become aware of something which expresses this in imaginative form: it is a letter, made of the softest green light, glowing and vibrating in your heart centre. It is the Sanskrit letter *tam*, and it stands upon a horizontal disc of silvery light like the full moon. You imagine the *tam* visually, and you can also hear the primordial sound-syllable which it represents.

The moon mat is in the calyx of a tiny flower—a lotus blossom, made of pure light—and the lotus is in the heart of a goddess, the beautiful and gently smiling Bodhisattva Tara. She is the quintessence of compassion—and she is also you.

You are Tara. Seated cross-legged as though in meditation, but with her right foot outstretched as though ready to rise to aid some troubled being, Tara is dressed in the silks and ornaments of a princess. Her right palm is opened outwards upon her knee in a gesture of giving. Her left is at her heart, its fingers expressing some quintessential point of Dharma. As you sit, and as the vision unfolds out of the voidness, you feel as though you yourself are formed of light, transparent and empty.

Around the *tam* at your heart, the letters of Tara's mantra (which contain her entire symbolic meaning, and which are associated with quickly-responding compassion) begin to revolve anti-clockwise. Peacefully listening, you can hear the sound of her mantra, *om tare tuttare ture svaha ... om tare tuttare ture svaha ... om tare tuttare ture svaha*, over and over again.

From the letters, which stand erect and dance gracefully around the seed-syllable, emerges a diaphanous rainbow radiance. Rainbows curl upwards and downwards like incense smoke, and slowly your whole body, outwardly Tara, inwardly fills with rainbow light. After a while her/your body is so pervaded with light that the rainbows overflow. From the crown of your head they emerge, eightfold, and at the tip of each rainbow is the tiny figure of a goddess, bearing an offering: water, flowers, lights, incense, perfume, delicious fruit, refreshing drinks, and music. The eight goddesses rise upwards, presenting their offerings to the zenith, far above your head.

As the rainbow light continues to rise there begins to pour down, from above, the purest snow-white light—pouring down in a stream of blessing which descends onto the crown of your head and enters your body. It flows into your heart, into the *tam*. And from your responding heart, the rays of light now flow outwards, towards all living beings—who are gathered, you now notice, all around you. You are sitting in the midst of a great multitude of beings, which stretches to infinity, all quietly reciting the Tara mantra, *om tare tuttare ture svaha*. Over and over again the mantra sounds, as the rays of light rise up from Tara's heart, as the rays of blessing pour down upon her heart and then out to help and heal the sufferings of all living beings.

This might seem to be a very different kind of meditation from the ones we have encountered up until now. In a way it is, but it still involves the elements we have been discussing. It still involves concentration, positive emotion, and reflection on the Dharma. The main difference is in the rich imaginative visualization.

VISUALIZATION IN THE CONTEXT OF SAMATHA AND VIPASSANA

This kind of visualization practice incorporates elements of both samatha and vipassana. Samatha is built up through concentration on the visualization and repetition of the mantra, the rich imagery helping to develop positive emotion. Many of these *sadhanas*, as they are often termed, also include the development of metta and the Brahma-viharas as a preliminary stage. There will often be a specific vipassana reflection, perhaps on shunyata, as a preliminary.

But the main vipassana elements are introduced through the medium of the visualization and its imagery. This is done in a number of different ways. Vipassana can be developed, for example, by reflecting on the conditioned nature of the visualization itself. An experienced meditator will be able to create a visualization that becomes very vivid indeed, yet he or she knows that it is all a mental creation; it has all been deliberately fashioned out of the void. A sadhana may incorporate Dharma verses which encapsulate insight in words which can be reflected upon; other elements of the practice will also contain insights in symbolic form. The clear blue sky from which the image emerges, for example, symbolizes the ultimate 'void' potentiality of all things; the mantra has an inner symbolic meaning which can be learned through constant reflection and repetition. The expression of the visualized image—hand gestures, form, clothing,

The forty meditation practices (kammathana) originally taught by the Buddha[64]

Ten kasinas (concentration upon discs of various colours)
Ten impurities (stages of decomposition of a corpse—as in impermanence meditation)
Ten recollections: (1) Buddha
(2) Dharma
(3) Sangha (community of practitioners of the Dharma)
(4) Ethics
(5) Generosity
(6) The gods
(7) Death
(8) The body (mindfulness of the body)
(9) Breathing (Mindfulness of Breathing meditation)
(10) Enlightenment
Four Brahma-viharas (Metta Bhavana meditation plus Karuna, Mudita, and Upekkha)
Four formless spheres (the arupa-dhyanas)
Reflection upon the loathsomeness of food (an antidote to craving)
Analysis of the four elements (similar to the six element practice)

etc.—all have symbolic significance, awareness of which grows and impresses itself on the mind over years of daily practice.

Without reflections such as these the practice remains a samatha practice, the beauty of the mantric sound, together with the form and colour, serving to integrate the mind and induce the rich calm of the dhyana state. Vipassana is brought into play when the visualization is 'embroidered' with discursive reflection on one of the vipassana elements within the sadhana.

THE MAGIC OF ARCHETYPAL IMAGES

The whole field of visualization practice is very large and complex. To us in the West, certain aspects, such as peculiarly Tibetan forms of visualization, may be obscure and difficult to relate to. It seems clear, however, that we naturally respond in a very positive way to certain archetypal images. In time, perhaps the traditional Buddhist visualization practices will incorporate images which arise out of our own cultural context—perhaps from our own mythology. This happened, for example, when Buddhism went from India to China and Japan. Some forms of visualization practice would therefore seem to have an important future in Buddhist meditation in the West.

VISUALIZATION IN RELATION TO THE BUDDHA'S ORIGINAL TEACHING—THE FORTY METHODS

How, then, did visualization develop from the original teaching? So far as we can tell, the Buddha never explicitly taught visualization meditation in this way. He presented forty methods of meditation, known as the *kammathanas* or 'work-places'.

Apart from the reflection upon loathsomeness of food (an antidote to craving), we have already touched on most of these practices in one way or another.

KASINA MEDITATIONS

The first ten *kammathanas* are varieties of the kasina meditations that were given as an example in Chapter Four. The inner perception of colour was used as a means of developing concentration and integration even in the earliest days of Buddhist meditation. Pure colour and light figure prominently in descriptions of mystical experiences of all spiritual traditions, and Buddhism is no exception.

The Tara meditation just described is one example out of thousands of subjects for visualization meditation, each one arising out of some meditator's visionary experience of enlightened qualities, seen in the form of Buddhas and Bodhisattvas.[65] Visualization of these Buddha- and Bodhisattva-forms, like visualization generally, seems to have a specific origin in the *kammathanas*—and, no doubt, in the 'visions' of the Buddha seen by his disciples during his lifetime.

RECOLLECTION OF THE BUDDHA

If we think strongly about a quality such as metta or compassion, we will actually evoke it in our mind. By recollecting the qualities of the Buddha, we may bring about a small reflection of his greatness in ourselves. And in creating this intense imagination of the Buddha's qualities, the meditator will probably imagine a visual image of him—this is probably how visualization practices developed.[66]

The first of the Ten Recollections is the recollection of the Buddha. The practice involves calling the Buddha's qualities to mind with some traditional verses:

Iti'pi so bhagava araham samma-sambuddho
Vijja-carana sampanno sugato
Loka-vidu, annuttaro purisa-damma-sarati
Sattha deva-manussanam buddho bhagava-ti

[Such indeed is He, the richly endowed: the free, the fully and perfectly
  awake—
Equipped with knowledge and practice, the happily attained,
Knower of the worlds—guide unsurpassed of men to be tamed,
The Teacher of gods and men, The Awakened One richly endowed.][67]

There is a visualization of pure two- or three-dimensional geometrical forms which is very akin to the kasina meditations. This is the visualization of the stupa, a symbolic representation of the six elements. The stupa is also symbolic of the Buddha's Enlightenment, and as such is often

VISUALIZATION OF THE SIX ELEMENT STUPA

erected in the East as a monument-like shrine.

The stupa visualization is generally a samatha practice, though clearly there are aspects which can be employed for vipassana reflection. (There is obviously an association with the Six Element Practice, the vipassana meditation mentioned earlier.)

The six-element stupa

(1) **Consciousness.** In the first stage, visualize an infinite blue sky, representing consciousness.

(2) **Earth.** When you have established this, imagine, in the centre of the sky ahead, a bright yellow cube (or square if you are visualizing in two dimensions). This represents the element earth.

(3) **Water.** Next imagine a pure white globe (or disc), above the yellow cube. This represents the element of water.

(4) **Fire.** Above the globe, imagine a bright red cone (or triangle), representing the element of fire.

(5) **Air.** Then, above the cone, imagine a saucer-shape (or crescent) of a delicate pale green, which represents the element air.

(6) **Space.** At the top of the stupa imagine an iridescent 'jewel drop', scintillating with all the colours of the rainbow. This represents the element of space.

The elements of the stupa, having been built up, are then slowly dissolved one by one. The jewel drop dissolves down into the saucer-shape, the saucer-shape into the cone, the cone into the globe, the globe into the cube, and the cube into the blue sky. Finally, the blue sky itself gradually fades, bringing the practice to an end.

BENEFITS OF THE STUPA VISUALIZATION

The stupa visualization has some special benefits. It can be a very good concentration exercise as a supplement to the Mindfulness of Breathing, especially if you are finding that practice a little dry. The stupa is colourful and attractive to concentrate upon; it engages the imagination.

As you get more deeply involved with it, you will find that the form of each element has a particular feeling quality of its own—for example the yellow cube, with its six sides, eight corners, and twelve edges, expresses something very different from the white sphere, which has one continuous 'side', and no corners or edges whatsoever. Each colour also has a feeling quality; as you practise, you should be receptive to the way each of the forms, and each of the colours, are affecting you.

The stupa visualization is an excellent method of releasing, stimulating, and purifying your inner energies. Each of the elements of the stupa represents a particular mode of energy, with the grosser energies at the bottom, and subtler, more refined energies towards the top. If you like, you may visualize each element with these energies in mind.

The **earth** element represents static energy, energy which is blocked and obstructed: rigid, solidified, unworkable energy, at present unavailable. It is as though you are bound hand and foot, unable to move.

Like physical water, which can be sloshed around from side to side but naturally flows only downwards, the **water** element represents energy which is just a little free. It operates narrowly, within strict limits. It tends to swing between one extreme and another, between love and hate, hope and fear. It is not very flexible, being confined to a small circle of interests. It is as though you are no longer tied up but allowed to move freely within a tiny room.

The **fire** element represents the stage when your energy begins to move as it were upwards. Things start 'happening' quite quickly—you are becoming liberated from the previous restrictions, and mental conflicts are being resolved. You are integrating previously unconscious, repressed, energies into consciousness, becoming inspired, entering higher states of consciousness. It is as though an opening had appeared in the roof of your room and you are able to float up and out of it by the power of your inspiration!

The **air** element represents energy which is not only freed in an upward direction but in all directions simultaneously, pouring inexhaustibly everywhere. It is as though you are so free that you can fly, not only upwards but everywhere at once, or as though you could multiply yourself into millions of bodies, each of which was travelling in a different direction towards infinity.

The **space** element represents energy which is in a different dimension altogether—it is the medium in which everything has so far taken place. Since you have become that medium, the same kind of analogy can no longer be applied—the imagination cannot easily encompass it.

JUST SITTING MEDITATION

'Just Sitting' is unique among meditation practices in that there is no object upon which to concentrate. We simply sit, mindfully experiencing the present moment.

Just Sitting is a formal meditation practice in itself, as we'll shortly see. It can also be seen as a principle to be applied within other meditation practices. An example of using Just Sitting as a principle could be preparing for a session of meditation by simply sitting quietly for ten or twenty minutes, tuning in and becoming more sensitive to ourselves. This

APPLYING THE JUST SITTING PRINCIPLE

enables us to disengage from the activities we have just left, take stock of our mental state, and consider how to work with it.

Another important application is to add a period of Just Sitting at the end of a session of meditation, in order to absorb its impact. Here we simply sit without trying deliberately to concentrate, but remaining mindful of the feeling tone of the experience, allowing it to be incorporated into ourselves. This allows us to disengage gently from meditation and make a smooth transition to ordinary activities.

THE METHOD OF JUST SITTING

The method of the Just Sitting practice itself is to remain as continuously mindful as possible. As we do this over a period of time, a general quality of concentration will develop as we get engaged with our bodily and mental states. This quality of concentration is more difficult to sustain than the usual method of bringing our mind back to one particular object. Yet difficult though it is initially, the method develops a broad and well-grounded quality of concentration which may include the whole breadth and depth of our experience.

If we are doing several sessions of meditation a day, it is a good idea to include some Just Sitting. When meditating on a specific object it is possible to find ourselves concentrating over-narrowly, in a way that does not fully acknowledge our broader dimensions. Just Sitting counteracts this tendency.

Whenever we find ourselves becoming distracted in the Just Sitting practice, we return to a general mindfulness rather than to a particular object. Of the four Foundations of Mindfulness, the most useful ones to remain in contact with are the body and feelings—especially the body, since it usually offers the most tangible and definite experience. Another way is to come back to awareness of breathing for a while, until concentration is re-established.

It is a good idea to set a time for the session: anything from fifteen to thirty minutes is fine as a start. This may sound rather short, but it seems best not to try for too long a session at first. If you feel like doing a lot of Just Sitting, it is usually more effective to have a number of short sessions.

Just Sitting may be practised with the eyes open or closed. With open eyes, you may find it helpful to sit facing a wall—preferably a blank, undecorated one (to avoid getting visually distracted)—or place your gaze on a particular spot, say a metre away, on the floor.

Just Sitting develops samatha by maintaining awareness and integrating whatever arises into the practice. It is also very effective as a vipassana practice. Without an object, our concentration tends to build up around a continuous sense of 'me'—the experiencer. But the experience of sitting with this 'me' eventually shows very clearly that it is something indefinite and fluid, not the concrete identity we usually assume. We realize that we cannot really identify with this 'me', and so are able to widen and even transcend our notion of selfhood.

Our experience is the same with all the mental events which arise in the course of a session of Just Sitting. Since they are ultimately impermanent and insubstantial, we cannot identify with them either. We may see that both subjective and objective experience are devoid of any lasting nature. Everyone who meditates, even relatively new meditators, can benefit from this practice in some way—though a sound basis in the fundamental practices needs to be established first.

WALKING MEDITATION

The Buddha spent the greater part of his life in the open air, and it seems from ancient records that a considerable portion of his time was taken up with mindful walking.

Walking meditation is a very useful variation to sitting practice, and an important method in its own right. The traditional way of practising is to find a straight path on a flat piece of ground, and walk mindfully up and down. An alternative method is to walk continuously in a circle.

Almost any of the practices that have been mentioned here can be adapted for walking meditation, though some are more suitable than others. The best are mindfulness of the body, mindfulness generally, Mindfulness of Breathing, Metta Bhavana, and simple vipassana reflection. Even apart from formal meditation methods, walking up and down is a very good way of relaxing and clarifying one's thoughts, and, like Just Sitting, it can also be used for consciously absorbing experiences, or as a preparation for meditation.

Mindful walking is an excellent practice. The regular, deliberate movement of walking has the effect of stimulating you physically while at the same time calming you down. It is ideal at times when sitting meditation would be difficult, for example if you are tired or emotionally unsettled.

BENEFITS OF WALKING MEDITATION

Of course, the fact that you are moving your body also involves definite restrictions: for example it is not usually possible to concentrate very finely. In this respect walking meditation is rather like Just Sitting; the concentration is more generalized, since you are constantly experiencing the movements of your body and the environment in which you are walking. Concentration of this kind also requires a certain amount of time to build up: you need to allow at least fifteen or twenty minutes for your awareness to become established in any kind of continuity. Some people will find this initial period boring or unsatisfyingly distracted. However if you persevere your state of mind will change and you will eventually feel more inspired.

The walking speed you choose depends on your state of mind and the specific practice you are doing while you are walking. If you are feeling dull it may help to walk more briskly, if you are restless it may help to walk more slowly—though it generally seems to be a good idea to walk a little faster at first, and gradually slow your pace as you become more concentrated. If you are very concentrated, the pace may be reduced—right down, if you like, to an almost imperceptible movement.

Walking more slowly and deliberately can induce a deeper concentration, though this won't come automatically. Sometimes it is tempting to walk extremely slowly in an attempt to force a level of concentration for which you are not yet ready, but the likely result is that you become 'stuck' in a narrow unfeeling concentration. It is important to maintain a breadth of mindfulness. So long as you do, you can move as slowly as you like—so long as you are physically relaxed and able to walk, even at your snail's pace, in a free, natural manner. If you feel tense, it may help to walk faster for a while and let the tension dispel itself.

Walking meditation is ideal when you feel like meditating but do not have a quiet room and a cushion immediately available. At work, for example, if you have half an hour to spare at lunch time, you could try using it for walking up and down a quiet street or corner of a park. In other circumstances walking meditation is useful when you do not feel like meditating, as when you are very agitated or restless.

Walking meditation can have a soothing, integrating effect. It can also have an invigorating effect that can transform slothful mental states. Or again you may be getting on very well with your sitting meditation—perhaps you are on an intensive meditation retreat—but your aching limbs will not allow you to sit any longer. In that situation it can be very useful to alternate periods of sitting with periods of walking meditation.

ADAPTING DIFFERENT MEDITATION METHODS TO WALKING PRACTICE

Taking that example of a lunch period, the best practice to choose would probably be to re-establish awareness of the four Foundations of Mindfulness. If you are agitated, with a lot on your mind, then a gentle Metta Bhavana, or mindful walking up and down, could be recommended.

On a meditation retreat, you could choose practices to complement your sitting meditations. Reflection, for example, is a very good application of walking meditation, whether in the *cinta-maya panna* sense or in the full vipassana sense. In the latter case, you could use the first ten or twenty minutes to establish concentration—if you are practising intensively, you may be able to establish yourself in access concentration—and then you can start turning over some point of Dharma in your mind. For example, the impermanence of the body might be introduced as a theme.

Mindfulness of the body makes a very good 'lead in' to walking meditation. Mindfulness can be established in a general way by simply walking up and down—or round and round—at a comfortable pace, not too fast or slow. Then, once you are used to walking, you can begin taking your attention to your feet as each takes the weight of your body, one foot after the other. In your experience of each individual footfall you may experience the transfer of weight from heel to toe, and feel the changing sensations in the sole.

USING MINDFULNESS OF THE BODY AS A 'LEAD IN'

As you become accustomed to paying attention to the changing sensations, you may gradually become more concentrated and relaxed, in just the same way as in sitting meditation.

This method of taking awareness to the point of contact with the floor has, quite literally, a 'grounding' effect, and is something you can return to whenever you become distracted. Once concentration is established in your feet, you can incorporate more parts of your body in to your mindfulness. Working up from your feet, experience the shift of weight in your ankles, calves, knees, thighs; then in the whole of each leg. Then you can move your attention to your pelvis, so that as you shift your weight from one leg to the other you will feel your pelvis supporting the free leg as it swings forward. You can also experience all the muscular adjustments which take place in your spinal column, and all the supporting muscles of your back, as they compensate for the change in weighting with each step. Finally, you can experience the subtler shifts in muscular adaptation in your head and neck.

You could take ten minutes or more to build up this awareness of your body, and then start to experience your body and its movements more as a whole. Once that is established, you could experience yourself less in terms of sensation and relaxation, and more in terms of movement. While you are still walking in a completely natural, relaxed manner, the meditation now becomes more dance-like—you experience yourself more in terms of a changing physical shape moving through space.

Then, having developed awareness of your body, you could move through the other Foundations of Mindfulness. At the same time as you experience the sensations of movement, you can also give attention to whatever feelings are present. You will be feeling pleasant and painful feelings at different times; each different sensation will have its own feeling tone. Having tuned into your feelings, you can then become aware of your emotional responses, and note the thoughts which are entering and leaving your consciousness. 'Noting' is the best approach here generally, since there is such an enormous amount of experience going on: if you try to remain continuously aware of each aspect of your experience you may just become tense. You should simply be aware that physical and mental states are arising and passing away.

You could do this in terms of the six elements, being mindful of the earth, water, fire, air, space, and consciousness elements in successive stages. The element of consciousness could be experienced as above, in terms of feeling, emotion, and thought, or, as an alternative, in terms of the senses. You could go through the sensations of sight, hearing, smell, taste, and touch which arise, aware both of the feelings which arise in dependence on these and your emotional response.

This could be a samatha, or 'mindfulness' practice. But if your concentration is very strong it could eventually turn into a vipassana meditation. For example, you could contemplate the impermanence of each element and each sensation as it arises; or you could contemplate the way your feelings, emotional responses, and thoughts are dependent on the sensations aroused by the contact of your body with the outside world.

APPENDIX

•

THIS SECTION IS INTENDED AS A REFERENCE FOR 'TROUBLE SHOOTING'
HINDRANCES TO MEDITATION.
It is not an exhaustive list—approaches to working with hindrances
are limited only by your imagination. However, it may sometimes be
useful to skim through a section on one particular hindrance to
stimulate a clearer understanding of its character.
There is a table towards the end of each section giving a quick guide
to possible ways of working against the hindrance concerned.

•

Appendix

METHODS OF WORKING
ON THE FIVE HINDRANCES

IN CHAPTER THREE we learned about five general antidotes to the hindrances. We found that once we know that a particular hindrance is present, we can work to dissolve it, using antidotes like reflecting on its consequences or cultivating its opposite quality.

Any of these antidotes can, theoretically, be applied to any one of the hindrances, but, in practice, each hindrance has its own peculiar character—some antidotes work very well for certain hindrances, but not for others. It is therefore useful to get a more exact idea of how specific hindrances work. So in this supplementary chapter we're going to go through each one individually, looking at the most effective ways of counteracting them.

The list is extensive. It is not necessary for you to know it all but there will probably be items which you find especially interesting or relevant. The principal idea behind this section of the book is to give an impression of the nature of the hindrances, their strengths and weaknesses. If you do not feel like reading the whole section, you can skim through it to get a general idea—it may perhaps be useful some time as a reference for checking your meditation experience.

Note on the categories: With each hindrance we will use the five categories of **cultivating, considering, sky-like mind, suppression,** and **outside meditation.** Some of these categories have now been extended in scope beyond the traditional antidotes covered in Chapter Three—any changes are explained when we first encounter them. For the sake of this summary the fifth category of 'Going for Refuge' has been dropped, and is replaced by methods to be adopted outside formal meditation practice.

SENSE DESIRE

Sense desire (*kamacchanda*) arises because we are drawn to a pleasant sense experience. From the point of view of developing concentration, this is a potential trap which will dissipate our energy and sense of purpose. We need to recognize that sense desire is to be avoided if we are to get any further with the meditation. The five methods below will help.

CULTIVATING

Note: This now extends beyond the 'cultivating the opposite' category. It consists of methods of *active* cultivation. These include methods of self discipline, or methods which direct or transform energy, or through which we deliberately move our mind away from a hindrance and towards something deeper.

Recognize that this is sense desire—it's a hindrance to concentration which you need to start working on immediately.

Simply to **concentrate more strongly** on the object of meditation may bring your energies together and disperse the distracted state of mind that you are in.

You can learn to **observe the quality of your breath**: once you know your typical patterns, the way you are breathing may indicate when you are distracted. If you concentrate on the experience of the breath in the lower part of the body—at the navel, for example—this may help stabilize your concentration, taking it away from thoughts towards a more 'grounded' experience of yourself.

You may be able to **refine your desire** by channelling your excitement towards a less gross and stimulating object—such as the object of your meditation, or the breath. In fact, you can develop as much 'greed' for meditation as you have invested in the object, thus channelling the emotion towards something positive.

CONSIDERING

Note: This category is no longer being used in the simple sense of 'considering the consequences'. It now also includes every kind of *reflection*, many of which are traditional vipassana-type contemplations.

With this method we reflect on the real nature of subjective desire for sense experiences, as well as the real nature of the object we happen to be desiring. By reflecting in these ways we may be able to sublimate our interest in the object claiming our attention.

Reflect on the nature of the hindrance of sense desire. You could simply ask yourself where you think this emotion (which is essentially what it is) is likely to lead you. If you consult your experience, you will probably find that such thoughts merely tend towards further distraction and attachment to sense experience. You could also reflect that indulging in sense desire does more than waste your precious time; it also deepens a particular kind of habit, and deepens your resistance to meditation in the future.

You could also **reflect on the impermanence of the hindrance**—remind yourself that this emotion will not last. Nothing ever does last, so you can be quite confident that the sense desire will dissolve in time. If you spend some time reflecting deeply on this you will become more firmly convinced that the hindrance of sense desire is not worth pursuing.

You could apply the fact of impermanence to yourself too. Reflection on death—and, in particular, the inevitability of your own death—may provide a very effective antidote to sense desire by putting your life into a clear perspective. Reminding yourself that you only have so much time shows how important your present efforts in meditation are. We often entertain sense desire when we forget the significance of what we are doing, and our thoughts, wandering from this interest to that, become more interesting than the meditation once the sense of urgency is lost. Reflection on death can re-establish that perspective, so that you lose your attachment to the thoughts and again become interested in the practice.

Then sense desire is clearly not 'yours' or even really a part of you—in reality, you cannot own anything for very long. By reflecting on the 'ownerlessness' of all things, you may eventually be able to let the hindrance go and continue with meditation. When it is seen in the lightness and freedom of this higher reality, craving may become less insistent.

Lastly, this feeling can obviously never bring lasting satisfaction. By reflecting on its ultimately unsatisfactory and frustrating nature you will see its nature more clearly, and so, perhaps, feel less interested in pursuing it.

Instead of the mental state of sense desire, you could **reflect on the nature of the object which is drawing your attention**. For example, you could ask yourself whether this thing which attracts you so much is really worth thinking about or listening to. Often, if we are honest, such things are rather trivial—and forcing ourselves to admit this may have the effect of resolving the conflict involved in our attachment to them.

You could reflect that in the ultimate analysis this object, though currently attractive, is impermanent. It may be surprising to see the change in your relationship with the object, which can be effected simply by introducing this reflection.

You might then go on to consider that since it is impermanent, this attractive thing actually has no real essence; it does not exist independently, in its own right. Your perception of it as an attractive object really depends on the various conditions which make up its existence—and your own too. Then, of course, because of its impermanence and conditionedness, it could never give you any full, complete sense of satisfaction!

You will probably need to be convinced in advance—through previous vipassana meditation—of the principles behind these reflections, otherwise they are unlikely to be very effective. But in combination with any already existing glimmerings of insight you have stimulated, these reminders will definitely begin to resolve your attachment to attractive objects.

You could **ask yourself**, finally, **whether this thing you are attracted to is actually beautiful**. Is it really attractive from an aesthetic point of view? You could compare it with the beauty of the dhyanas, or with the beauty of Enlightenment.

SKY-LIKE MIND

It is possible to apply the 'sky-like' attitude to sense desire by adopting a passive, observational attitude while at the same time scrupulously avoiding the tendency to give extra attention to the distracting object.

This may be somewhat demanding, but in the right circumstances it can be a very effective method. In the same spirit—perhaps as a more long-term strategy—you could try to increase your awareness of the objects which come into your mind in meditation. This will tend to broaden your experience out from the narrow grasping which characterizes sense desire.

SUPPRESSION

Suppression simply means saying 'no' to the sense desire. Sense desire can be very strong and passionate indeed—the stronger the hindrance, the more difficult it is to suppress, so generally it isn't to be recommended. But if your tendency to distraction is not so much a passion as a general habit, then suppression could work quite well, especially if you are definitely convinced that you want to get beyond it. Suppression can be a good antidote to apply after using a 'consideration'-type reflection.

OUTSIDE MEDITATION

Note: In this category we look at how we can work with the causes of hindrances outside meditation.

If you are prone to sense desire, then in your life generally you need to

Cultivating (Cultivating the opposite quality; re-direction of attention or energy)	• Recognize that what is happening is a hindrance • Concentrate more on the object • Watch breathing • Watch breathing low in body • Channel excitement to more refined object • Refine/sublimate desire for the object	
Considering (Considering the consequences of sense desire, and other methods of reflection)	**Nature of hindrance of sense desire**	• Where do such thoughts usually get us? • Further distraction • Waste of time • Deepens tendency • Deepens resistance • Sense desire does not last • It is not me or mine • It cannot satisfy completely
	Nature of specific distraction	• Is it worth thinking about? • It is impermanent • It is not me or mine • It cannot satisfy completely
Sky-like mind	Observe passively, without giving extra attention	
Suppression	Say no	
Outside meditation	• Guard the gates of the senses • Monitor speech—less about sense-based topics, more about Dharma • Be less self-indulgent in appetites • Develop friendships	

Working on the hindrance of desire for sense experience

observe the effect of different sense objects and avoid those which stimulate greed and craving—in other words, you need to **guard the gates of the senses**. You need to be quite uncompromising with yourself as to whether something really does stimulate craving or not. Your speech, too, very much affects your mental state, so it may lessen your tendency to this hindrance if you **talk less about attractive sense objects**. Perhaps you could speak more in terms of the Dharma. Obviously you are also affected by what you think about, and, if you can, it may help counteract sense desire if you **try not to indulge thoughts connected with craving**.

As a general rule, we re-fuel the desire for sense experience whenever we indulge it; so you may be able to reduce it if you **cultivate a little healthy restraint**. Generally, it may help to be a little more moderate in appetites: you could pay special attention to your investments in food and sex, which make the strongest demands.

These demands are so strong that fast progress is unlikely. Indeed, it is probably unwise to deny yourself too much too soon—if you are unrealistic about your capacities for restraint there is very likely to be an emotional reaction. Take things gradually. You probably just need to be a little more moderate in your grosser pleasures—it is possible to enjoy life in moderation!

Coupled with this, you could also **refine your sources of emotional satisfaction**. You could, for instance, cultivate an interest in the arts, which may create a new appreciation of beauty—one less based in craving. Contact with other people is another area in which you could possibly channel your responses away from craving. See if you can improve the quality of your friendships and communication with others, and especially cultivate friendship with those who like you and support your efforts. Craving is partly the outcome of a feeling of insecurity, so if you can make sure your emotional needs are met, you may experience far less desire for external sense experiences. A traditional suggestion is to develop friendships with people who seem less sense-oriented.

ILL WILL

Ill will (*vyapada*) is similar to sense desire in that the *object* of the hindrance is its dominant feature; this is not the case with the other three hindrances. In both sense desire and ill will we are strongly attached to an object which we are reluctant to let go. With sense desire we are trapped through our craving; in the case of ill will we are trapped through our aversion to it—yet the fascination of the object, the power of its spell over us, is no less strong.

CULTIVATING

You should **recognize that this is ill will**—a hindrance to meditation—and that right now you want to meditate, not to be irritated! Recognition is the primary antidote to any hindrance—sometimes recognition alone is sufficient to weaken it—but recognition can also be very difficult, since we often do not want to acknowledge that this is an unskilful state of mind.

We are very often attached to mental states, whether they are skilful or not, and this attachment is particularly common with ill will: we often feel justified in being bad-tempered. But even without discussing the issue of whether it is possible to justify some forms of anger from an ethical point of view, it is certain that we can never meditate in this state: ill will is simply not compatible with skilful concentration.

Having recognized ill will you can try to **develop the opposite quality**: developing some metta is an obvious antidote. In fact, if ill will persists in your meditation, and is hard to eradicate, then it is generally advisable to spend extra time, perhaps a lot of time, on the Metta Bhavana practice.

You might be able to 'cool' the ill will if you **physically relax and calm down**. You could pay attention to the breath lower in the body, especially in the belly—or to your bodily posture generally. The hindrance of ill will is largely fuelled by thoughts, and this kind of method takes your attention away from your head.

It is important to **keep checking your progress** against this hindrance, because it is difficult to eradicate once it has a hold. You should not be satisfied with just a little progress, but keep checking to see whether the ill will has really gone.

CONSIDERING

Turning to more analytical methods, you can **reflect on the nature of the emotion** itself (we will consider the *object* of the ill will later). Ill will can be a very difficult hindrance indeed to counteract, and reflection on its nature may help you to see through it.

First of all, you are indulging in ill will; you do not want to let it go. **Ask yourself what the emotion feels like**. Is it enjoyable? Ill will is often a very painful, barbed emotion. Some people feel that they actively enjoy mentally criticizing and inflicting imaginary harm. But the nature of this enjoyment can be questioned—look deeply and see if it is not a mixed pleasure. In any case while this hindrance is present you cannot settle down and relax. So why, you might ask, hold on to it?

You might also **question what the likely result of ill will is**. The result is likely to be more pain and suffering: ill will just worsens painful situations and relationships. Life can produce nothing but bitter fruit without some degree of metta, love, and friendliness. It is far better to do nothing rather than indulge ill will, because the more you indulge the more your ill will tends to escalate, and the more damage you do. Ill will is, indeed, very damaging; it is well worth doing whatever you can to combat this hindrance.

You could **consider your own experiences in the past**. Ill will separates you from others; no one is attracted to an angry person. Most people experience irritable people as unattractive, frightening, painful to be with. So as an antidote, you may consider how much you would like to overcome ill will, since it has never helped you, or brought you any worthwhile satisfaction. On the contrary it has brought shame and remorse, and complicated your relationships with others.

You could **consider the outcome** of ill will for the person with whom you are angry. It is likely that your dislike of them will continue, together with all the difficulties in your relationship with them. Surely you would prefer to reconcile the difficulties? This question may reveal the extent of your attachment to the ill will, since you may find out that you do not really want to be reconciled. Probably you think that you are right and they are wrong. But until you can see that there are rights and wrongs on both sides, there can be no lessening of the hindrance of ill will; you must be able to forgive, or at least forget for the time being, the other person's faults.

If you take a wider perspective and consider this emotion according to the Dharma, you can **reflect**, first of all, **that the nature of your ill will is an irrational aversion**. It is an unrealistic rejection of something you find threatening, yet which, were you more able to acknowledge it, would probably make you more balanced and happy.

You might try to analyse your emotion a little more deeply, and **reflect that underneath the ill will is craving**. Somewhere or other you feel deprived of something that you want; it may possibly be some sort of recognition or attention, or even some actual possession. Whatever it is, you can ask yourself whether it is worth craving for, and whether you really want to be in the narrow state of mind the emotion creates. You may even discover some genuine need that could easily be met.

You might try to **analyse yourself at the deepest level**, looking at ill will's basis in primordial ignorance. At base, *ill will is your natural refusal to acknowledge things as they really are*. If you can reflect on this quality, examining its connection with your present ill will, you may see through it; you may experience how utterly limiting it is.

Look at the situation in terms of the principle of conditionality—that you inherit the conditioning set up by your past actions, and that your present actions condition your future experience. You know that your present ill will is conditioned by some painful experience. Consider to what extent the experience has been, in some respects at least, of your own making. When you react with ill will, you are feeding a tendency which only creates further suffering for you in the future.

You can apply this to others too: other people also inherit the conditioning of their own actions. They may have faults which you find painful and irritating, but actually they suffer from them too. If you reflect, with compassion, on what this conditioning must be doing to them, how limiting it is, your ill will may dissolve.

You can **consider your attitude towards difficult situations generally**. You must be prepared to accept some things in life which you do not immediately like, otherwise you could never make any progress. In fact sometimes painful situations can even help you to develop stamina, strength, and patience. Some Buddhist teachers go so far as to say that you should feel grateful for the difficulties which other people make for you—feel glad that you have enemies—because it is only possible to develop patience in those testing situations!

From the ultimate point of view *your emotion of ill will is impermanent*. It is a reaction, on your part, to a painful feeling—and painful feelings, like pleasant ones, are conditioned by your actions. They are conditioned by the general trend of your way of life, or by specific actions which 'set you up' for such a feeling. If you indulge the reaction, allowing yourself to get more angry in response, you are 'setting yourself up' again; you are increasing the likelihood of painful feelings. But if you do not indulge it, but simply experience the painful feeling as it is, it may eventually subside, along with the temptation to react with ill will.

You can **contemplate the hindrance of ill will from the point of view of non-selfhood.** Ill will has no fixed nature of its own, but consists merely of the changing conditions which set it up. It is not 'your' ill will, either, except in the conventional sense, because your own nature is equally fluid and unfixed.

You can also **reflect on the nature of the *object* of your ill will.** This 'object' will usually be some person who has wronged you, either in your imagination or in actual fact. You could first of all be honest, and consider how much of your irritation with this person has to do with objective reality. It is probably mainly subjective, to do with you rather than them.

You can check whether or not this is so by trying to separate what has actually happened from your personal response to it. You may find that it is your subjective response which is causing you all the suffering, not the objective facts. You are attached to your *view* of the person concerned, and even though it causes you pain, you do not want to let go of your view of them, even if you grudgingly acknowledge that they have some good points.

Probably, what you basically want to do is *vent* your ill will; you want to think about that hateful person, and about the things they have done which have harmed you. If you can only recognize your attachment and its futility, you may then lose interest in ill will and be able to interest yourself once again in meditation (which, you may need to remind yourself, is what you are trying to do at the present moment!).

Remember that however strongly another person hates or is angry with you, **their dislike cannot harm you**; it is your own reaction which will do the damage.

Even a person who is definitely acting badly has some good qualities. This applies even when someone causes suffering to you or others you love. Your acknowledgement of their good nature doesn't mean that you have to accept them uncritically, but you should strive for objectivity, trying to see them as they really are. If you are indulging in ill will, your view is inevitably one-sided and cannot be trusted. You can only see a person as they actually are by looking for and acknowledging any positive qualities they possess. Your emotional response towards them may then become more balanced and objective.

It is important to **be clear that you are meditating,** and that for the time being you are concerned only with your own state of mind—you do not have to be concerned with what another person should or should not do.

Then there is the possibility that you could **develop compassion.** The person you have in mind may have caused another person suffering—or even harmed many people. But human beings have an almost infinite potential for negativity, and you also are constantly causing harm to others. The result of unskilful behaviour, which sets up certain predispositions and tendencies of mind, is inevitably going to be unpleasantness, both for you and the hated person. So even if the person you are hating really has been behaving badly, compassion is the appropriate emotion, not ill will. They really harm only themselves, so ill will is quite out of place.

The above reflections might seem rather involved. Simply to **ask yourself if you have things in perspective** can be very effective. Could you possibly be taking it all too seriously? Just that thought might be enough to burst the whole bubble.

From a wider point of view, you could quite effectively apply the same considerations to the *object* of your ill will as you applied to the *hindrance* of ill will. This person is just an impermanent, conditioned human being, devoid of permanent selfhood, and was never capable of giving you any permanent satisfaction anyway! In this way you can strive to view them with the eye of wisdom, and the heart of compassion.

SKY-LIKE MIND

Sometimes this method can work with ill will, especially if the emotion is persistent and you are fairly convinced that you do not want to be in an irritated state. If you are so convinced, then you can simply observe its effect on your mind in a detached way. It is important not to get involved, to let your thoughts come and go quite freely, yet without attachment. Eventually, if you are patient and truly non-reactive, the ill will may lose its power and dissipate itself.

Cultivating (Cultivating the opposite quality; re-direction of attention or energy)	• Recognize this mental state as a hindrance • Develop metta, forgiveness, patience, peacefulness • Relax physically • Be aware of the breath, and breathe low • Keep checking that you are working on the hindrance	
Considering (Considering the consequences of ill will, and other methods of reflection)	**Nature of hindrance of ill will**	• Is ill will enjoyable? • What is the likely outcome • For you • For the other person • We inherit the fruits of actions—and so do others. If they have acted badly they will suffer, whatever we think or do • Difficult situations are opportunities to develop patience • Ill will is impermanent
	Nature of specific distraction	• Is it worth thinking about? • In this situation, what is subjective reaction and what objective fact? • Their hatred (of itself) cannot harm you • Even an evil person has good qualities • You have the same faults, or others as bad • Are you taking this all too seriously?
Sky-like mind	Observe thoughts and feelings, let them burn themselves out	
Suppression	Just stop it	
Outside meditation	• Develop friendships with loving, positive people • Spend less time with 'hate types' • Avoid hateful, spiteful, cynical speech	

SUPPRESSION

Suppression will probably not work for strong ill will, but it might in the case of persistent, habitual, rather weak negative thoughts which you are already convinced are useless.

OUTSIDE MEDITATION

If you often experience the hindrance of ill will in your practice, you must be prepared to do some work. It may help if you deliberately try to develop some counteractive qualities outside meditation—qualities such as forgiveness, patience, peacefulness, faith, and inspiration—in order to redress the balance. Developing these may involve your activities at home, at work, and in every part of your life.

It is especially valuable to **pay attention to your speech**. If you do your best to speak in a helpful, harmonious, graceful way, you will avoid encouraging your irritable side. Cynicism, or rough, crude speech, even in the form of little asides and comments, has a strong effect, as do habitual grumbling and complaining, or expressions of resentment. You could try to avoid these, as well as criticisms of others, and malicious gossip.

You would also be well advised to develop friendships with people who are positive and loving, rather than 'hate types'. Buddhism makes a rough-and-ready division into psychological types: there are 'greed types', who are primarily motivated by their desire for enjoyable experiences, and tend to be emotional rather than intellectual; 'hate types', who are motivated by their aversion to pain and tend to be more intellectual; and 'deluded types', who sometimes seem motivated in one way, sometimes another. In fact people are usually rather a mixture.

If you are predominantly a 'hate' type (which might well be so if the hindrance of ill will is persistent), it could go rather against the grain to make friends with those whom you may find unbearably jolly, friendly, positive people. People tend to be attracted to their own type on the whole. Yet if you are prepared to open up, put aside your prejudices, and enjoy such company (at least sometimes), it will certainly do you good by helping to balance your personality. This is part of the aim of the Buddhist ideal of spiritual community. Contact with spiritually committed people brings you into contact with very different temperaments to your own, and this can radically change your habitual attitudes.

RESTLESSNESS AND ANXIETY

CULTIVATING

The first thing to do is actually to **recognize that you are restless and/or anxious**. A few facts about restlessness and anxiety may help with the recognition.

The two aspects of this hindrance, restlessness (*uddhacca*) and anxiety (*kukkucca*), may each arise independently of the other. 'Restlessness' means physical restlessness and turbulence, or arousal; the more 'physical' antidotes may well work on it. 'Anxiety' is excessive associative thinking which is essentially irrational; it often returns to the same topic repeatedly, but does not think matters through, and in fact avoids doing so.

Having recognized the hindrance, you can then recall that restlessness and anxiety is a hindrance to meditation, and that since what you really want to be doing is meditating, you need to work to counteract it.

Since restlessness and anxiety is such a persistent mental state, you should **still continue to check** even when you feel it has been eradicated.

One characteristic of restlessness and anxiety is that it pulls your attention away from the object of meditation; so you can sometimes counteract that if you **make a stronger effort to concentrate**. In doing so, you need to take particular care to work appropriately and avoid a hard, forced effort; there is a tendency to become tense with this hindrance, so this antidote needs to be accompanied by receptivity and kindness towards yourself.

Indeed, it might help you to calm down if you **focus on contentment and acknowledgement** of yourself as you are now, perhaps with the aid of the Metta Bhavana practice. You could try focusing on one calming thought to achieve this, perhaps with the aid of a phrase like 'let yourself relax'.

It may also help to **bring the focus of attention** (perhaps with the aid of the breath) **down more into the body**, and away from the chaotic mind. In your imagination, look for the quality that is missing, and anticipate enjoying the simplicity of concentration in contrast to the present complex chaos.

Another very good antidote can be to **pay special attention to your posture**, being mindful of every bodily tension and small movement. It is especially effective to sit very still. In order to do this you could resolve to sit motionless (apart from inner relaxation and adjustment of posture) for the whole of the session, resisting every impulse to move.

Your mind and body may be racing if you have been exerting yourself with work, travel, or exercise immediately before the meditation session. The effects of these efforts can last for some time afterwards, perhaps for an hour or more in the case of strenuous exercise, and for considerably longer if you have been travelling. In these circumstances it is almost impossible to concentrate the mind until some time has passed, so allowances should be made. On intensive meditation retreats it is important to allow time for adjusting to the effects of travel, and wise to avoid heavy work and strenuous exercise.

CONSIDERING

You could first of all **reflect that** very often with this hindrance **you are not actually worrying about anything specific**. It is just a habitual state of mind which is looking for an object to fasten on to and worry about. Once you see that this is what is happening, you can acquire the confidence to move beyond it. Sometimes the mere act of seeing that it is a habit will enable you to leave it behind; at other times, having seen, you can move on to using a different antidote.

If you do have something specific that is worrying you, **remember that there is nothing you can do about it while you are meditating**. The best thing to do is put it aside for the duration of the meditation, and think about it later.

If the restlessness is manifesting physically so that you are full of nervous tension, you could **try to see the cause of the tension**. There could be many causes; perhaps some thought in your mind at present, or the result of something you have done or which has happened. If you can discover the cause of the restlessness, you may be able to counteract it either now, outside the meditation, or both.

Reflecting from the broadest possible perspective, *restlessness and anxiety is impermanent*; it will go away eventually. It depends on its 'fuel' of previous actions for its present existence, and if you don't provide it with any more fuel, perhaps by using the 'sky-like' method in conjunction with this consideration, it will eventually dissolve.

You can also **consider**, of course, **that this hindrance is unsatisfactory**. While it is perfectly obvious that anxiety is not 'satisfying', it can nonetheless be worthwhile reflecting on the universality of its unsatisfactoriness: that it is unsatisfactory in the same way that all other conditioned things are. You could think about the potential satisfaction of unconditioned reality and in that way create a truer and more inspiring perspective from which to work with this hindrance.

Like other conditioned, changeable things, *restlessness and anxiety does not have any essence*; neither is it part of us. All these considerations will gradually provide you with the means of letting go of this anxiety and restlessness.

SKY-LIKE MIND

If it is very strong, the 'sky-like' approach can work well for the mental aspect of this hindrance. Anxiety tends to create a narrow prison-like world consisting only of thought. By being aware of every thought, feeling, and emotion which enters your mind, without trying to hold on to any of them, and also by being mindful of physical sense-experiences, you will eventually develop a broader awareness of yourself that extends beyond this mental prison.

SUPPRESSION

It may sometimes be possible to stop this hindrance through the power of resolve alone. However, it will probably be rather difficult unless the restlessness is relatively weak.

Cultivating (Cultivating the opposite quality; re-direction of attention or energy)	• Recognize that this state of mind is a hindrance • Keep checking progress • Make stronger efforts to engage—in a balanced, not a tense, way • Develop inner contentment • Use a phrase to calm yourself • Breathe low in the body • Pay attention to posture • Resolve to sit very still • Meditate very regularly		
Considering (Considering the consequences of restlessness and anxiety, and other methods of reflection)	• You can do nothing about your specific worry at present (i.e. when you are meditating) • Look for causes for present mental and/or physical state		
	Nature of restlessness and anxiety	• It is impermanent and dependent • It is unsatisfactory • It is not 'you' or in any way yours	
Sky-like mind	A good antidote. Just observe what happens		
Suppression	Probably not possible		
Outside meditation	• Do not exercise just before sitting • Exercise can *help* at other times though • Develop less hectic life-style • Spend time with people possessing dignity, calm, and restraint • Avoid useless and frivolous speech • Develop your thinking faculty • Tackle confusion through Dharma study • Understand ethics—see the relationship between cause and effect		

Working against the hindrance of restlessness and anxiety

OUTSIDE MEDITATION

When this hindrance predominates it shows an unsettled, possibly an un-disciplined, disposition; it can therefore be counteracted if you **pay special attention to regularity of practice**. You could try, for example, to meditate at exactly the same time, and preferably the same place, every day.

You could try to **lead a more regular life-style** generally: doing basic things, like getting up and eating, at the same time every day helps meditation generally. A restless life-style certainly tends to create a restless mind.

If you are chronically 'speedy', you perhaps ought to consider what else you could do to become more steady and grounded. For example, you could deliberately **spend more time with friends who are not restless**, but who are calm and self-possessed.

In your speech, you can especially try to **avoid frivolous, useless**

speech, speaking only when you have something to say, and then only when that is going to be useful and helpful to the situation generally. It is always difficult to make major changes like this, but any progress at all will make a substantial impact on your mental state and your meditation. Working with your speech is a very powerful method.

You might then try to **develop more steadiness and regularity in your thinking**; a restless mind is superficial, unable to go beyond its concern with surface appearances. So trying to be more mindful of your thoughts will have the general effect of calming you down and taking you deeper. This will require some dedicated work—writing down your thoughts is a great help, perhaps by keeping a journal. Once you are more aware of your thinking, you can try to be less at the mercy of your thoughts, less passively driven along by them.

A fundamental condition for this hindrance is basic mental confusion—something we all suffer from in varying degrees—and a very good way of tackling it is through the study of Buddhism. It is best to study regularly, and also to study with others, so that your understanding is tested. The main thing you need to **be clear about** is **your understanding of the principles of ethics**. If you can gain a clearer understanding of the relationship between causes and effects—between your actions and their results—you will then become less confused in your thinking; you will become happier, less agitated, and less anxious.

SLOTH AND TORPOR

CULTIVATING

The hindrance of sloth and torpor consists of two aspects: physical sloth (*thina*) and mental torpor (*middha*). Its antidotes are a range of methods, from the subtle to the gross, of getting yourself to WAKE UP!

For mental torpor, which is a dull, sleepy, stiff, rigid state of consciousness, you can first of all try to **counteract it by stimulating energy**. You could reflect on the inspiring quality of sympathetic joy, for example. Or if need be you can interrupt your current practice and start actually practising Metta and Mudita Bhavana. Or you could try to **make your experience of the object more vivid** and energizing: if you are visualizing a form, for example, you could imagine it as shining and vibrating with light and colour. If you are concentrating on a sensation such as the breath, you could pay attention to its more stimulating aspects, for example, finding the place in the body where the sensation is strongest.

For physical sloth—which may range from a slight lack of vitality, through head-nodding, to complete collapse and sleep—strong medicine is often required. You will have to make a very strong resolution not to give in to drowsiness, because it could take all your energy just to keep awake. The very nature of sloth is to avoid working in meditation; the desire to do absolutely nothing is remarkably strong.

For this reason it is vital to **recognize this hindrance** right from the beginning. Recognition can be a major step, even a breakthrough! Even though you recognize sloth and make efforts to work against it, sloth will still persist in 'hiding' from your awareness.

Even when you begin to get it under control, you need to **keep checking** to see whether sloth is still there.

It may help if you **have your eyes open**, at least enough to let in sufficient light to stimulate you.

You could also **have as much light around you as possible**—at night, for example, you could have all the lights switched on. What is more, you should not hesitate to break your meditation to get up to switch them on, provided your action will not disturb others meditating with you. Getting up will not harm your meditation—under the power of this hindrance you were not meditating anyway. On the contrary, by opening your eyes and switching on the lights you are doing something to enhance your practice.

If staying awake gets very difficult, you could try gazing at a source of light, for example a candle; or, if it is daytime, try gazing into the sky (not, of course, directly at the sun) and meditating.

You could **open a window**: you could get up, interrupting the meditation, and open a window, and breathe fresh, cool air. Perhaps you could wear less clothing, too—if it keeps you awake, it is better to be a little cool rather than let sloth get the better of you (though for some people coldness encourages sloth—so they need to get warm).

It may also help if you **concentrate on the breath high in the body**, for example at the nose or imagined at the top of the head—this can work very well. Indeed, paying attention to your body can be a very effective method indeed.

If the sloth is very strong, you may be able to prevent yourself from completely 'going under' if you **concentrate entirely on your posture**.

The tendency with this hindrance generally is to sit very slackly, with very little bodily awareness; in particular there is a tendency to lean too far forwards, with the head bowed and nodding. A good physical antidote is to **lean slightly backwards**, and to tilt the head back a little.

If you are definitely sleepy, you can stop meditating for a while and **stimulate yourself physically**. You can rub and massage your limbs, change your posture, pull your earlobes (a traditional recommendation), or pinch yourself!

Something of this kind may revive you—but if it does not, it is best to **give up for the time being**, have a break, and sit again later. You could take a short break, perhaps washing your face in cold water before returning almost immediately, or walking mindfully up and down outside for half an hour or so.

In the last resort, you will have to **conclude that you need sleep**! So then you should lie down and sleep, continuing the meditation later when you are refreshed.

Taking another approach, sloth can often be transcended if you **chant or recite out loud**, which is both physically and emotionally stimulating. For example, you can chant traditional verses, of which there are some very beautiful ones in the Buddhist tradition.

There are also a number of visualization techniques traditionally recommended for dissolving sloth and torpor. You can, for example, **visualize light**—brilliant white light—inside your body and head, and then imagine it glowing and radiating outwards from your body. Tibetan teachers sometimes recommend visualizing a point of white light inside your heart which shoots upwards out of the crown of your head, merging with the sky.

But finally, if the standard antidotes do not seem to be working, you can **try calming down and relaxing**! Sometimes sloth and torpor is caused by underlying tension: you may not be allowing yourself to experience some emotion, so that the effort of repressing it is absorbing all your energy. If this is the case you should try to relax and experience whatever emotion is there, releasing the tension and bringing back your energy.

CONSIDERING

The hindrance of sloth and torpor is not a very suitable basis for Dharmic reflection. Theoretically it is possible to contemplate the impermanence, unsatisfactoriness, and insubstantiality of sloth and torpor just like the other hindrances, but it cannot be generally recommended. Anyone who wishes may try reflecting in this way if they like—if they can!

Sloth and torpor probably requires a much more down-to-earth course of action. You are half asleep, stuck in dullness—so you need to wake up; you really need to **give yourself some kind of positive shock**. Traditional Buddhism can provide a number of suitable reflections.

You can reflect, for example, on the shortness of your life, and on how precious the opportunity of life is. Readers of this book have probably been born into a very favourable situation. Not only are you alive and in a position to develop yourself spiritually, but you even have some idea how important spiritual development is. How few people have this—how few are in a position even to think about it! Most people have little time to think of anything but supplying their immediate wants and needs. But you are able to function more fully as a human being; in our present world that is a privilege, not a right.

What is more, you have actually come into contact with the spiritual path, something that most human beings are unlikely to do. Moreover, you could hardly be in a better position to put its teachings into practice. You may, perhaps, be relatively healthy, and with the political freedom to practise as you wish. For most readers, Buddhist literature and Buddhist teachers will be widely available. If you do not practise the Dharma now, when else will you have such an ideal opportunity, when else will you be able to make any progress?

Traditional Buddhism would point out that if you neglect these opportunities, you are likely to forget that they exist, and become even more immersed in the endless round of cyclic existence—you are unlikely to come across something like this again for many lifetimes, and, even then, are you any more likely to take advantage of it, since at this moment you are responding lazily to an insignificant difficulty like this hindrance?

You may not accept the traditional Buddhist idea of rebirth, but these arguments do not really depend on the idea of future lives in any case. There would be no point putting things off to some future life, even if it did exist, because if you don't make an effort now, when will you? There really is no excuse for laziness once you have accepted the need to develop yourself.

Another approach to the 'positive shock' is to **consider the inspiring qualities of others**, in particular their heroic qualities of energy. The Buddha, for example, was a wonderful example of energetic dedication to his work. From his youth he worked on himself, until at the age of thirty-five (some say twenty-nine) he gained Enlightenment. After that he simply gave himself for the benefit of others, travelling and teaching constantly, often in very trying circumstances, right up until his death at the age of eighty. Even on his deathbed he gave an ordination, and immediately before his death the few last words he uttered, in front of a great crowd of disciples, summed up his entire teaching. He said, 'Monks, all conditioned things are impermanent. With mindfulness, strive on.' Together with the cultivation of awareness, he clearly regarded the putting forth of effort as absolutely vital for human progress.

Working against the hindrance of sloth and torpor

Cultivating	Mental torpor
(Cultivating the opposite quality; re-direction of attention or energy)	• Recognize that this is a hindrance
	• Decide to engage with the practice
	• Stimulate energy, e.g. through metta
	• Pay extra attention to the object and try to experience it more vividly
	Physical sloth
	• Recognize it as a hindrance!
	• Keep checking!
	• Have lights on full
	• Have eyes open
	• Breathe fresh air
	• Don't be too warm—remove some clothing (some physical types)
	• Breathe high—nose or top of head
	• Pay attention mainly to posture
	• Physically stimulate yourself—move, change your seat, take breaks
	• Take a nap
	• Do some chanting
	• Visualize bright light in body
	• Calm down and relax!—if sloth is caused by tension
Considering	• Life is a very precious opportunity. You should use it to the utmost. There is no excuse for not trying!
(If you *can* think in this state!)	• Consider the energetic qualities of others, e.g. the Buddha
Sky-like mind	• Not usually to be recommended!
Suppression	• There's nothing there to suppress! Create some energy instead!
Outside meditation	• Exercise—the right amount and the right kind
	• Food—the right amount and the right kind
	• Avoid passivity and dullness in speech—speak energetically and positively
	• Spend time with, and emulate, energetic people
	• Reflect on your motivation
	• Study the Dharma

SKY-LIKE MIND

Some people might possibly be able to use this method for sloth and torpor, but since the most likely outcome is simply an increase in the hindrance it cannot be generally recommended.

SUPPRESSION

Sloth and torpor is generally a 'passive' hindrance; there isn't really anything there to be suppressed. Suppression is brought about by actively cultivating an antidote.

OUTSIDE MEDITATION

If you are habitually slothful or torpid, there are bound to be factors at work in your life which are encouraging it. You could look at the traditional classification of body, speech, and mind: as far as your physical body is concerned you need to **get enough but not too much exercise**, so you are neither sluggish nor constantly tired.

You should **be aware of how much you eat**; again, the ideal is not too little, not too much. The type of food can also be important; it is a good idea to avoid too much stodgy, fatty food.

You also need to **get sufficient—though not too much—sleep**. Too much will make you dull and dreamy, but too little will have a similar effect; either extreme can cause sloth.

Regarding speech, it may help if you try to **avoid being passive and dull in speech**. You could have a policy of always saying what you think, and of not being afraid to speak out. Perhaps you could also try to speak more energetically, and only get involved in lively conversations! Avoid speaking dully and pessimistically.

Mentally, you might be able to alter the tendency towards torpor if you **cultivate the friendship of energetic, active, lively people,** and **motivate yourself through Dharma study**.

DOUBT AND INDECISION

CULTIVATING

First of all—as always—one must **acknowledge that this is indeed the hindrance of doubt** (*vicikiccha*). In the case of this hindrance, it is the implications of recognition that are important, because as soon as you have recognized that the hindrance of doubt and indecision is present, that it is a hindrance, and that you do not want it—you must decide, firmly, that you are going to do something to change things.

You can recognize doubt and indecision by the fact that you are holding back; you are not really putting yourself into the practice. It is as though you do not trust the meditation—which probably means that you lack confidence in your own potential. Possibly, you are a little afraid of your own power. But anyway, whether this is the case or not, you certainly lack trust in either the practice or your ability to engage in it. This lack of trust causes you to hold back from committing yourself to a line of action; and your not engaging has the effect of laying you open to the other hindrances. You can sometimes see this ability of doubt to 'underlie' other negative states when you successfully ward off a hindrance such as restlessness, only to discover doubt lurking underneath.

Since this hindrance is essentially a lack of resolve, to **develop a positive sense of resolve** is an important counteragent. You might be able to develop this by impressing upon yourself the seriousness of what is happening to you. Doubt and indecision is certainly a very serious obstacle to your progress: its nature is to maintain a chronic state of unresolvedness, in which you actively resist the idea of clarifying your attitude. You continually allow yourself to avoid facing up to and clarifying important issues. This is why most of the methods recommended are either of the consideration type or are to be employed outside meditation.

CONSIDERING

The hindrance of doubt and indecision could be worked on with the more 'vipassana'—like considerations of its impermanence, nonselfhood, and unsatisfactoriness, which have been applied to some of the other hindrances. These can certainly be experimented with, but in practice it seems more useful to work more 'psychologically'. Your basic need is to develop confident resolve, so you can consider ways of clarifying the unconscious confusions which sap your confidence.

You could try to **discover**, through conscious reflection, **whether anything is not clear** to you—perhaps something to do with the practice you are doing, or something about Buddhism, or the path of development generally.

Having isolated a specific doubt, you can then **put it aside**, deciding to think it through later. But if it seems there is no chance of getting into the meditation otherwise, you might as well think it through now.

You could try to **develop**, through conscious reflection, **a sense of confidence in yourself**. You need to believe that you are justified in having confidence in yourself. Many people find this almost impossible, so to overcome this obstacle you must assess yourself quite objectively—that is, not negatively ('obviously I'll never be able to meditate'), nor over-optimistically ('I really am wonderful')—both are clearly unreal. In Buddhism it is considered a great virtue to rejoice in objective merits and good qualities—including your own. You might well need others to verify your self-assessment in order to believe it yourself; you can then encourage yourself much more.

You can reflect that through practising meditation you develop yourself, and that there is no limit to the extent you can develop. Buddhist teachers say that you can never be sure of the results of any worldly undertaking—but spiritual practice inevitably has good results! The sincere will to develop always produces fruit, because that is the way of human development: intention is everything. If you have been meditating for a while you can ask yourself—and your friends—whether you have actually made any progress. You will inevitably find some improvements in your life, however small.

You can ask yourself whether it is objectively possible to grow and develop. The answer has to be 'yes'. Then you can ask, well—do you yourself want to develop? If again the answer is 'yes', then the obvious thing to do is decide to make a little effort towards it! As soon as you accept that you want to grow (emotionally accept it and its implications, not merely acknowledge the idea), then you have begun to clarify your confusion and are in a position to make a decisive effort. Then, if doubt rises up again (as it probably will), you can again work through these reflections. But if the answer to either of the questions above is 'no', you have not thought it through clearly!

Or perhaps you are stuck in the present moment; perhaps right now you are not in the mood. But even that really evades the issue, for in the long term, if you understand what personal development is, you surely want it. Or perhaps that is the problem; you don't know what it means to 'grow and develop'. But that is a manifestation of doubt too! You need to work at it again and again until you see more clearly. It will obviously help to talk with friends (positive ones, not cynics) about the issues it raises.

SKY-LIKE MIND
This can be a useful way of *experiencing* your doubt and indecision, once you have recognized it. It can be useful to 'size up' its character by allowing it some space.

SUPPRESSION
This is similar to sloth and torpor in that there is nothing to suppress—except your resistance to doing something. So to suppress doubt and indecision, be decisive!

OUTSIDE MEDITATION
Generally, you need to **understand your doubt and indecision more deeply**; you need to become more aware of its nature and its effect on your life.

All its manifestations are merely the products of a mental state, not rational thoughts—it is not that you genuinely do not understand something, not that there is a definite reason you are unsure. The hindrance of doubt and indecision is an emotional state which always looks for reasons to doubt things. If you **look more rationally at the doubts themselves,** you may be able to see the deep irrationality of this most poisonous hindrance.

In doing this it is necessary to generate a special mindfulness of the way that you think and use ideas. It is especially interesting to **observe how you receive new ideas**. In what ways do you accept or reject them? When they seem true to you, do you really accept them, or are there further reservations? And if there are, do you examine what the reservations are, and voice them to others?

Keeping ideas to yourself, to avoid the risk of having them challenged, is a typical ploy of this hindrance. So as a counteragent, you can **make a practice of speaking out** when ideas do not seem right to you. Even if at the time you cannot articulate your objection precisely, a lot may be gained by mentioning that you are not sure about something, or that you feel that something might be wrong. When you practise thinking more critically like this, you should not be closed-minded either, but open to discussion.

Through this practice you learn to monitor your thinking and to notice the emotions which lie behind your thoughts. It is the uncomfortable emotions which cause you to hold back from decision-making, so having realized this you can try to **unify your thinking and your feeling**, both by bringing more clear thought into your actions generally and by trying to have more emotion in support of your decisions.

Another approach you could take is simply to **be more decisive** outside meditation—you can do this by being more aware of your indecisiveness, recognizing symptoms like wavering, dithering, and lack of clarity.

It will also help combat this hindrance if you **form associations and friendships with people who are helpful and encouraging**. You should recognize that you need support—you need friendship and the confidence that friendship gives. A lot might be said about how to acquire friends, but the most effective method is simply to be one.

You can also try to **make a connection with an experienced spiritual teacher**. This need not be some famous 'guru'; all you need is as frequent contact as possible with somebody a little more developed and experienced than yourself.

It will also increase your confidence in yourself generally if you **think less about yourself—and**, instead, **affirm and give your support to others**. You can let them know how much you appreciate them, praising them for their virtues, and surprising them with your expressions of esteem! 'Rejoicing in merits' can be astonishingly powerful. Many people never seem to receive any appreciative comments about themselves from anybody.

Cultivating (Cultivating the opposite quality; re-direction of attention or energy)	• Recognize that this is a hindrance • Decide to engage with the practice	**Working against the hindrance of doubt and indecision**
Considering (Considering the consequences of doubt, and other methods of reflection)	• Is there something about the practice, or about the Dharma, which is unclear to you? • Develop confidence through objective self-assessment	
Sky-like mind	• Can be used to experience the nature of doubt (once it is clear that is what it is)—but beware mental wandering	
Suppression	• Be decisive!	
Outside meditation	• Watch clarity of ideas and thoughts— do you really think something or not? • Express doubts and lack of clarity to others • Be aware of emotions behind thoughts • Be decisive in actions. Watch dithering • Develop positive self-affirmation • Learn to appreciate others • Spend time with encouraging people • Improve intellectual understanding of principles of Dharma • Develop faith through ritual, chanting, contemplation, or visual images	

It will definitely help your clarity of thought to **develop a better intellectual understanding** of the principles of Buddhism. You need to be quite sure that your understanding is correct, so that you can trust and use it. This can be achieved particularly through discussion and by formulating questions.

Finally, you can **view the need to overcome doubt in terms of developing trust or faith in the spiritual path.** Faith in Buddhism is never 'blind' faith; it is always based on a modicum, at least, of experience. So faith is developed through reflection—but once that has been awakened, even to a tiny extent, it can also be greatly strengthened if you **perform devotional practices** such as pujas and chanting, in which you not only celebrate your understanding of the Dharma, but try to contact the potential for Enlightenment within yourself directly. Devotional ceremonies exercise your more artistic, playful, imaginative energies. As an antidote to your chronic doubt and indecision, you could perhaps be really lavish with them, with special shrines, offerings, or whatever else appeals to your imagination.

NOTES AND REFERENCES

1 Trans. John Stevens, *One Robe, One Bowl: The Zen Poetry of Ryokan*, Weatherhill, **PREFACE**
  1984, p.65.
2 Trans. Wai-tao, 'Dhyana for Beginners' in *A Buddhist Bible*, ed. Dwight Goddard,
  Beacon, Boston 1970.
3 *A Buddhist Bible*, p.437. **INTRODUCTION**
4 *The Dhammapada* I, 1.
5 Shunryu Suzuki, *Zen Mind, Beginner's Mind*, Weatherhill, 1983, p.34.
6 Thich Nhat Hanh, *The Sun My Heart*, Parallax, Berkeley 1988, p.62.
7 Trans. Nanamoli, *The Path of Purification*, Buddhist Publication Society, Kandy (Sri **PART ONE**
CHAPTER ONE
  Lanka) 1975, p.300.
8 Trans. Ayya Khema, *Being Nobody, Going Nowhere*, Wisdom, London 1987, p.96. **CHAPTER TWO**
9 *Metta* (Pali) or *maitri* (Sanskrit), kindness or friendliness. *Bhavana* means 'making to
  become', 'development', and even 'meditation'. Pali is the language of one of the main
  sources of Buddhist scriptures, and is used for most of the technical terms in this book.
10 Trans. H.V. Guenther, *The Jewel Ornament of Liberation*, Rider, London 1970, p.16–19.
11 *A Buddhist Bible*, p.479.
12 *A Buddhist Bible*, p.482. **CHAPTER THREE**
13 Lewis Carroll, *Through the Looking Glass*.
14 C.M. Chen, *Buddhist Meditation, Systematic and Practical*, published privately,
  Kalimpong 1962, p.72.
15 With acknowledgements to Sangharakshita, *Vision and Transformation: An Introduction
  to the Buddha's Noble Eightfold Path*, Windhorse, Glasgow 1990, p.132.
16 These are simplified renderings of the traditional Pali terms used in the *Satipatthana
  Sutta* (the classic source for the Buddha's teaching on mindfulness). The four
  Foundations of Mindfulness given there are body (*kaya*), feeling (*vedana*), mind or
  mental state (*citta*), and mental object (*dhamma*). My rendering of the first two (body
  and feeling), is in accordance with the traditional list. 'Emotion' is also a reasonably
  straightforward rendition of the third foundation, since the sutta's description of *citta* is
  mostly given in terms of emotional responses ('Herein a monk knows the mind with lust,
  as with lust … with hate, as with hate …' etc.). In describing the fourth foundation, the

Buddha exhorts the practitioner to check the contents of his mind. Are they useful for development or not? The practice of mindfulness of *dhammas* is described in terms of the objects of thought, rather than the faculty of thought itself. It is concerned with cultivating the capacity to apply insightful analysis to the mental objects arising in one's mind. Yet since this capacity must be developed through mindfulness of thought it seems reasonable, for the sake of simplification, to describe the foundation itself in terms of thought.

17 Walt Whitman, 'I Sing The Body Electric', in *Leaves of Grass*, Penguin, London 1986, p.116.

18 D.H.Lawrence, 'Thought', In *Selected Poems*, Penguin, London, p.227.

19 For practical purposes, Buddhism regards the thinking mind as a sixth sense—it grasps onto an idea in more or less the same way as our eyes fix onto an object of sight.

20 These three key aspects are known as the Three Jewels, or most precious things.

21 Trans. Sangharakshita, from the *Mangala Sutta*, in *The Enchanted Heart*, Ola Leaves, London 1978, p.155.

22 See also Note 29.

23 *Zen Mind, Beginner's Mind*, p.21.

PART TWO
CHAPTER FOUR

24 *The Enchanted Heart*, p.5.

25 *A Buddhist Bible*, p.454.

26 Trans. T.W. Rhys Davids, Samanaphala Sutta, *Digha Nikaya I*, 74, Pali Text Society, London 1977.

27 We will come across this term again in Chapter Ten.

28 I would not recommend taking up one of these practices on a regular basis until a good foundation of Mindfulness of Breathing and Metta Bhavana are established. Without a qualified teacher, it may be more difficult to sustain this kind of exercise long term. But if you are curious, there is no harm in trying it out.

29 There is a considerable difference in quality between the reflex image and the *samapatti* phenomena referred to in Chapter Three. The *samapattis* are generally somewhat coarse and often feel a little odd, though not unpleasantly so. The reflex image is definitely 'friendlier', and indeed can be extremely inspiring in character.

CHAPTER FIVE

30 Whatever we think of the Buddhist doctrine of rebirth, our present life is obviously the important one! References to previous and future lives should not be taken to mean that a belief in rebirth is a necessary requirement for practising meditation or developing spiritually. However, most Buddhists do believe in rebirth, and there is convincing evidence to support their view. For a good analysis of this issue which includes a review of other relevant literature, Martin Willson's *Rebirth and the Western Buddhist*, Wisdom, London 1987, is highly recommended.

31 C.M. Chen, *Buddhist Meditation, Systematic and Practical*, published privately, Kalimpong 1962, p.26–7.

32 Note that the first four dhyanas (i.e. those within the rupa-loka) are known as the *rupa-dhyanas*.

33 *A Buddhist Bible*, p.439.

34 *A Buddhist Bible*, p.468.

35 *Samadhi* is quite a well known term. In Buddhism it is used differently in different contexts. It may refer simply to dhyana (samatha), but it often refers to a state of very deep dhyana that is also imbued with a particular vipassana realization. Accordingly some suttas refer to many varieties of samadhi.

36 *A Buddhist Bible*, p.455–6.

37 H.D. Thoreau, *Walden*, Harper & Row, London 1961.

38 *A Buddhist Bible*, p.444–5.

39 Adapted from *Samatha*, (Chen's Booklet series XIV), published privately, Kalimpong 1963.

40 In the UK write to the Society for the Teachers of Alexander Technique at 10 London House, 266 Fulham Road, London SW10 9EL. They will send an address list of all AT teachers.

41 from 'Burnt Norton', the first section of T.S. Eliot's, *Four Quartets, Collected Poems*, Faber & Faber, London 1963.

42 *The Path of Purification*, p.103.

43 *A Buddhist Bible*, p.458.

44 *The Path of Purification*, p.161.

45 This and the next four terms are in Pali. Together with *passaddhi*, these are known as the six qualitative factors, figuring in a list of nineteen *sobhana cetasikas* (beautiful mental states) in the Theravadin *Abhidhamma*.

46 from John Lennon, *Imagine*, Wise, 1981.

47 From *The Jewel Ornament of Liberation*, p.39, quoting the *rDzogs chen kun bzan bla ma*.

48 These are hatred, egoistic pride, greed, envy, and spiritual ignorance.

49 From *The Jewel Ornament of Liberation*, p.38, quoting the *rDzogs chen kun bzan bla ma*.

50 List according to Gampopa, who seems to have the fullest. (Detailed at length in *The Jewel Ornament of Liberation*.) Each of the four Tibetan schools has a slightly different approach. This list is from the Kagyupa School.

51 Sangharakshita, 'Advice to a Young Poet', in *The Religion of Art*, Windhorse, Glasgow 1988, p.135.

52 Trans. F.L. Woodward, *Udana V*, v. from *Minor Anthologies of the Pali Canon* Part II, Oxford University Press, London 1948, p.67.

53 From the Mettanisamsa Sutta, *Anguttara Nikaya* V. 342.

54 The Theravada commentarial tradition. See *The Path of Purification*, p.348.

55 *Dilgo Khyentse Rimpoche*, Editions Padmakara, 1990, p.12.

56 The 'Great Way', or the tradition that encourages the pursuit of Enlightenment for the sake of all beings, rather than just for one's own personal spiritual development.

57 See Mettakatha of *Patisambhida-magga* and Vajiranana Mahathera, *Buddhist Meditation*, Buddhist Missionary Society, Malaysia 1975, pp.288ff.

PART THREE
CHAPTER SIX

CHAPTER SEVEN

CHAPTER EIGHT

CHAPTER NINE

CHAPTER TEN

58 *Bardo Thodol*, composed by Padmasambhava, 8th century CE. Translated by W.Y. Evans-Wentz as the *Tibetan Book of the Dead*, Oxford University Press, London 1984, p.202.

59 The Trikaya doctrine involves three (*tri-*) levels of perceiving the the Enlightened consciousness. *Kaya* literally means 'body' or form. The *Nirmanakaya* is the human historical Buddha as perceived by ordinary sense-based consciousness, the *Sambhogakaya* his deeper qualities as perceived by visionary, dhyanic consciousness (in terms of archetypal, ideal form), and the *Dhammakaya* (Sanskrit *Dharmakaya*) as the essential Buddha-nature perceived with transcendental insight.

60 Extracted from the 'Song of Transience with Eight Similes', trans. G.C.C.Chang, *The Hundred Thousand Songs of Milarepa*, Shambhala, Boulder (USA) 1989, pp.204ff.

61 *The Path of Purification*, p.700–1.

62 Trans. F.L. Woodward, *Some Sayings of the Buddha*, Oxford University Press, London 1960, p.213.

63 The cyclical nidanas are explained in detail in Sangharakshita, *A Survey of Buddhism* (6th edition), Tharpa, London 1987, pp.94ff. The spiral nidanas are explained in Sangharakshita, *The Three Jewels*, Windhorse, Glasgow 1991, pp.110ff; see also Alex Kennedy, *The Buddhist Vision*, Rider, London 1992. One source in the Pali Canon for the spiral nidanas is the *Nidana-vagga* of the *Samyutta-Nikaya*.

64 Collated and systematized by Buddhaghosha from the Pali Canon. See *The Path of Purification*, p.112.

65 Bodhisattvas are either Enlightened already, or beings who are established 'on course' for Enlightenment.

66 See Paul Williams, *Mahayana Buddhism*, Routledge, London 1989, pp.217ff.

67 Trans. Sangharakshita.

INDEX

A

absorption factors 174

access concentration 66ff, 75, 76, 86, 91, 164, 166, 168, 173

acknowledgement 54, 154

acquired image 76

actions 6, 81, 108, 110, *see also* karma

activity 119

addiction 206, 218

agility 175

ahimsa 107

alcohol 107

Alexander Technique 135, 144, 265

alienation 34

anger 82, *see also* hatred

ankles 133, 136

antidotes 54, 157, 237ff, *see also* working

anxiety 72, 92, *see also* restlessness and~

appana 205

applied thought 70, 72, 89, 174

archetypal images 226

archetype 83

arching 129

art 110

arupa-dhyanas 85–6, 96

arupa-loka 85–6

asanas 140

assimilation 117

associative thinking 178

atmosphere 112

attachment 221

attention 13

authority 108

Avalokiteshvara 186

avijja 220

awareness 44, *see also* mindfulness of the body 48, 124

B

back 122–3, 129, 142

balanced concentration 173

balancing effort 56

bardo 210

beauty 240, 242

becoming 81, 221

behaviour 64, *see also* actions

benefits (of meditation) 37, 57, 194, 231

bereavement 92

bhava 221

bhavana 263

bhavana-maya panna 186

birth 218, 221

bliss 63, 71–2, 220

Bodhichitta 185

Bodhisattva 82, 224, 266

bodily awareness 48, 124, *see also* mindfulness of the body

body 45, 49, 122, 166, 249, 257

body language 45

Brahma-viharas 96, 192, 203, 225

breadth 156, 188

breath 14ff, 167

Buddha 33, 67, 69, 75, 83, 226

Buddhahood 81

Buddhism 32, 79, 80–3, 108–9

Buddhist centre 39

Buddhist terms 192

c

calm 220

chair 127, 134

change 82, 94, 210

chanting 261, *see also* mantra

characteristics of existence 91

Chen, C.M. 114

chest 130, 133

Chi-I 1, 3

Christianity 94

cinta-maya panna 183

classes (in meditation) 38, 132

cobbler's pose 142

colour 228

communication 113, 115, *see also* speech

compassion 69, 195, 246

complacency 84

conceit 211

concentration 13, 49, 66, 76, 98, 106, 134, 156, 164, 171, 220, 230–1

concentration object 15, 205, *see also* meditation object

conceptual understanding 90

conditionality 80, 244, *see also* dependence

conditioned co-production *see* dependent origination

conditioning 103, 108

conditioning factors 217

conditions 111, 114

confidence 9, 21, 24, 34, 123, 257, 258, *see also* faith

conscience 108

consciousness 7, 63, 65, 69, 85, 86, 214, 216, 220, *see also* higher~ consciousness element 214

considering the consequences 54, 238, 243, 249, 254, 258

contact 28, 221

contemplation 238, *see also* reflection of conditionality 217 of impermanence 206

contentment 107

counterpart image 76

craving 96, 207, 218, 221, 244, *see also* desire

cross-legged posture 137, 142

cruelty 197

cultivating the opposite 55, 238, 242, 248, 252, 257

cushion 129, 134

cyclic existence 218 nidanas 220

D

dakini 93

dana 107

death 82, 207, 221, *see also* impermanence

decomposition 207

dependence 111, *see also* conditionality

dependent origination 218

desire 52, 72, 82, 238, *see also* craving

devas 83

development *see* spiritual development

development of friendliness 23ff

devotional practice 261

Dharma *see* Buddhism

Dharma seeds 185, 219

dhyana 56, 63–76, 84–5, 89–90, 118, 174, 201

dhyana factors 70–6, 91, 153, 166, 201, 220

Dhyana for Beginners 1, 263

diary *see* meditation notebook

difficult person 26, 30

difficulties 58, *see also* hindrances

directed thinking 179

discomfort 123, *see also* pain

discussion 185

disentanglement 223

disinterested emotion 96

dissatisfaction 219

distractions 13, 20, 43, 49, 66, 117,
   see also hindrances

divine being 83, *see also* God

doubt 72, 215, 257

doubt and indecision 53, 257ff

dreams 7, 117

drifting 165, 169, 171, 173

drugs 94

drug abuse 107

duck walk 136

dukkha 219, *see also* unsatisfactoriness

dullness 111, 114, *see also* sloth, torpor

E

earth element 212

effort 157, *see also* balancing~

ego 95

elements *see* Six Element Practice

emotion(s) 33, 34, 46, 49, 96, 124
   see also feelings

emotional attachment 93

   investment 73

   satisfaction 242

   truthfulness 34, 35

emptiness 97, *see also* shunyata

ending (the meditation) *see* finishing

enemy *see* difficult person

energy 117, 124, 166, 228, 255

enjoyment 41, *see also* happiness,
   joy, pleasure

Enlightenment 4, 69, 82, 184, 223

enthusiasm 148, 151

environment *see* place

envy 200

equanimity 73, 74, 201, 204

ethics 106, 108, 252

example 161

excitement 114

exercise(s) 110, 116, 134, 257

experiences 57

external conditions 41, 104, 106

eyes 253

F

faith 54, 154, 219, 261, *see also* confidence

far enemy 193, 197, 200, 202

fear 92

   of feeling 199

feeling(s) 28, 34, 46, 48, 49, 59, 218,
   219, 221, *see also* emotions

finishing (the meditation) 19, 40

fire element 213

first dhyana 68

fitness 116

five hindrances *see* hindrances

five poisons 191

flexibility 142

focus 156, 188

food 116, 257

formless absorptions 86

   dhyanas 201

forty methods 226

Foundations of Mindfulness 44, 48, 230,
   232, 233, 263

fourth absorption 87

   dhyana 69, 74

freedom 107, 223

friendliness 23ff, 195, *see also* metta

friends 64, 80, 110

friendship 33, 79, 184

full lotus 128, 134

G

generosity 107

goal 8

God 94, *see also* divine being

gods 84, 96

Going for Refuge 55

good friend 26, 29

greed *see* craving

guarding the gates of the senses 109, 241

guilt 54, 68, 107, 108, 154

H

habit 94, 221

hands 130, 133

happiness 36, 69, 82, 85, 106, 199,
    see also enjoyment, joy

hatha yoga 135, 140

hatred 96, 193, *see also* anger

head 124, 130

heart 121

hell-being 83

higher states (of consciousness) 63ff, 67,
    71, 85, 119

hindrances 51, 66, 72, 76, 89, 124, 237ff,
    see also distractions

Hinduism 94

hips 137, 140, 141, 142

horizontal integration 65

horrified anxiety 198

hungry ghost 83

I

ignorance 90, 92, 217–8, 220

ill will 52, 72, 242ff

images 29

impermanence 81–2, 89–93, 184, 207,
    210, *see also* death

indifference 202

individuality 95

information 117

initial thought 70, 72, 89, 174

initiative 109

inner conditions 119

insecurity 82

insight 81, 87, 90, 93, 96–9, 187, 195,
    201, 204

    meditation 88, *see also* vipassana

inspiration 41, 59, 69, 110, 158, 255

integration 63ff, 69, 71, 86, 88, 95, 96, 165

intellect 99

internal conditions 104, 113

introspection 148, 150

irrational guilt 108, 154

Islam 94

J

jara-marana 221

jati 221

joy 199, 219, *see also* happiness

Jung, C.G. 66

Just Sitting 229

K

kama-loka 77, 85, 86

kamacchanda 238

kammannata 175

kammathanas 226–7

karma 109, *see also* actions

karma-formations 220

karma-vipaka 109

karuna 195, *see also* compassion

Karuna Bhavana 195, 204

kasina 75, 227

knees 133, 136, 138, 140, 141, 142

knowledge and vision… 220

knowledge of the destruction… 223

kukkucca 248

L

lahuta 175

lakkhanas see characteristics of existence

Lankavatara Sutra 99

legs 140, 142

levitation 71

life-style 104, 106, 251

limitations 118

listening 181

loving kindness *see* compassion, metta

lungs 121

M

magical powers 70

mana 215

mantra 186, 225, *see also* chanting

martial arts 136

material needs 112

meditation notebook 151, 159

meditation object 74, 158, 170, 173, 229,
  see also concentration object, *nimitta*

mental health 69
  poisons 191

metta 32, 35, 193, 209, 225, 263

Metta Bhavana 23ff, 88, 96, 104, 173,
  192, 249

middha 252

mind 6, 169

mindfulness 27, 42ff, 64, 111, 114, 120,
  178, 188, 230–1

Mindfulness of Breathing 13ff, 76, 88,
  104, 173

mindfulness of the body 122, 233,
  see also bodily awareness

motivations 7

motive 110

mudita 199

Mudita Bhavana 199, 204

muduta 175

mystical experience 94
  state 69

myth 83, 86, 94

N

namarupa 221

nature of existence 80

near enemy 193, 194, 197, 200, 202

neck 124, 130

negative emotion(s) 35, 154

negative self-view 154

neutral person 26, 30, 202

neutrality 202

nibbida 223

nidanas 219, 266

nimitta 74–6, 86–7,
  see also meditation object

non-selfhood 93, 97, 216, 245

nonviolence 107

O

object *see* meditation~, concentration~

old age 221

one-pointedness 70, 72, 74

operational concepts 79

opposite quality *see* cultivating the ~

outside meditation 240, 247, 251, 257, 259

P

padding 133

pagunnata 175

pain (physical) 34, 46, 48, 52, 82,
  129, 132, *see also* suffering

pamojja 219

passaddhi 71, 74, 175, 220

path 79, *see also* spiral

path of (ir)regular steps 98ff

pelvis 122, 129, 137

pema 194

personality 64, 69

pharana 204

phassa 221

physical exercise *see* exercise
  training 135, 136

PIPER 148, 154

piti 220

pity 197

place 41, 112

plane of exceedingly subtle form 85, 86

  of pure or subtle form 85, 86

  of sensuous enjoyment 85, 86

pleasure 34, 46, 48, 51, 52, 71, 82,

  see also enjoyment

pliancy 175

poisons 191

polar oppositions 169

positive emotion 33

  mental states 73

posture 121ff, 148, 149, 249, 253

preliminary concentration 114

preparation 39, 42, 44, 54, 104, 105,

  114, 148, 208, 229, 231

preparatory concentration 75–6

  image 76

proficiency 175

progress 98

psychological types 248

psychophysical organism 220

puja 261

purification 74, 228

purpose 148, 150

R

radiation 204

rapture 71, 72, 220, *see also* bliss

rational guilt 108

reading 117, 187

realm of the gods 84

rebirth 264

receptivity 173

recognition 67

recollection of the Buddha 227

reflection 89, 172, 177–188, 215, 225, 232,

  see also considering

reflex image 76, 77, 264

reflexive awareness 27

  consciousness 7

regular practice 37–8

rejoicing in merits 199

relaxation 140, 144, *see also* rest

religion 79, 95

religious conditioning 83, 94

resentment 200

resolve 148, 152, 258

rest 116, *see also* relaxation

restlessness 72, 111, 117

restlessness and anxiety 52, 125, 172, 248ff

restraint 241

retreats 39, 67, 111

Root Verses 209

rupa-dhyanas 85, 264

rupa-loka 77, 85, 86

S

sacca 107

saddha 219

sadhanas 225

salayatana 221

samadhi 76, 220, 265

samapatti 58, 65, 264

samatha 88–97, 192, 216, 220, 225,

  228, 230

sankharas 220

santutthi 107

sati 107

scientific world-view 83

second dhyana 68, 73

security 92

self 94–5

self-awareness 7

  -confidence *see* confidence

  -discipline 38

  -discovery 118

  -image 118, 123

  -view 215

senses 28, 109, 218

sense desire 72, 238ff

  experience 90

  organs 214, 221

sentimental attachment 194

sex 107–8

shock 254

shoulders 124, 130, 133

shrine 41

shunyata 97, 225

silence 116

simple consciousness 8

   life 111

sin 108

sinking 165, 169, 170, 173

sitting faults 129, *see also* posture

Six Element Practice 211ff, 234

six sense organs 214, 221

skeleton 122

skilful 106

sky-like (mind) 55, 240, 246, 250, 256, 259

sleep 116, 257

sloth 72, 252

sloth and torpor 52, 54, 124, 171ff

slumping 129

solitary retreat 111ff

solitude 111, 188

soul 94

space element 214

speech 115, 247, *see also* communication

sphere of infinite consciousness 87

   of infinite space 87

   of neither identity... 87

   of no-thing-ness 87

spine 129, 130

spiral nidanas 218–9, 223

spiritual development 81, 82, 84

   friendship 79, 184

   ignorance *see* ignorance

   life 85

stimulation 109–110

stool 127, 134

strain 98, 122, 123

strategy 150

stray thoughts 169, 172, *see also* thoughts

study 90, 118, 187

stupa 227, *see also* Six Element Practice

sub-personalities 64

subject-object distinction 96

subtle hindrances 165, 169

subtle sensation 18

suffering 195, 196, 244, *see also* pain

sukha 220

suppression 55, 240, 247, 250, 256, 259

surroundings 41

suta-maya panna 182

symbolism 225

symbols 186

sympathetic joy 199

T

t'ai chi 135, 138

tail-bone 129

tanha 221

Tara 224

teacher 260

technique 176

tension 123, 130, 166, *see also* anxiety

thighs 133, 137, 138, 141

thina 252

thinking 47, 252, *see also* thought

third dhyana 69, 74

thought(s) 47, 49, 50, 68, 71, 89, 119,
   169, 172, 178, 264, *see also* thinking

thought-free awareness 50

Tibetan Book of the Dead 209

Tibetan Wheel of Life 83

timing 20, 42

tiredness *see* sloth, torpor

Titan 83

torpor 72, 252

transcendental consciousness 8

travel 116

triangle pose 141

trikaya doctrine 266

truth 107

U

uddhacca 248

ujjukata 175

unconscious mind 109

understanding 261

unsatisfactoriness 91, 92, 184,

 see also dukkha

unskilful 106

upadana 221

upekkha 74, 201, 203, 204

Upekkha Bhavana 201

upright 175

V

vedana 221

vertical integration 65, 69, 74

vicarious enjoyment 200

vicikiccha 257

views 180

vimutti 223

vinnana 220

vipassana 88–97, 176, 185, 192, 206,

 215, 216, 220, 225, 230, 234

viraga 223

visionary experiences 65

visualization 75, 173, 224, 225, 227

vyapada 242

W

walking meditation 211, 231

water element 212

Wheel of Life 83, 84, *see also* nidanas

wisdom 69

withdrawal 223

workability 175

working 54, 147ff, 152, 155, 158,

 see also antidotes

Y

yoga 144